Dear Bill

Thanks for your support *private system*

Regards
Silvia

SB — policies { Gas Peron { private system
{ Vargas { cap
but w/o

Vital
Connections

Why is the 1924–1964 period "populist"?

p. 35   3 explana. of inflation, w/o monetauss
SB — mon in Chile in 70s

Compares performance of Pinochet +
SS reform & 1978 not 1973
p. 197

p. 145   cites Prat Report (1958–64

RECENT TITLES FROM THE HELEN KELLOGG INSTITUTE FOR INTERNATIONAL STUDIES

Scott Mainwaring, *general editor*

Michael Fleet and Brian H. Smith, eds.
The Catholic Church and Democracy in Chile and Peru (1997)

Robert Pelton, C.S.C., ed.
Small Christian Communities: Imagining the Future Church (1997)

A. James McAdams, ed.
Transitional Justice and the Rule of Law in New Democracies (1997)

Carol Ann Drogus
Women, Religion, and Social Change in Brazil's Popular Church (1997)

Víctor E. Tokman and Guillermo O'Donnell, eds.
Poverty and Inequality in Latin America: Issues and New Challenges (1998)

Brian H. Smith
Religious Politics in Latin America, Pentecostal vs. Catholic (1998)

Tristan Anne Borer
Challenging the State: Churches as Political Actors in South Africa, 1980–1994 (1998)

Juan E. Méndez, Guillermo O'Donnell, and Paulo Sérgio Pinheiro, eds.
The (Un)Rule of Law and the Underprivileged in Latin America (1999)

Guillermo O'Donnell
Counterpoints: Selected Essays on Authoritarianism and Democratization (1999)

Howard Handelman and Mark Tessler, eds.
Democracy and Its Limits: Lessons from Asia, Latin America, and the Middle East (1999)

Larissa Adler Lomnitz and Ana Melnick
Chile's Political Culture and Parties: An Anthropological Explanation (2000)

Kevin Healy
Llamas, Weavings, and Organic Chocolate: Multicultural Grassroots Development in the Andes and Amazon of Bolivia (2000)

Ernest J. Bartell, C.S.C., and Alejandro O'Donnell
The Child in Latin America: Health, Development, and Rights (2000)

Vikram K. Chand
Mexico's Political Awakening (2001)

For a complete list of titles from the Helen Kellogg Institute for International Studies, see http://www.undpress.nd.edu

VITAL CONNECTIONS

Politics, Social Security, and Inequality in Chile

SILVIA BORZUTZKY

University of Notre Dame Press

Notre Dame, Indiana

Copyright © 2002
University of Notre Dame
Notre Dame, Indiana 46556
All Rights Reserved
http://www.undpress.nd.edu

Manufactured in the United States of America

Library of Congress Cataloging-in-Publication Data
Borzutzky, Silvia.
  Vital connections : politics, social security, and inequality in Chile /
Silvia Borzutzky.
    p. cm.
  "From the Helen Kellogg Institute for International Studies"—CIP galley.
  Includes bibliographical references and index.
  ISBN 0-268-04356-6 (cloth : alk. paper)
  ISBN 0-268-04357-4 (pbk. : alk. paper)
  1. Social security—Chile—History—20th century. 2. Chile—Politics
and government—20th century. 3. Chile—Social policy. I. Helen Kellogg
Institute for International Studies. II. Title.
  HD7156 .B67 2002
  368.4'00983—dc21
                                                          2001004914

∞ *This book is printed on acid-free paper.*

Contents

Acknowledgments   vii
Introduction   ix

Chapter 1   Politics and Policies at the Beginning of   1
            the Twentieth Century

Chapter 2   Populist Politics, 1924–1964   19

Chapter 3   The Social Security System, 1924–1964 *important*   45

Chapter 4   Frei's Revolution in Liberty: 71
            The Social and Political Crisis of the 1960s

Chapter 5   The Politics of Social Security Reform   97
            under Frei, 1964–1970

Chapter 6   The Failed Road to a Socialist State: Politics   121
            and Social Security Policies during the Allende Regime,
            1970–1973

Chapter 7   Authoritarianism and Neo-liberalism: 153
            The Making of a Capitalist Society

Chapter 8   Winners and Losers: The Privatization   203
            of Social Security

            Epilogue: The Limits of Chilean Democracy   241

            Notes   257
            Index   291

Acknowledgments

My interest in social security policies can be traced back to my years at the University of Chile's Law School. However, I was not able to fully develop those interests until I became a graduate student in the Political Science Department at the University of Pittsburgh. I joined the Pittsburgh program at a time when Carmelo Mesa-Lago and James M. Malloy were developing the first set of analytical and coherent studies of social security policies in Latin America. My intellectual debt to both of them is enormous. From Jim Malloy I learned a great deal not only about Latin America, but about social sciences in general. Carmelo Mesa-Lago's pathbreaking work in social security has been widely recognized. I am deeply grateful for his constant support and friendship.

My experience as a graduate student at Pittsburgh was also marked by the presence of an outstanding human being, Richard Cottam. He was a great teacher and a superb scholar. I owe a lot to him and I will always cherish our friendship.

Brian Loveman is not only an outstanding scholar, but a dedicated reader. His knowledge of Chilean history and politics is exceptional. I am truly thankful for the comments and suggestions he made to an earlier version of this book. His careful reading and comments made the book much better. My thanks also to James Midgley for reading the entire manuscript and for his valuable comments. Jim Midgley has enthusiastically supported my scholarship during the past ten years and I am very grateful for that.

A number of institutions and people have contributed to this project in different forms. The Center for Latin American Studies at the University of Pittsburgh has provided not only research money, but most importantly has been an intellectual home for Latinoamericanists in Pittsburgh for the past thirty years. Teaching at Carnegie Mellon University during the past twelve years has been a truly rewarding experience. I very much appreciate the support I have received from both the administration and my colleagues in the Social and Decision Sciences Department and The Heinz School. Thanks also to the Tinker Foundation for providing me with travel grants. The staff at the University of Notre Dame Press has contributed much appreciated thoughtfulness and expertise. My thanks to Jeff Gainey for his enthusiastic reaction to my manuscript and to Carole Roos for her excellent editorial work. Rosa Stipanovic, from Carnegie Mellon University, helped me prepare the manuscript with her usual diligence and speed.

This book is the product of a number of deeply personal experiences. My parents' love for Chile and their interest in social and political issues instilled in me a desire to understand the society and its political system. My husband Carlos has always been an enthusiastic supporter of my academic endeavors and my daughter Claudia has been a source of inspiration. I am especially indebted to my son Danny. Because he is a writer I have had the luxury of his editorial help. He edited the entire manuscript with love, patience, and thoughtfulness. My husband's and my children's support and enthusiasm for my work have always been vital to me. They have contributed to this book with their love and encouragement.

I know that I was able to write this book because of the unconditional support of all those I love and I dedicate this book to them.

Introduction

In Spanish the word *política* means both politics and policies. Consequently there is a close relationship between *la política* (politics) and *las políticas* (the policies). It should not be a surprise then that the specific policies generated by a given political system look very much like the political environment that generated those policies. This book is about the connections that exist between política and políticas, between politics and policies. Specifically, it is about the vital and intimate connections that exist between Chilean politics and social security policies in the mid- and late twentieth century. To achieve this goal I have pursued a comparative analysis of the political system and of the social security policies during a seventy-five-year period.

The book contains an analysis of the central characteristics of the political and economic systems of Chile at times when the society experienced major crises. These crises manifested themselves in the transformation, or attempt to transform, the political and economic organization and the social security system. In the case of Chile, the problem of order and of restructuring socioeconomic and political relations has been a recurrent one. However, I do not attempt to discuss the entire evolution of Chilean politics, but only those critical processes which led to a change in the socioeconomic functions of the state, and consequently to a major change in the social security system. The crises of 1924, of the mid-1960s, and of the early and late 1970s produced this kind of impact and resulted in complex processes that led to a change in the relations between the society and the state, a change in the nature of politics and in the social security policies.

These crises manifested themselves in new constitutional arrangements that attempted to end a host of social, political, and economic problems. In each case the larger goal was to structure a new political legitimacy, to redefine the nature and role of the state, and to restructure state-society relations. In each case the social security policies were either totally changed or there was a serious attempt at changing them.

The discussion and analysis of social security policies during three different stages—the mid-1920s, the late 1960s, and the late 1970s—will illustrate the nature of the political system, the activities of the state in a specific policy area, the nature of the relations between state and society, and the complex relationship between policies and politics. I have chosen to focus on these critical stages because they are indicative of the form in which social security policies were used to resolve, or to try to resolve, major political crises. Following Hugh Heclo, "I shall look at proximate sources and causes. How have issues of social policy arisen; where have the substantive ideas about what to do come from; what is the process by which they have been politically accepted and changed through time—in short how have governments come to do the specific things they do?"[1]

In Chile, as elsewhere, the state has been most active when the society and the government were in crisis, when there was a perception that the existing problems could only be solved by the public authorities.[2] The focus will be on the actions of the state geared to regain legitimacy at a time in which the society was experiencing a major crisis. A preferred form of action of the Chilean politicians between 1924 and 1973 was to grant social security benefits in order to deal with the problem of legitimacy and to satisfy the socioeconomic demands of the most vocal sectors of the working class.

The diachronic comparison of social security policies includes an analysis of the main components of the system: pensions, family allowances, and health benefits. In the ensuing pages there is an analysis of the principles and ideas that inspired those policies and the form in which they reflected a set of sociopolitical structures. However, the process does not end there: the policies, once in place, affect the existing socioeconomic organization and the political system, generating the foundations for a new set of policies and political processes. In brief, the comparative analysis of a set of public policies across time will serve to describe the role of the state, its interactions with a set of social groups, and the way in which the political system both incorporated and excluded important socioeconomic groups. Ultimately, the social security politics also affected the politics of the country—just as much as the children change and affect the life of the parents and the entire family.

Chapters one, two, and three deal with the late nineteenth and early twentieth century. They contain an analysis of the socioeconomic situation at the end of the nineteenth century, the crisis of the early 1900s, the social security policies of 1924, and the political system created by the 1925 Constitution. The Constitution involved the adoption of ideas developed in western Europe during the late nineteenth century which dealt with the functions of the state in rapidly industrializing and changing societies. The state was expected to provide for certain public needs and the expansion of state functions between 1925 and 1973 precisely followed this principle.

The provision of benefits to satisfy some pressing public needs served, also, as a tool to resolve social conflicts and legitimize a political and economic system based on huge inequities. The basic socioeconomic structure remained unfair and unequal, but the partial benefits granted through the social security system sustained the illusion that the state was there to serve the needs of the people, and that sooner or later one's needs will be satisfied.

From the societal standpoint what needs to be stressed is the impact that the rapid process of political development had on a society characterized by extremely unequal distribution of wealth and income. In this context a number of processes took place, including the fragmentation of the societal actors and the use of clientelistic linkages to obtain the satisfaction of basic demands. The constant growth of the number of power contenders and the constant inability or unwillingness of the policymakers to fully satisfy those demands led to a fragmentation of the pressure groups and to an endless cycle of partially satisfied demands and partially acceptable policies. At the core of the analysis is the concept of *clientelism,* a very salient and not very much studied characteristic of Chilean politics. The distinguishing feature of the traditional patron-client relationship is a broad spectrum of mutual obligations based on the belief that the patron should display a paternal concern for the needs of the client, while demanding that the client display filial loyalty to him.

The expansion of state functions and the expansion of the social security system were responses to societal pressures exercised through the political institutions and through informal clientelistic channels. In Chile, as in other societies, the appearance of modern political structures did not produce the disappearance of traditional forms of interest aggregation; on the contrary, traditional clientelistic arrangements penetrated the political parties and the different branches of governments.

While most studies on clientelism focus on local politics, the focus here is on its impact on national politics, specifically on the general expansion of the state functions and on the growth the social security system during the mid-twentieth century as seen in chapter three. The state, and more specifically the politicians, became the *patrón* that had the ultimate control over the national resources while the development of dyadic ties between political groups and those that controlled parts and parcels of the state became the leitmotif of political activity. The provision of social security benefits and exemptions through legislative riders was at the core of the growth and expansion of the social security system and ultimately it created the conditions for a massive financial crisis, which is analyzed in chapter six.

Chapters four and five contain an analysis of the socioeconomic crises of the late 1960s, and President Frei's attempts to solve those crises through a set of constitutional and political reforms and a new approach to social security policies. The 1970 Constitutional Reform as well as the major socioeconomic reforms that formed President Frei's programs were based on the notion of the communitarian state. This notion stressed an organic concept of the state. Its primary function was to integrate the society through policies geared to ameliorate the impact that the market economy had on the society, particularly on the poorest groups, and to avoid any further social fragmentation. The reforms called for the establishment of corporatist forms of interest aggregation, the strengthening of the executive branch, and the expansion of the social and economic functions of the state among those groups that until then had remained at the margins of the society. The attempts to create a communitarian state, an organic society, and to reform the social security system failed.

The failure of these attempts, the further fragmentation of the society, and the inchoate expansion of the functions of the state during the Allende government played an important role in the destruction of the political system. Chapter six analyzes both the main characteristics and policies of the Allende regime, as well as the expansion of social security policies to specific sectors of the society. The chapter concludes with a discussion of what I have called the parallel crises experienced by both the political system and the social security system. This section shows once again the vital connections between politics and policies.

The military coup of 1973 marked the beginning of a new era in state-society relations and a new process of statecraft. The nature as well as the functions of the Chilean state were radically transformed by the 1980 Constitution and the major socioeconomic and political reforms implemented by the government of General Pinochet. The neo-liberal ideology inspired the economic reforms, which involved a reduction of the state functions in the area of social and economic policies, while the authoritarian ideas of General Pinochet provided the foundation for the new political system. In spite of the drastic nature of the reforms, the state continued playing a guiding role in the economic arena. The political arena was reduced to a handful of interest groups associated with the regime, while the rest of the society bore the brunt of the repression. It is my argument that there was a complementary relationship between the economic changes and the repressive nature of the regime. Human rights abuses were a central feature of the political system established by General Pinochet and an intrinsic part of the regime's socioeconomic policies. Chapter seven contains an analysis of the nature of the Pinochet regime from both an economic and a political dimension. This chapter also traces the transition to democracy. Chapter eight discusses the privatization of social security and its impact on the society, emphasizing the regressive nature of the system, the reduction in coverage, and the enormous costs involved in the transition from a public to a private system. The transition to democracy has not produced any substantial change either in the economic or in the social security system.

The epilogue contains a brief overview of Chile's new democracy.

Finally, there is a limited attempt to incorporate into the analysis the notion of social narrative. Although a full-fledged analysis of the question of social narrative lies beyond the scope of this research, I argue that the social security system was part of and played an important

role in sustaining an official story and an official history that emphasized the uniqueness of Chilean politics. Just as *política* means both
politics and policies, the term *historia* in Spanish means both history
and story. In the case of Chile this intimate connection between both
terms was used to create a story out of the history. The "official" story
in turn provided legitimacy to historical actions and processes, medi-
ating the differences between the ideology and the reality.

According to the official history/story, Chile was unique among
the Latin American countries because of its ability to forge a united
and orderly political system at a time when the rest of Latin America
was submerged in chaos and internal wars. The official history and the
story also stress the early development of stable "democratic" institutions and respect for the laws. In fact, I believe that although it is true
that Chile had a stable political system by the 1830s, that stability was
built upon authoritarian institutions and an unequal social structure.
I also argue that the emphasis placed on this uniqueness served governments and politicians to bind together this very unequal and divided society. Nonetheless, these accomplishments served to forge
what Loveman and Lira called the myth of national unity.[3] The story
as it was developed in the 1920s and 1930s stressed the importance of
Chilean democracy and the role that the state played in creating a
more egalitarian, harmonious society. The "official story" not only gave
the society an identity, but served to manufacture consent and disguise a system that in fact was characterized by truly profound inequalities.[4]

In the case of Chile, this myth satisfied needs that neither the
state nor the policies were able to satisfy. The myth bound the society
together, and in the process of unifying a very unequal society it legitimized the political system, strengthening the power of those with
power. Confronted with major crises of legitimacy or situations in
which the differences between rhetoric and reality had become too
apparent, the Frei and Allende administrations attempted to narrow
that gap through political and economic reforms. However, those policies threatened the interests of those who had developed the myth in
the first place. General Pinochet had to intervene to restore that
broken "national unity." In order to achieve its goals the regime destroyed the existing political institutions, tortured, and killed. The new
regime redefined the functions of the state and developed a new nar-

rative: they both stressed individualism and self-reliance, despised democracy, equality, and the most basic rights of the people.

What this book shows is that, between 1925 and 1973, while the "official" myth stressed democracy, unity, and harmony, Chilean society was characterized by profound divisions and inequalities.[5] Given the nature of this work I can only show the impact and importance of this official myth in the area of social security. Between 1924 and 1973 social security polices were presented as trying to ameliorate the inequalities and benefit the poorest sector of the society. In practice, these policies were just like the rest of the society, highly stratified and unequal, because they were the product of a highly stratified and unequal society and political system. In fact, I suggest that one of the social security system's central functions was to sustain a set of political and economic institutions that were designed to maintain or increase that very inequality. The basic foundation of social security policies was rooted in nineteenth-century ideology and the policies served to re-create that ideology. The fact that the policies were developed during the mid-twentieth century did not make them more egalitarian or democratic.

The Pinochet regime destroyed all that and developed a new narrative. The society was told that the old political system was unfair and inefficient, and that it was leading the society toward Marxism. That system had to be replaced by one that emphasized individualism and the power of the market as regulator of socioeconomic activities. The privatization of the social security system, the retrenchment of the state, and the emphasis on individualism has only deepened inequality.

CHAPTER 1

Politics and Policies
at the Beginning
of the Twentieth Century

In the early years of the twentieth century, Chile, as well as the other Southern Cone countries, experienced a long period of social and political crisis. This crisis was solved through the transformation of the state and the enactment of a new set of laws that changed the relations between state and society. A crucial element in the solution of the crisis, and an integral part of a larger process of social and political reform, was the enactment of a set of policies toward labor. Those policies established the right to unionize and strike and created the first social security funds. These laws were followed by a new constitution which transformed Chilean politics and the nature of the state.

The social and labor policies, a state response to a major crisis that threatened the socioeconomic system, were the result of actions of sectors of the elite. They perceived the need to rid Chile of its colonial political structures in order to modernize its political system and to restore support for a social narrative that stressed the importance of unity. They found in the military the support and force needed to break the political deadlock and to carry out the policies required to transform the state. This chapter presents the background of this crisis and the political changes that occurred in 1924–1925.

The Political Development of Chile during the Nineteenth Century and the Origins of the Social Question

In Chile the anarchical period was shorter than in any other Latin American country. Political stability was obtained through the perpetuation of colonial structures under a republican form and was accomplished by institutionalizing the power of the landowners of the Central Valley, the richest agricultural area.[1] The task was performed by Diego Portales, and the power structure he created was formalized in the 1833 Constitution. Mario Góngora argues that "the political regime created by Portales was based on the aristocracy . . . but this class had to be obedient to the government in order to protect its own interest as well as the public order."[2]

Social peace resulted not only from an early institutionalization of the political system, which consolidated the power of the aristocracy, but from a process in which the traditional land-owning class merged socially with the new elites created by the process of economic development. As a result, in Chile, the land-owning and the bourgeois segments of the elite merged socially and retained a large degree of economic identity throughout the nineteenth century. A century later it was very difficult to distinguish among the merchant, the agricultural, and the mining elite, who all maintained the values of the rural society.[3] Social peace was disrupted only on three occasions during the nineteenth century, twice in the 1850s and in 1891. In these cases, as Zeitlin argues, the antagonists did not represent separate classes, "but distinctive segments of the dominant class itself, torn apart by contradictory interests and political requirements."[4] The 1891 civil war put an end to the reformist government of President Balmaceda, reestablished the power of congress, and established a de facto parliamentary system built upon the existing constitution.[5] The civil war lasted seven months and produced more than 10,000 casualties. The parliamentary period lasted until the military intervention of 1924.

Like other Latin American countries, Chile's economy was based on exports, which gave the country sustained economic growth throughout the nineteenth century. Both agricultural and mineral products inserted Chile into the international economic system, but it was the mining sector that provided the growth. The political economy of the system created by Portales was designed to insert Chile in the world markets through the export of commodities, while manufactured products were imported from Europe. From the Pacific War (1879) until the Great Depression, nitrate was the primary export product. Both the industrial and the urban development of Chile were closely tied to nitrate exploitation. Roads and railroads were built to allow the movement of nitrate from the desert to the ports, and electricity and other infrastructural projects were undertaken to satisfy the needs of the industry. An entire financial and banking system developed in Santiago and Valparaíso as a response to the industry's fiscal demands, which in turn allowed the development of small consumer goods industries in those two cities. The process of economic development was possible due not only to the entrepreneurial spirit of the Chilean elite involved in the nitrate exploitation and capitalist agriculture, but to state involvement through fiscal policies that transferred resources from mining to the pre-capitalist agricultural sector and invested in roads and railroads in the Central Valley. The state also established the legal and juridical framework that could facilitate economic exchanges, giving the country a body of law that was later adopted by several other countries in Latin America.[6]

The 1833 Constitution involved the application of the centralist, conservative tradition inherited from the colonial administration. Political power was concentrated in the executive branch, which was in the hands of the Conservative Party during most of the nineteenth century. However, from an economic perspective, both the Constitution and the Civil Code established a set of principles geared to protect private property. The elite was represented by two political parties—Conservadores and Liberales—which held contrasting views regarding the nature and functions of the state, relations between state and society, and the economic role of the state. The power of the Chilean elite remained unchallenged until the early twentieth century, when the social classes generated by economic development began to demand participation in the political system.

By the 1860s the development and growth of the nitrate exploitation and the mining of coal and copper began to have an impact on the social and political fabric of the nation. The mine owners of the North, the small landowners in the South, and some of the businessmen of the cities appeared as a new bourgeoisie who sought active political participation and attempted to restructure the functions and role of the state, challenging the power of the land-owning families. After the insurrections of 1851 and 1859 these groups attempted to express themselves politically through the creation of the Radical Party, which advocated a reform to the 1833 Constitution and the expansion of the political system, while maintaining an openly anti-clerical position that soon became the trademark of the party.[7] Its leaders were "the lions of the society, happy destroyers of all traditions, democrats and free thinkers."[8] But the oligarchy was not ready to reform since their power was not really threatened. The radicals, as well as the rest of society, had to wait another sixty years to see those reforms enacted.

The process of economic development initiated in the mid-1860s took a new force after the Pacific War against Peru and Bolivia (1879). The mining wealth acquired by Chile during the war added to the exploitation of nitrate and generated a period of sustained economic growth and industrial and commercial development which, in turn, created a large labor force and an important urban sector. Between 1908 and 1918 the number of factories and shops increased approximately sixfold, while the number of nitrate workers grew to 57,000 by 1918. By 1920 there were an estimated 33,000 railroad workers and almost 80,000 people were employed in the manufacturing industries. To these numbers we must add copper, dock, and coal workers, commercial and bank employees, and the government bureaucracy. By 1920 the economically active population was 1,355,000 persons.[9] The bulk of the working class was formed by former peasants uprooted during the Pacific War or "hooked" by company agents in the countryside. The urban workers, on the other hand, had a very strong foreign component, which impinged upon their future political organization.

Working and living conditions were deplorable. Many Chilean and foreign writers have described the sad situation of the working force and especially of the nitrate workers. Stressing some aspects of the nitrate exploitation, James O. Morris writes:

Gambling, drinking, prostitution and political radicalism all flourished, but this was due as much or more to the psychological consequences of isolation, distance and the bareness of the land as to the companies, wages and other social problems. For drama, perhaps nothing could match the natural geographic setting and unusual climatic conditions of the Northern pampa. A dry, flat, end-less and uninhabited desert expanse hundreds of miles and several exhausting days away from the lush Central Valley, it was by comparison a little Chilean hell which devoured huge daily quantities of human labor and gave up little for the soul in return.[10]

In 1910 *El Mercurio*, Chile's most traditional newspaper, acknowledged that "25 percent of Santiago's population lives in inhuman conditions. 100,000 people are living in small, narrow, dark rooms in which the body becomes atrophied; another 100,000 persons occupy 25,000 rooms, this is an average of 4 persons in a room."[11] Poor living and working conditions were reflected in Chile's death and infant mortality rates, which were among the highest in the world.[12] From an economic perspective, throughout this period the country underwent two parallel phenomena: substantial inflation that greatly reduced the real income of the working class, and upward redistribution of income due to the elimination of most internal taxes, made possible by the revenues generated in the export sector.[13]

Most of the analysts have traced the roots of inflation to a deliberate policy pursued by the Chilean landowners who cheapened the currency in order to settle mortgage debts in depreciated currency, while at the same time selling their products in England for sterling pounds.[14] The inflationary process bore directly on both the very low living standards of the working class and the formation of a working-class movement, making the economic situation worse and anti-capitalism stronger.

Inflation and the redistribution of national income in favor of the upper class continued until World War I, when the economic model came to an abrupt end with the entrance of synthetic fertilizer into the world market. The appearance of synthetic nitrates threw the economy into a profound crisis. At the nadir of the recession, in 1922, some 47,000 nitrate workers and thousands of copper and coal miners were jobless.[15]

Thus, in Chile, the social question, that is, the social and economic consequences of emerging urbanization and industrialization, was exacerbated by an immobile, exclusionary, and inefficient political system; by an economic system based on the availability of cheap labor and the exploitation of primary export products; by the use on the part of the bourgeoisie of monetary policies favorable to its own interest; and by a social system based on the dominance of the land-owning class. It was the unwillingness and inability of the majority of the upper class to comprehend the seriousness of the social situation that forced the events of 1924 and their consequences.

The Workers Movement and Its Impact

The first workers organizations in Chile were formed in the 1850s and were structured as mutual aid societies or *mutualidades*. These multi-class organizations were created solely for the purpose of forming resource pools to aid members in case of illness and death.[16] Although these organizations developed fairly quickly in the early and mid-1850s most of them survived only until the end of the decade. After the civil war of 1859 a large number of new mutual aid societies were created. They were followed by the *filarmónicas* which combined co-operative and recreational functions. In some cases the mutual aid societies organized strikes, anticipating the more militant organizations that were created later in the nineteenth century.[17]

The passive attitude that the mutual aid societies had toward most social and economic problems moved the miners and dock workers of the North to create the first *mancomunal* or fellowship. Their purpose was to defend working-class interests, particularly to improve the standard of living and the education of workers. *Mancomunales* spread rapidly throughout the other industrial centers of the country.

A third form of workers organization, called the "resistance societies," was formed by the anarchists. This movement, initiated in the last years of the nineteenth century, reached its peak around 1912 with the arrival in Chile of foreign anarchists, among them a few Russians, followers of Kropotkin and Bakunin. University students acted as leaders and instructors, proclaiming the disappearance of the existing social order and its violent replacement by a free, classless society. At its peak the organizations had 9,000 members.[18]

The resistance societies disappeared without leaving important traces, while the *mancomunales*, before disappearing, served as the base upon which Luis Emilio Recabarren organized the first national labor movement. According to Grez, "the web of mutual aid societies expanded through all the important cities, incorporating the members of almost all the urban trades and it was beginning to expand among the blue-collar workers. . . . [T]hey pushed the popular movement toward the formation of coordinated structures."[19]

Founded in 1909, the Federation of Chilean Workers (FOCH) was a hybrid between a mutual aid society and a *mancomunal* with limited syndicalist aims, such as a minimum salary, a working day of eight hours, and the creation of a government office to deal with the basic problems of the working class. During the following ten years the organization suffered a radical transformation, becoming a revolutionary organization that aimed at the destruction of the capitalist system. Luis Emilio Recabarren, who later became the leader of the organization, argued that the working class had to pursue a twofold fight against the oligarchy: one of a *reivindicative* nature,[20] geared toward obtaining, in the near future, an improvement in working and living conditions, and a second one, of a political nature, aimed at the destruction of the capitalist system and carried on not by the working-class organization itself, but by a popular political party.

Recabarren, originally a Democratic Party militant, founded in 1912 the Socialist Workers Party, which rapidly evolved into a radical organization and became the Communist Party of Chile in 1922.[21] Recabarren's influence and his role in the Chilean labor movement are crucial parts of Chile's labor and political history. Particularly important was his tactical approach, which established the formal division between party and union, stressing that the workers had to be active in both, as well as his concern with morality and education.[22]

Under the guidance of Recabarren the workers attempted a two-pronged strategy: the short-term improvement of their socioeconomic situation through strikes, and the long-term destruction of the capitalist system through the actions of the Communist Party. In practice, they could only implement their short-term strategy. The long-term political strategy had to be postponed.

Although the earliest strikes date from the 1840s, they were a rare occurrence until the 1860s. During and after the 1860s workers began to resort to strikes more often.[23] By and large, they were non-violent strikes and had purely economic goals. During the 1880s the frequency and intensity of the strikes increased rapidly. Grez lists about eighty strikes taking place during the decade, most of them during 1888. The strikes took place mostly in the ports and mines, and in most cases they resembled more a mutiny than a modern organized strike.[24] The first general strike took place in 1890. It began among the dock workers of Iquique and spread rapidly throughout the nitrate-producing area, involving some 10,000 workers. Jobet reports that the strike wave spread throughout the country reaching the coal mines of the South.[25]

The first decades of the twentieth century were full of violent events that reflected the seriousness of the social situation. In 1903, Valparaíso was paralyzed for several weeks by a dock workers' strike, which culminated when the workers set fire to the building of the largest shipping company. In Santiago, in 1905, workers protesting against a new tax on imported beef took control of the city for two days. Some 400 people were killed in this incident. The following year, a similar event in Antofagasta produced about 150 deaths and over 300 wounded.[26] Generally known as the Massacre of Iquique, the most violent and tragic incident took place in 1907 when 20,000 workers protesting against economic and working conditions in the nitrate fields took possession of that city. The refusal of the workers to abandon the school in which they had taken refuge and surrender to the military produced a carnage in which men, women, and children were killed by the military. The government, which initially had tried to mediate the conflict between the workers and the nitrate companies, quickly became the right arm of the companies. The actions of the government and the military sent a powerful message throughout the society and the incipient labor movement.[27]

The years between 1908 and 1918 were of relative social peace, but the economic depression caused by the reversal of the nitrate market following the end of World War I exacerbated the already deep socioeconomic cleavages, and strikes and violence again dominated the social picture. Throughout this period the labor movement increased both in size and organization. Unionization had spread through the export sector of the economy, as well as through the transportation sector. By 1925 there were 214 unions with a total of 204,000 members, 100,000 of which belonged to the FOCH.[28]

The leadership of the labor movement was concerned with political and economic issues. The political issues were related to the role of the labor movement in the revolutionary process, the opposition to the capitalist system, and the opposition to the state. But these were mainly rhetorical problems. The bread and butter issues were the overwhelming problems of the working class and these constituted the strikes' objectives.[29] Thus strikes were geared toward obtaining basic economic benefits and solving fundamental working-class issues such as the length of the working day, the recognition of the union, and minimum safety standards in the workplace. By and large, strikes and violence did not produce the desired effect, and the workers obtained an improvement in neither their standard of living nor in their working conditions.

The Chilean power elite remained adamant in the protection of its prerogatives and in an unwillingness to accommodate even the most basic worker demands. As a very prominent member of the Chilean elite declared: "Inequality is the law of God . . . the only equality that exists is everybody's love of God."[30] Loyal to this belief in inequality, the elite rejected workers' demands for better wages and working conditions and refused to accept legislation dealing with either contractual relations or the right to unionize. Salary increases were consistently denied, and real wages continued to decline. The workers' violence was met with police and military violence.

Nevertheless, the workers were able to attract the attention of some sectors of the elite. The Executive and Congress responded by establishing the Labor Office in 1907 and the Committee on Social Legislation in the Chamber of Deputies. Congress also enacted a few laws dealing with working conditions.[31] Two major breakthroughs in the legislative area took place after 1910. In 1911 a system of old age pensions for the powerfully organized railroad workers was established, making this group the first blue-collar workers to obtain such a benefit. In 1916 an occupational accidents law protected the blue-collar workers against accidents in the workplace. This law was an improvement over the Civil Code since it shifted the burden of proof of responsibility to the employer.[32]

Labor and the actions of the labor movement had an impact on an important sector of the society: the intellectuals. While neither the actions of the labor movement nor the writings of the intellectuals had a direct impact on the Chilean political organization, both set the stage for the reforms that occurred in the next decade. As James M. Malloy argued in the case of Brazil, "while labor represented an important challenge to the system, the full impact of its challenge did not rest in labor's political power alone, but on the other challenges the system faced."[33] Rather than dealing with the central grievances of the working class, the limited social legislation passed before 1920 was mostly a mechanism used by the elite to mollify some of the workers' concerns, such as occupational hazards and inadequate housing.[34] Labor remained excluded from politics and from exerting any direct impact on the political system.

The Election of Alessandri
and the Passage of the Labor Legislation

By 1920 the social question involved more than improving working and living conditions. It entailed a fundamental change in the political system—a change in the nature of the state, the enfranchisement of the working class, and the acceptance of the newly formed political parties. Not only was the political organization challenged, the social organization and the structure of property that it represented was challenged as well. Arturo Alessandri, one of the presidential candidates in the 1920 elections, recognized the explosive potential of the situation.

During a period in which the repercussions of the Russian and the Mexican revolutions were felt everywhere, Alessandri had become convinced that capitalism was going to survive only by making profound transformations in the functions of the state and fundamental concessions to the working class. It was necessary to create a more effective and open political organization, one that could deal with the pressing socioeconomic problems of the nation, and one in which the organized sectors of the working class could participate. Alessandri stated his position very clearly in his speech at the Presidential Convention of 1920:

> At the present time, the whole world is going through a period of profound social change: we are seeing the birth of a new era; those that do not want to see it or feel it are blind and deaf. From one end of the planet to the other there is an imperious cry, already heard by all the thinkers and by the brightest statesmen, to resolve with justice and equity the rights demanded by the proletariat, in the name of solidarity, and for the harmony of the society.[35]

Three years later, President Alessandri, faced with the inability of Congress to legislate on social and political matters, restated his position:

> It is necessary to promptly pass legislation aimed at protecting the interests of the employers and the workers as an antidote to those spirits that are working for the dissolution of the social order. If we establish some social equilibrium through fair laws that take into account the demands of the proletariat, we will prevent anarchic and subversive elements from predicating their theories. You will see how those theories crash against the wall erected by social justice.[36]

Alessandri's observations in 1920 and 1924 could not have been more accurate. Undoubtedly, the world was going through a period of social, economic, and political reorganization. In Chile, the impact of that convulsion was being felt by a depressed economy, an inefficient and static political system, and a divided and demoralized society. An American observer, John Stevenson, vividly described the situation of the Chilean society at that time.

> The Chilean sociopolitical scene in the first two decades of the twentieth century was similar in many ways to Mount Aconcagua, the highest peak in the Andes. This majestic granite block appears as still and immobile as death itself, but actually, beneath its snow covered exterior, molten lava is constantly seething and may some day boil over.[37]

The 47,000 unemployed nitrate workers and the 10,000 unemployed copper workers abandoned the isolation of the northern provinces and dispersed throughout the country, taking with them their well-developed notions of unionization and political action.

In the political arena, the economic crisis and the government's inability to deal with it made possible a new alliance formed by the Liberal, Radical, and Democratic parties. The program of the Democratic Party reflected the sociopolitical and economic concerns of those who advocated reforms. The party's leader Malaquías Concha proposed the effective inclusion of 85–90 percent of the population, free universal education, gender equality, and social policies to improve the living conditions of the peasants, miners, and urban workers.[38]

The program of the Democratic Party set the stage for the election of Arturo Alessandri, the Liberal Alliance candidate. Alessandri's campaign was centered around a deep criticism of the current system and recommendations for its replacement, as well as a new approach to the social question. Shortly after he was elected, Alessandri introduced a Labor Code bill and a bill creating a pension fund for civil servants. Despite his repeated pleas, the Congress acted on neither the president's bills nor the labor bill introduced by the Conservative Party. Instead it procrastinated for the next four years, endlessly discussing both.[39]

The conservative bill involved the application of the social principles of the Catholic doctrine, and especially those laid out by the encyclicals of Pope Leo XIII. Thus the Catholic intellectuals, led by Juan Enrique Concha, believed that the origins of the social question were traceable to a breakdown in social morality, which caused the "natural order" of unity and harmony between unequals to disappear. As a result, labor was pitted against the entire capitalist class. The solutions to the problems stemming from this social breakdown were industrial stewardship or *patronato*, religious education, and social legislation. *Patronato* involved a number of economic and moral obligations that the employer, or *patrón*, had toward his employees. Labor legislation was needed to limit the rights and correct the abuses of the wealthy and to protect the weak who are oppressed by complete liberty. In this scheme, "the State was a great father who could teach wayward employers their duty toward the workers so that peace, order and harmony could reign in the workplace, in industry and in society."[40]

The Liberal Alliance bill reflected the thoughts of nineteenth-century liberals. Their Chilean counterparts, led by Eleodoro Yañez and Benjamín Vicuña Subercaseaux, argued that the social question was a product of industrialization and that it reflected real problems in the workplace which forced the state to expand its role beyond the borders established by traditional liberal thought to provide the workers with the basic rights demanded by industrialization but denied by the employers. The liberal bill was written entirely by Moisés Poblete, a professor of labor law, the first director of the Labor Office, and a prolific writer on social, labor, and political matters.[41] The Labor Code bill comprised four major sections: craft unions at the local and the national level; conciliation, arbitration, and the right to strike; working conditions; and social security.

Opposition to social legislation came from sectors within both parties, which effectively obstructed the passage of either the liberal or the conservative bill. But obstruction and inaction were not, by any means, limited to labor legislation. Throughout this period the Congress was totally paralyzed—a paralysis which reflected a profound split within the elite between those who argued for the conservation of the autocratic, exclusionary system of government, and those who thought that Chile should move along with the civilized countries, adopting a more modern political system. Alessandri's election was a victory for the modern bourgeoisie, which, since the 1850s, had been demanding the elimination of the autocratic state. Military action was the only available resort.[42]

The Military Intervention
and the "Solution" of the Social Question

The military movement of 5 September 1924 began as a nonviolent, spontaneous protest by junior and middle rank military officers against the failure of the government to deal with the serious social, economic, and political problems of the post–World War I period. Despite the fact that the movement was conceived in the national interest, professional considerations prompted military actions.

The military had not been a passive element in the evolution of the social question. Throughout the century the army had been directly involved in it, protecting the status quo by repressing the workers. But the status quo and the general social crisis had also adversely affected the military itself. Poor economic conditions and low morale had taken a heavy toll within the army.

In September 1924, the Congress failed to act upon an imminent budget crisis, which left the state without the funds needed to pay public servants, including the military. The failure prompted the young officers to intervene, demanding from Congress and President Alessandri not only the immediate passage of the budget bill, but also the passage of the Labor Code and other social laws, and the approval of the income tax law. Alessandri responded by naming the Commander-in-Chief of the Army head of his Cabinet and accepting the military intervention. Congress responded by passing all the legislation requested by the military in a few hours.[43]

The laws approved by Congress on the night of 8 September covered three different areas: the national budget, the army, and social laws. In the budgetary area, the Congress approved the pending budget bill, an income tax law, and also legislation rectifying the budget deficit as requested by the President. Regarding the army, the Congress passed four basic laws: one dealing with salaries and wages, a second that increased military personnel, a third that reformed the already existing pension system for army and navy personnel, and a fourth law that gave legal existence to the army's Industry of War Materials.

In the area of social legislation, the Congress approved several laws that dealt with working conditions and the working contract, unions, conciliation and arbitration, occupational diseases and work injuries, old age pensions and maternity benefits for blue-collar workers, and old age pensions and life insurance for white-collar workers.

Why did the Congress legislate on these specific topics and not on the total package of social legislation as proposed either by Alessandri or by the Conservative intellectuals? According to President Alessandri, the Joint Congressional Commission charged with the study of the labor bills had examined and approved only certain sections, and those were the ones enacted by the Congress. Thus, the legislation approved under military pressure reflected neither the conservative nor the liberal approach to the social question, but a compromise worked out by the Commission.

It is not clear whether the military knew the exact content of the social legislation approved by Congress on the night of 8 September. Given the speed of the events, it is very likely that they assumed that the Congress was approving the whole bill. What is clear is that the country had the desired legislation as a result of military pressure.[44] Because of their relevance to this work, among the bills approved by Congress, the unionization and social security bills deserve special attention.

The Joint Congressional Commission had spent two years deliberating the matter of unionization. Both the conservative and the liberal bill proposed a restricted and controlled union structure. However, the conservatives argued for a plant union system dependent on the employer, and the liberals argued for a craft union structure controlled by the state. The 1924 law was a compromise between these two bills. For the blue-collar workers, it established a hybrid system of plant unions dependent on the employer and the state, and for the white-collar workers a system of craft unions dependent only on the state. Thus the basic organizational distinction between blue- and white-collar workers found in all the future labor and social security legislation was the result of a compromise between the political elites. Consequently, the more radical and combative blue-collar sector was permitted to unionize only under a very well-controlled situation, while the middle-class white-collar worker was allowed a larger degree of freedom.

By establishing the plant union as the basic unit of the blue-collar workers organization, the legislators ensured the creation of an atomized system. It depended on the state, which had to authorize the existence of the union, and the employer, who had to provide part of the funds. Moreover, by establishing the division between blue- and white-collar workers, and by creating a craft-based system for the latter, the legislators ensured that the two groups could never organize under the same banner. As one observer put it:

> It is most striking how [the law] faithfully combined the most viable restrictive features of each of the original proposals. Thus, the corporate features of obligatory unionism, weighted voting by workers with seniority, compulsory arbitration, and the prohibition of industry-wide federations in the conservative proposal was combined with the ban on public employees unionization, division of workers into separate industrial and employees unions and meticulous state control of union elections, finances and strikes procedures drawn from the liberal proposal.[45]

In brief, the 1924 legislation created an atomized union system, divided along social and occupational lines. Under the system the national federations could exercise only limited functions and were prohibited from negotiating labor contracts or declaring strikes.

Three of the 1924 laws established the basis of the subsequent Chilean social security system. Law 4051 established the Caja de Seguro Obligatorio, the Obligatory Insurance Fund. It created a compulsory social insurance system for blue-collar workers that provided old age and disability pensions, medical benefits, and burial expenses. Law 4052 created the Caja de Empleados Particulares, the White-Collar Workers Fund, which provided retirement pensions and life insurance to all white-collar workers in the private sector. Law 4053 reiterated the employer's responsibility in cases of occupational accidents, and his obligation to bear the burden of proof, adding the same provisions in cases of occupational diseases.

Summary

The economic growth generated by the "outward-oriented export model" created a large working class and set the basis for the growth of a new urban-based middle class. Following changes in the world market for nitrate, this model challenged the power of the oligarchy and its unity, bringing the government to a total standstill while the entire social fabric was being eroded by the crisis.

The need for change was manifest in 1920 with the formation of the Liberal Alliance and the election of Arturo Alessandri, a candidate who had campaigned for constitutional and labor reforms, which would effectively transform both the role and functions of the state. But in order to carry out these reforms it is imperative to have control of the state, and Alessandri—just like Salvador Allende in the 1970s—only controlled the Executive branch. Furthermore, the division in Congress did not run along party lines, but among those who perceived the need for reform as the only avenue available to avert the entire elimination of the capitalist state, and those who wanted to maintain the society frozen in the colonial structure. Just like in the 1970s Congress was polarized and paralyzed.

As was going to happen some fifty years later, social forces outside the state, such as labor and the intellectuals, had been able to set the stage for the reforms by publicly stressing the seriousness of the socioeconomic problems. In both the 1920s and the 1970s these forces were able to alter and obstruct social life and the production process through strikes and violent actions. However, neither the intellectuals nor the labor movement had the strength to shift the balance of power in their favor.

In the final analysis the shift in the balance of power resulted from military action, namely from forces within the state structure, which pressured Congress to pass the social and economic legislation of 1924 and the constitutional reform of 1925. These laws were, nevertheless, the product of an oligarchic congress guided by its desire to maintain an exclusionary political organization. As will be shown in the following chapters, the application of these exclusionary laws in a competitive, pluralist political system determined a very particular form of interaction between the working-class organizations and the state.

As Stephen Skowroneck has argued in his study of the United States, "State building is a process basic to any nation's political development. Government officials seeking to maintain power and legitimacy try to mold institutional capacities in response to an ever-changing environment. Environmental stimuli, official responses and new forms of government are the basic elements of the state building process."[46] Chile, during the first twenty years of this century, experienced this type of process. The analysis of this period shows how the combined effect of international economic changes, class conflict, and political paralysis led to the crisis of the 1920s. This crisis, in turn, prompted a process of state building formalized in the 1925 Constitution and in the social and labor policies of this period.

The crisis had also threatened the narrative and consequently the power of those who had forged that narrative. The Chilean family was divided. It was critical then

> to include millions of people previously defined as 'huachos' (illegitimate children) by the elite: peasants, agricultural workers, miners, urban workers, artisans, and the new middle class which were not in the mythical 'conciliación original'. The conflict could no longer be restricted to the struggle for the control of the state and its prebends, nor could it be restricted to the factions or parties of the 'gente decente' (the decent people), nor to the debates about the political power of the Catholic Church. What was required now was a much broader social and political reconciliation than the one that existed in the nineteenth century. A political reconciliation that was sought after all throughout the twentieth century and that was never fully achieved.[47]

The new social legislation played a pivotal role in this process. To the extent that the Chilean elite was not ready to fully share power with the *rotos*, the policies were an effective way of restoring order and social peace and of including the emerging groups into the political system without losing economic power. The narrative was expanded as well. According to the new rhetoric the benefits of the state should be expanded to all. How much the rich and the poor would get was another matter.

CHAPTER 2

Populist Politics, 1924–1964

The modern political system of Chile was created by the 1925 Constitution, which in practice involved the establishment of a populist form of state and the adoption of the import substitution model of economic development. This chapter will examine the functions of the Chilean state after the 1930s and its interactions with major social forces, especially the labor movement and the political parties.

Populism, which was the dominant political model in the region during this period, was characterized by the formation of a broad multi-class coalition based on the selective incorporation and co-optation of sectors of the bourgeoisie, the middle, and the working classes. In Chile, unlike Argentina and Brazil, populism developed within the framework of a democratic political regime based on a representative political party system. Thus, selected incorporation of different social groups took place through multiple political parties and the formation of political alliances, and not through one multiclass party or political movement, as was the case in the other Southern Cone countries.

Regularly held elections and multiple parties and coalitions made Chile's populism more flexible than that of its neighbors, and in the long run, the representative system gave groups within the urban coalition the chance to participate. This type of populism, however, led to two related political and economic phenomena: the growth of the socioeconomic functions of the state and a continuous inflationary process. The state expanded its functions because it had the obligation to provide for certain public needs, while multiple pressures exercised

19

by the different groups generated a constant increase in public expenditures. In an economy of limited resources, inflation, the further fragmentation of the pressure groups, and the continuous growth of the socioeconomic functions of the state were unavoidable consequences.

From 1924 until 1973 the ever-expanding functions of the state were at the center of the sociopolitical narrative. The expansion of political and socioeconomic rights were defined as a form of political and economic inclusion. The state through its social policies was asked to fulfill the myth of social unity and harmony, but the very nature of the system determined that the myth could only be partially fulfilled.

The Political System of Chile

The military action of 1924, which started as a movement aimed at improving the economic situation of the military, soon became a movement geared toward solving Chile's major social and political problems. The military demanded a total reform of the constitutional structure. After the passage of basic socioeconomic legislation, Congress was dissolved and President Alessandri resigned, only to return from exile the following year after the military movement came under the control of Major Carlos Ibañez. Both Alessandri and Ibañez, even when they held different views about the nature of the political regime, were committed to constitutional reform as the only way to prevent the collapse of the existing structure of domination. Since only a few politicians understood the real dangers of the situation, the process of constitutional reform was plagued by the same political problems that had paralyzed the Congress in previous years. Only threats of continued military intervention stimulated changes in the political structure.

Despite the democratic nature of the new constitution, the military, and especially Carlos Ibañez, dominated Chilean politics for the next ten years. According to Nunn, "the new Constitution and the return to full constitutionality had all been the result of Army actions. The new legislation affected only the paper on which it was printed; the Constitution meant little more."[1] Ibañez had put an end to oligarchic politics in Chile, replacing it with a populist system which operated on the basis of an urban, multiclass, political alliance.[2]

The Constitutional Framework

In 1925 a commission appointed and chaired by Arturo Alessandri wrote a new constitution which shifted the balance of Chilean political power from the Congress to the Executive. It was approved in a plebiscite supervised by the Armed Forces and, not surprisingly, opposed by the political parties.

Several legal restrictions reduced the power of the Congress. Deputies and senators were prohibited from accepting Cabinet positions and individuals employed by the national government were barred from sitting in the Congress. Congress lost the power to overturn the Cabinet and to immobilize the government by refusing to enact the budget, which had been a common occurrence under the 1933 Constitution. Only the President could propose amendments to the budget, changes to the political or administrative division of the country, and increases in the gratuities to the personnel in the public administration, government agencies, and semi-public institutions.

Other significant political reforms were the direct popular election of the President, extension of the presidential mandate to six years and the prohibition of consecutive terms, the enfranchisement of all literate males over twenty-one years of age, and the creation of a constitutional tribunal to review election results.

Despite the shift of constitutional power toward the Executive, both branches of Congress retained important prerogatives that allowed them to keep a central role not only in the legislative process, but in conducting affairs of the state in general. Furthermore, the new Constitution recognized the role of the political parties in national politics, establishing an electoral system based on overlapping and varied terms for elected offices. In practice, this assured that the same political party could not control the executive and the legislative branches at the same time. Elections were governed by a system of proportional representation, and in the presidential elections, if no candidate received an absolute majority of the popular vote, the Constitution assigned Congress the responsibility to choose the President from the two candidates who had received the highest number of votes.

The new Constitution provided a stable framework for the Chilean political system. It allowed new social forces to be represented and new political participants to be included through the political party system, while allowing the old ones to retain a large degree of political and economic power. Stability, a major feature of Chile's political system during the following years, resulted from the formal organization of the government, which combined a presidential system and a congress that retained a central political role.

Political stability and democracy also rested in a complex legislative process that allowed both branches of government, and both chambers of Congress, to intervene repeatedly in the legislative process. While this process facilitated political accommodation and compromise among contending parties and interest groups, it also contributed to the inefficiency of the system, creating large amounts of often incoherent and particularistic legislation. In the long run, these "checks and balances" contributed to the durability of the democratic system, but paralyzed effective government, obstructed reforms, and allowed, at best, incremental changes. The process of conciliation and accommodation which this system involved explains the survival of the political organization for almost forty years; hence the growth of the functions of the Chilean state.

Underneath the formal political stability, however, there was constant tension between the two branches of government and among the different societal groups. Tensions between the branches of government were mostly the result of the manipulations of the electoral system purposely carried out by the political right—formed by the Conservative and Liberal parties—and the nature of the electoral system adopted by the Constitution. In fact, the right managed throughout the period to maintain control over the Congress through two mechanisms that gave the traditional parties a large congressional representation, the control of the rural vote and the apportionment of congressional seats.

Direct control of the peasant vote was an uncontested reality until the 1958 electoral reform that established a single ballot system. Before 1958 each party printed its own ballots and distributed them among their supporters. The landowners gave the peasants already marked votes favoring the landowner's candidate, denying them access to other ballots.[3] Such coercion assured the Liberals and Conservatives a strong representation in Chile's Congress and power to veto presidential programs.

Manipulation of apportionment further enhanced the significance of the rural vote. The Constitution established that one deputy be elected for every 30,000 inhabitants, obligating Congress to reapportion itself after each new census. Fearing that as a consequence of urbanization, the right's rural strongholds would lose their majority representation to the leftist-controlled cities, the parties of the right, with the support of the radicals, stopped approving the census in the 1930s. For the purpose of congressional apportionment, the distribution and number of deputies that existed in the 1920s were thus maintained until 1973. The distortion between representation and distribution of the population resulted in the gross under-representation of the urban industrial areas and the over-representation of the rural areas. For instance, in the third district of Santiago, an area densely populated mainly by industrial workers, the ratio was one deputy per 195,000 inhabitants.[4]

The modified D'Hont system of proportional representation used in municipal and congressional elections was another facet of the electoral system that fostered conflict between the branches of government. Since it encouraged electoral pacts and coalitions on which the Executive had to rely for passage of legislation, it constituted a de facto limitation on presidential power.[5]

In brief, while presidential elections tended to reflect the existing political realities, congressional representation reflected the realities of the past and served as a bastion of the right, impeding socioeconomic and political reforms.

Political Parties: Ideologies and Clientelism

Much has been written about the political party system of Chile, its complexity, depth, and relationships with interest groups. Although a detailed history of the system is well beyond the purpose of this work, it is important to stress the scope of this system and its impact on the political economy of the country.

The Chilean party system covered the entire political spectrum. To the existing Conservative, Liberal, Radical, and Communist parties of the nineteenth and early twentieth century, two other parties were added during this period: the Socialist Party, founded in 1933, and the Christian Democratic Party, founded in 1957.

Founded by a group of middle-class intellectuals under the leadership of Salvador Allende, the Socialist Party competed with the Communists for the representation of the working class. The socialists stood for anti-imperialism, anti-capitalism, and anti-communism; they were Marxists and nationalists, and they embraced a populism of a very special nature.[6] In the words of Paul Drake, "There was a constant tension between socialism and populism which was revealed in their incessant contradictions, conflicts, and divisions over ideology, membership, and methods. . . . Never resolved was the party's ambivalence toward the means to reach power and create socialism."[7] As the experience of both the Popular Front government and the Allende government demonstrated, once a party beset by all these contradictions achieved power, the tensions destroyed the party itself, not to mention its ability to conduct the government.

The Christian Democrats owed their birth to a group of young Catholics who had abandoned the Conservative Party in disagreement with its social policy. The group found theological inspiration in the writings of the Church, especially the encyclicals *Rerum Novarum* and *Quadragesimo Anno*, and in the French Catholic thinker Jacques Maritain.[8] The ideology of the party is clearly stated in its *Declaración de Principios*, which holds that "the state is not the concentration of one class in the center of power, but the juridical expression of all the communities that form the society."[9] The document also points out that both the professional associations and the unions are essential to the common good and for full development of the human person, and it gives these organizations the responsibility for transforming the structures of society while maintaining a respect for the law and the democratic system. The final goal is to obtain a society in which work becomes a vehicle for human fraternity and not a sign of injustice.[10]

Thus, the Chilean political spectrum had parties ranging from the far right to the far left. Paraphrasing Charles Anderson, one can say that the political system of Chile became a paradigmatic case of a "living museum," "because all the forms of western political authority in western historic experience continue to exist and operate"; and because "politically pragmatic democratic movements devoted to the Constitution and the Welfare-State ideals of the 20th century, stood side by side with a traditional, and semi-feudal landed aristocracy";

and because "new power contenders could always be admitted to the system, as long as they did not jeopardize the position of the established contenders."[11] But Chile fits only partially in the framework sketched by Anderson. A distinctive feature of Chile's political order was that social struggles took place within the political system and not outside its boundaries.

In a context characterized by a narrow economic base, a growing social base, and a political order that absorbed social struggles within itself, the political organization became flexible and adaptable. In turn, this resulted in large amounts of legislation created to satisfy the contenders' needs, and ultimately was responsible for the growth of the state. In a nutshell, the containment of social struggle within the political system produced an overdeveloped political organization, characterized by a sophisticated juridical structure and the overexpansion of state activity in the economic and social spheres. This process reached a critical point in the late 1960s and early 1970s when the economic structure proved unable to cope with the demands generated by the increasing number of power contenders.

Examining the party system relations with the society at large, it is important to note that the parties were basically coalitions of various clienteles; they constituted crucial links between given groups, or even certain individuals, and the state. Each party could be broadly classified in terms of specific social classes: the left with the blue-collar workers; the right with the land-owning class and the industrial bourgeoisie; and the center with the white-collar workers, civil servants, and other urban, middle-class groups. But political clientelism was a very complex phenomenon, since the clienteles of a given party or faction could not be collectively characterized by occupational or class lines. They penetrated the entire social fabric. As J. Samuel Valenzuela argues:

> The overall clustering of clientelistic linkages along class lines were by no means clear cut. The intensity of electoral competition led the parties to attempt an expansion of their bases of support by establishing new clientelistic ties. This was done, first, by articulating new demands and interests. Party militants, for example, would mobilize previous disorganized segments of the population in order to obtain a specific goal. . . . Second, clientelistic ties

were expanded by capturing the representation of "vindicationists" demands of existing groups. This was done, for instance, by legislating certain benefits in the particularistic manner (typically in social security areas). . . . These differential attachments offered convenient channels for a party in power to grant benefits, which could not be given to all the groups due to the budgetary limitations.[12]

To a large extent, then, the relationships between political parties and social groups were determined by the nature of the Chilean economy. Particularly important was the unequal distribution of income, which precluded large sectors of the population from obtaining the minimum resources required to subsist. Every individual had to use all possible resources to get a larger share of the economic pie, which reinforced the multiple societal divisions captured by the political parties. The lack of a clear clustering of clientelistic ties created an internally unstable political system in which parties could not maintain their strength for a long period of time since they could not satisfy the expectations of all the groups co-opted by the party. Dissatisfaction with the behavior of the victorious party prompted groups to move elsewhere within the political organization in search of better luck, creating a constant political turnover.[13]

Distinctive to the Chilean party system was a combination of ideology and clientelism. Ideology gave each party a program and a blueprint to solve all the problems of society; these programs were reproduced in all the party organizations. Clientelism gave the parties their political support. The best example of the combination of ideological and clientelistic commitments was provided by the parties of the left which, at the rhetorical level, paid due respect to Marxist ideology and the notions of class struggle and revolution, while at the political level pursued the same clientelistic, co-optive practices of the other parties.

Clientelistic politics were reflected in the legislative process, which by the end of this period had become almost entirely devoted to the solution of particular problems, the concession of special benefits, or exemptions to general obligations. Social security policies, among others, became an intrinsic part not only of the clientelistic political organization, but also of the entire political system facilitating the continuation of the political game.

The Growth of the Chilean State in the Mid-Twentieth Century

Although the origins of the economic role of the Chilean state can be traced back to the 1850s,[14] in its modern form it was initiated in the late 1920s and was closely linked to the actions of the two most important political figures of the time, Arturo Alessandri and Carlos Ibañez. While Alessandri's ideas had been at the core of the new constitution, its implementation was carried out by Major Carlos Ibañez. A political conflict between Alessandri and Ibañez, his Minister of War, made Alessandri decide six months after his election, that since he could not control his cabinet he would leave the country for Europe. In October 1925 Emilio Figueroa, a member of the traditional political elite, was elected president, but Ibañez remained as Minister of War and as the real power behind the throne. In 1927, Ibañez forced Figueroa's resignation and became president in a carefully orchestrated election.

Ibañez' "populist authoritarianism" combined limited repression and developmentalist policies. He eliminated the FOCH, reorganized the workers into state-regulated syndicates, put down communist and anarchist movements, and sent political enemies of both the right and the left into exile.[15] He saw himself as a "modernizing *caudillo*" along the lines of Mussolini and Primo de Rivera and launched a large number of public works programs, a dramatic expansion of the educational system, and a tariff and credit policy geared to promote industrial and agricultural growth.[16] Ibañez' policies were geared to support the middle class and to destroy the power of the elite. He believed that the state had the responsibility of transforming the society and that the "government existed to organize the productive forces that are the only solid bases for regenerating a national economy."[17] The initial success of the program kept unemployment low and wages rising, but the country's vulnerability to the changes in international markets put an end not only to Ibañez' developmentalist approach, but also to his regime. Ibañez left power in mid-1931 in the aftermath of a massive strike movement. The stock market crash engulfed Chile and the rest of Latin America in the largest economic crisis of the twentieth century and resulted in political instability throughout the region.

The full implementation of the developmentalist approach began during the Pedro Aguirre Cerda administration (1938–1941). The adoption of the import substitution model of economic development and the creation of the Chilean Development Corporation (CORFO) entailed the application of what the Radical Party called the national developmentalist approach. This, in turn, was combined with the political approach symbolized by their slogan, *"pan, techo y abrigo"* (bread, roof and protection), which was geared to expand the base of the party among the lower and middle classes.[18] In the words of the president of the party at the time, Florencio Duran, the party's most important accomplishment had been to initiate in 1938 a new process of both political and economic democracy.[19] However, this attempt was incomplete at best.

By the late 1960s the state had acquired a preponderant economic role, owning either totally or partially some of the most important sectors of the economy such as copper, steel, petrochemicals, telecommunications, petroleum, and electricity. The role of the Chilean state went well beyond the ownership of key industrial activities. The state, through the Central Bank, controlled imports and exports. Through the State Bank it controlled over half of the credit available to the private sector. The state set minimum wages and salaries as well as prices for most consumer goods. The public sector invested heavily in infrastructure and utilities and provided a wide array of social services. By the late 1960s the state controlled 40 percent of total GDP and over 70 percent of Gross Domestic Investment.[20] But neither public investment nor public capital accumulation remained in the public sector; instead they were transferred to the private sector.

The state also had a tremendous importance as both a direct and an indirect source of employment. Given the expansion of state activities, the size of the bureaucracy tripled between 1925 and 1965, and by 1969 the public sector employed some 250,000 persons, almost 10 percent of the labor force. This sector experienced steady growth, especially during the years of the Popular Front and of the Radical governments (1938–1952), and during the Christian Democratic period (1964–1970).[21]

The hyper-growth of the state was a byproduct of the growth of the middle class in a context of expanding educational opportunities, an environment which provided limited economic opportunities, and an active political party system. It was also a byproduct of the ideology that had inspired the 1925 Constitution which called for the expansion of the functions of the state in response to the changing demands from the society. The bureaucracy continued to grow despite the promises of every president to reduce it.

What is most striking is that the bureaucratic structure reproduced within itself the general characteristics of the society. In practice, the bureaucracy was divided in two categories or classes: the "privileged services," *Servicios Privilegiados*, and the "postponed services," *Servicios Postergados*. The Privileged Services were those that controlled key economic activities, i.e., Minister of Finance, Central Bank, and the Internal Revenue Service. Given the importance of their activities, and the reduced number of people involved in them, their employees enjoyed higher salaries and better social security benefits. Typical Postponed Services were the Postal Service and Education, which employed large numbers of people, did not have direct access to the law makers, and consequently provided lower salaries and benefits. Moreover, just as in the society at large, the differences between the groups generated constant pressures on the political organization for an improvement of economic conditions. This process was known as *nivelación de salarios*.

A similar process of stratification occurred in the decentralized sector of the bureaucracy, comprising those institutions that administratively belonged to the public sector, but operated with an independent budget. The decentralized institutions did not obey any uniform criteria, but were the consequence of the expanding state adapting itself to various social and economic activities. In order to be effective and competitive, the state had to create agencies that, without losing the character of public institutions, could also achieve the heterogeneous objectives typical of the private sector.[22] The multifarious Chilean bureaucracy became the focal point of political, social, and economic development, providing both services and employment to the middle class, which was the central faction in the urban coalition that sustained successive governments throughout the period. Here it is important to note that the social service administration was the fastest growing sector in the bureaucracy.

From an economic viewpoint, the role of the state was equally important. It performed all sorts of economic activities, becoming the engine of the process of import substitution and of industrial development. In the process, the larger goal of social integration through the actions and policies of the state was forgotten and became more a myth than a reality. Instead, the state began to reinforce the social cleavages.

Import substitution industrialization was the central economic policy, but unlike other Latin American countries, in Chile, the process of import substitution was carried out with the support of the bourgeoisie since it reinforced their preponderant economic position. The analysis of the creation of CORFO, the central economic agency in the industrialization process, shows the kind of arrangements that became typical of Chile's populist state.

The Popular Front government of President Aguirre Cerda wanted, initially, to create a development institution financed only by new taxes and managed and controlled by the state, but this project was soundly rejected by Congress. A second proposal, which relied on presumed foreign loans instead of internal financing and had an administrative structure that incorporated the private sector, received the support of the right and was approved by Congress. The new structure did not involve an outright expansion of state power, but took a compromise form in which the enterprises created by CORFO would be managed by a tripartite board comprised of government representatives, private sector representatives, and a minority representative of labor.[23] The key problem, nonetheless, was the financing of the new activities. As Michael Monteón asks, how was Chile going to realize its nationalistic hopes while depending on U.S. government loans?[24]

The approved plan marked the beginning of a very special relationship between the private and public sectors. The private entrepreneurs, through their representatives in CORFO, and later in the enterprises created by CORFO, exercised a large degree of influence in the formulation and implementation of economic policy in general, and industrial policy in particular. Moreover, the law which created CORFO stipulated that once the enterprises had become profitable, the board could decide between maintaining them in the public sector or transferring them to the private sector. Good examples of the form in which CORFO operated were the steel and energy industries. The steel industry was developed by the state with foreign capital, managed by CORFO until profitable, and then transferred to private control during the second Ibañez administration. In the energy area, CORFO devised a permanent association between the public and the private sectors through the creation of two different enterprises: ENDESA, a public corporation charged with the production of energy, and CHILECTRA, a private corporation charged with the distribution of energy throughout the country. ENDESA provided energy at cost to CHILECTRA, which in turn could distribute it to its customers at a profit.[25]

In brief, the process of import substitution neither excluded nor reduced the power of Chile's economic elite. On the contrary, a symbiotic relationship developed in which the state became responsible for the accumulation of capital while the private entrepreneurs could control and profit from the state activity.[26] President Aguirre Cerda summarized the situation in 1941, saying that Chilean working classes were "just as poor . . . and just as miserable as when I became President."[27]

Chile's Economy and the Nature of the Inflationary Process

Few economies in the world were studied as much as the Chilean economy. Its poor performance and often contradictory problems received multiple and contradictory prescriptions, ranging from purely macroeconomic solutions to broad sociopolitical ones and from the exclusively domestic to the international. At the center of this debate was a persistent set of economic problems which, in the long run, undermined the economy and the polity.

Basic economic problems such as inflation, low rate of economic growth, low rate of capital accumulation, dependency on copper, dependency on foreign capital, and unequal distribution of income remained the same during this period. Aggregate economic growth, for instance, was among the lowest in the world. After a tremendous decline during the Great Depression, the growth of the per capita GDP averaged only about 2 percent a year between 1937 and 1952; it decreased to 0.3 during the mid-1950s, then increased to 2.3 percent in the mid-1960s, well below the average rate of growth for the less developed countries.

Other structural problems remained equally refractory. The share of the agricultural sector in the total GNP remained very low and declining, while the service sector kept growing. Chile maintained a continuous dependence on copper and continued to rely on a system of high tariffs, quantitative restrictions, and other protectionist devices. The external sector of the economy was constantly distorted by an overvalued exchange rate that necessitated a number of exchange controls.[28] Overvaluation impaired the growth and diversification of exports and encouraged imports, reinforcing the reliance on a complex system of trade tariffs.

In the area of public finance, tax collection lagged permanently behind expenditures; borrowing from the Central Bank became the way to finance the deficit. Mamalakis argues that Chile's poor economic performance was the result of the upper and middle classes' refusal to finance public expenditures. From 1952 to 1973 the Congress repeatedly rejected tax reforms and tax increases proposed by the Executive.[29] Constant deficits created a chaotic fiscal environment, which was further degraded by a non-existent monetary policy. Aside from the financial requirements of the state, the growth of the money supply was never a concern. Thus the central government deficit, the decentralized agencies, and the public enterprises were financed in large part via monetary expansion. This, in turn, permitted the public sector to obtain from the private sector the resources it was unable or unwilling to tax away directly.[30] In spite of the seriousness of these problems all of them were secondary to the socioeconomic issue perceived as central by all Chileans, the issue with the greatest direct impact on their pockets and their minds: inflation.

Inflation also had stable and unstable aspects. Stability was reflected in the fact that for thirty years Chile had double-digit inflation every year, except 1960 and 1961. Inflation also followed a very predictable pattern within different administrations: in the first two years of each administration between 1932 and 1973, inflation either remained under control or declined, only to soar near the end of the first half of the administration. Instability was found at the policy level as well as in consumer prices. Expansionary policies were followed by stabilization programs; new policies and theories were easily adopted and abandoned.

Modern inflation made its appearance in Chile during the Popular Front administration of Pedro Aguirre Cerda. At this juncture two significant phenomena were taking place: economically, the country was readjusting its economic structure to changes in the international economic system; politically, the 1925 Constitution was being fully applied for the first time. As a result of the latter, the repressed sociopolitical pressures latent since the beginning of the century found expression in a number of socioeconomic policies designed to employ and protect the urban groups. Containing massive wage and salary increases, bank credit expansion, and Central Bank credits to state-sponsored development agencies, these policies were geared to benefit both the entrepreneurial sector and the working class. In turn, these policies created large fiscal deficits and generated greater inflationary pressures.[31]

The complete lack of an anti-inflationary policy during the entire period can be explained by the same socioeconomic factors. Aguirre Cerda's commitments to urban groups made anti-inflationary policies unthinkable. Furthermore, the President believed that the best way to increase production was to increase effective demand through wage and salary increases.[32] In fact, instead of pursuing anti-inflationary policies, all the radical governments tried to counter only the effects of inflation. Government interventions in the pricing system set minimum wages and salaries for the urban workers and established automatic wage and pension readjustments for specific sectors of the working class.

Toward the end of the Radical years the Gónzalez Videla government tried to control the labor movement through the imprisonment and exile of its leaders and at the same time halt inflation. These attempts were violently resisted by the blue- and white-collar workers and particularly by civil servants whose ties to political parties allowed them to undermine the stabilization policy as Congress granted them automatic salary and pension readjustments. Ultimately the government's right center political alliance was replaced with a left center coalition.

Ibañez' massive victory in 1952 was founded on hopes that he would control inflation with the same forcefulness he had shown in dealing with other problems in the past.[33] These hopes were unfulfilled. Inflation reached a record high of 80 percent in 1955. At that time the country was suffering the impact produced by the end of the Korean War and the resultant depression in the copper market, a situation that the Chilean government had not anticipated and which produced a large deficit in the budget. Politically speaking, the Ibañez victory had been the result of his personal appeal and popularity. However, once in power, he had only two alternatives, either to assume dictatorial powers and deal with inflation in an authoritarian manner or to follow the rules of the democratic game, which in this case involved satisfying the demands of the numerous groups that formed his constituency. Ibañez, a master of the political game, was able to buy time for a while through the manipulation of political friends and enemies alike. But in the long run, the pressures proved to be uncontrollable; inflation soared and violence increased. Rumors of plots and counter-plots dominated the political scene. In the final analysis, both the political and the economic crises were solved through the formation of a new political coalition, the arrival of a foreign economic mission (the Klein-Saks Mission), and the formulation of a stabilization program. The new economic program brought inflation under control but the costs of the program were borne by the working class. Throughout the period Chile had neither growth nor stability.[34]

The victory of Jorge Alessandri (son of former president Arturo Alessandri) signaled a return to power of the Liberal and Conservative parties and a new attempt to change Chile's political economy. The two main goals of the Alessandri development program were stabilization and growth. The Alessandri team understood inflation not as the result of excessive demand, as argued by the Klein-Saks Mission, but as a result of insufficient supply and excessive state intervention. The solution, then, was to free the economy of the controls imposed in the last twenty years, reduce state intervention, decrease taxes, and provide incentives to increase production and productivity.

Despite a firm belief in the capacity of the private sector to reactivate the economy, the government expanded public investment to provide the initial stimulus. Again, foreign loans and public borrowing from the Central Bank provided the money for the public investment program which was implemented by the private sector. After a short successful period, the program began to show some major flaws. By October 1962 it had to be abandoned because it generated new inflationary pressures, creating the stimulus for another political realignment.[35]

The economic crisis left serious social and economic consequences in its aftermath. Two years away from the end of the presidential term the political forces began to realign and prepare for the upcoming elections. The major political moves took place around the Christian Democratic Party (PDC), the winner of the 1961 congressional elections. After the right's inability to solve the basic economic ills of the country, key urban groups such as professionals, businessmen, and entrepreneurs began to look upon the PDC and its program as the best alternative

What produced inflation in Chile? One can distinguish at least three different schools of thought. To some inflation was the result of structural conditions of the economy, such as the low productivity of the agricultural sector, dependent industrial production, and the inflexible and regressive nature of the tax system. Consequently, anti-inflationary policies involved the implementation of structural reforms such as land and tax reform, and ultimately a readjustment of the pattern of integration in the international markets.[36] In the opinion of others, inflation was produced by the contradiction between a developed political system and an underdeveloped economic base, which, in the words of Anibal Pinto, "could not guarantee the fulfillment of the expectations produced by the democratic system." Thus, "the concrete economic manifestation of the aspirations generated by the democratic process is the urge of the ascendant groups to increase their income. The most probable consequence, in the case of a productive system that does not expand proportionately, is price increases."[37]

Moreover, in a context of *empate social* (social tie), in which there is an equilibrium of forces among the different political contenders (labor, landowners, industrialists) and a political structure which represents that equilibrium rather than any of the contending social groups, that structure is inevitably as weak as the labile, dynamic interplay of forces underlying it. The "system stimulates different groups to increase their nominal income, through different mechanisms, at different times, or to try to recuperate a former level [of income] from which they had been expelled by the pressure of other groups."[38]

Consistent with this approach is the notion of inflation as a substitute for civil war. The Chilean state, in this vein, mitigated the effects of those contradictions through a constant expansion of its activities and of the benefits it granted to the key political contenders. The central battles of this war were thus fought in the congressional arena and involved the distribution of wage readjustments and social security benefits for the working class and tax exemptions and credits

for the entrepreneurs. In this context, truly anti-inflationary policies
fully restructured the political organization and/or led to a profound
transformation of the economic base.

The socioeconomic history of Chile indicates that inflation produced permanent economic dislocations and constant political crisis.
Inflation created rigidities in the price system and impaired the formation of a capital market. Inflation brought about the proliferation of
exchange controls and protectionist measures which, in the long run,
only reinforced the inflationary spiral. Inflation produced in Chile a
distorted, chaotic, and expensive social security system. Inflation was
at the core of the political economy of each administration.

During this period inflation was closely tied to the nature of the political and economic system and the growing gap between a mythical
economic democracy and a very undemocratic economic reality, between the social narrative and the social reality, and between the imag-
ined and the real distribution of power. In this context, the policies that
generated that persistent inflation were not the result of a "social tie."
They were aimed at creating an image of democracy and equality, while
in reality the social and economic cleavages remained the same, or were
getting worse.

weak

Labor, the Unions, and Labor-State Relations

The labor law system created in 1924 neither responded to labor demands nor represented a unanimous desire to incorporate the working
class into civil society. Instead, it was a reaction on the part of the
state to the changing socioeconomic and political circumstances. If,
in the long run, labor acquired enough power to exert pressure over
the political system, this pressure was indirect and the result of unforeseen political events. The union structure and the industrial relations system created in the 1920s set the stage on which the Chilean
labor movement performed for the next fifty years.

The fragmented nature of the unionization system had a large
impact on Chilean politics and on the social security system. The 1924
law established a very complex and highly regulated union organization
characterized by vertical and horizontal divisions and by a large degree
of state control over the unions. The law distinguished between plant

unions formed at the factory or firm level and craft or professional unions formed by workers in a similar trade. By and large, plant unions were the organizational unit of the blue-collar workers, while craft unions were the organizational unit of the white-collar workers.

A plant union was formed by workers in each enterprise and its central function was to negotiate collective contracts with the entrepreneur. The unions could form federations, but the federations were not permitted to negotiate collective contracts or interfere with the relations between the plant union and the employer in any form. White-collar workers did not belong to the plant union, but to an appropriate craft union. This legal distinction between plant and craft union and the prohibition of the federations to negotiate collective contracts constituted the main weaknesses of the Chilean labor movement. The division reflected the desire of the ruling elite in 1924 to control and divide Chile's labor force.

Furthermore, the law closely regulated the aims of the industrial unions, indicating that "they will be institutions of mutual collaboration between the factors of production and, therefore, those organizations whose procedures impede discipline and order in the workplace will be considered contrary to the spirit and norms of the law."[39] The law adds that the unions can pursue social welfare objectives as long as they do not damage the interest of the enterprises. State control of union activities was exercised through a special Labor Inspection Office that dealt with the formation, functions, finances, elections, and termination of the unions.

The 1924 legislation was concerned also with the creation of an elaborate system of collective bargaining and conciliation designed to limit as much as possible the right to strike. In practice, the long conciliation process not only limited the right to strike, but made most strikes illegal. When they did occur, therefore, the labor leaders were legally liable. This system was also incorporated into the Labor Code and a new system of Labor Courts was created in 1931.

Inspired by a nineteenth-century paternalistic philosophy, the labor relations system created in 1924 effectively prevented the formation of a unified labor movement and disallowed any direct channel of communication between the labor movement and the political system. However, these measures did not eliminate the labor movement as a political contender, they only forced it to search for indirect routes to political influence. In the long run, and despite the formation of a unified confederation of workers, each of the multiple units that formed the labor movement developed its own connections with the state through the political parties.

The incorporation of those laws in the Labor Code in 1931 during the Ibañez administration did not change the basic principles and implications of those laws. The Labor Code incorporated in one text all the existing labor legislation, including Laws 4053–4059 passed on 8 September 1924. The new code expanded the scope of the laws by incorporating agricultural workers and domestics who had been excluded from the previous legislation. Over the years, none of the basic benefits provided by the Code were suppressed, but many were increased.

In fact, the enactment of the Labor Code in 1931 only reinforced the paternalistic nature of the labor legislation passed in the 1920s. This time the laws were reinforced by the authoritarian tendencies of the 1930s. However, despite the restrictive character of most of the labor legislation, the laws had managed to transform dramatically the relationship between workers and *patrones*. No longer was this a private contractual relationship between those two agents, now it was tripartite relationship in which the state played a significant role.

The Symbiotic Relationship: The Labor Movement and Political Parties

The initial reaction of the Federation of Chilean Workers (FOCH) to the enactment of the 1924 laws was negative. However, after Recabarren's death in December 1924 his successor, the communist leader Luis Cruz, argued that the workers should make use of the beneficial aspects of the laws such as regulation of working conditions, minimum wages, and social security benefits. The following ten years were very difficult for the labor movement. Political repression during the Ibañez administration, the effects of the stock market crash, chaos and instability, and a new Alessandri administration (1933–1938) which was quite unfriendly to the interest of labor excluded FOCH from having any real impact on Chilean politics. In 1936 the movement reappeared under a new umbrella organization, the Confederación de Trabajadores de Chile (CTCH).

The CTCH soon became the organized workers' arm of the newly created Popular Front, whose candidate, Pedro Aguirre Cerda, obtained the presidency in 1938.[40] But the life of the Popular Front was short. In January 1941 the socialists demanded the ousting of the communists from the Front. The refusal to expel them resulted in the withdrawal of the socialists. The CTCH, divided between the two parties, finally voted by a narrow margin to leave the Front. A few months later the president was abandoned by his own party. President Aguirre Cerda died while in office in 1941. The next president was Juan Antonio Ríos (1942–1946) who formed a coalition with the right-wing parties and maintained a strong anti-communist and anti-labor position. His successor Gabriel González Videla (1946–1952) managed to form a coalition with both the liberals and the communists, but soon veered to the right.

By 1947 the growth of the Communist Party, which had obtained 20 percent of the vote in the municipal elections, and its combative attitude at a time when the Soviet forces were consolidating their positions all over Eastern Europe and while the rest of the world was feeling the impact of the Cold War, prompted the passage of the so-called Law of Permanent Defense of Democracy (Law 8987), which outlawed the Communist Party and "cleansed" the labor movement from its "antisocial" elements. Law 8987, popularly known in Chile as *Ley Maldita* (the damn law), disintegrated the labor movement and, in the words of one analyst, "reflected the integral relationship between the Cold War, American foreign policy, and Chile's domestic developments."[41]

Syndicalism was reactivated years later by the white-collar workers who formed the Confederación de Empleados Particulares, which rapidly acquired significant power, in part due to their relationship with the government party (the radicals) and in part due to the vacuum left by the destruction of the CTCH by the government.[42] The civil servants also began a process of mobilization and organization during this period. Despite the fact that they were forbidden to form unions, they organized around associations, forming the Asociación de Empleados Fiscales and the Asociación de Empleados Semi-fiscales, representing the centralized and decentralized sectors of the bureaucracy respectively. Their close relationship with the Radical Party allowed them to define economic and social demands, especially social security benefits and automatic wage readjustments, and in general to have a large degree of political muscle.

The reunification of the blue-collar workers took place in 1953, after Ibañez' election, in the form of a new organization, the Central Unica de Trabajadores de Chile (CUT). After a short honeymoon in which the labor movement secured the passage of several laws granting social and economic benefits to blue-collar workers, relations between CUT and the government deteriorated rapidly. By 1954 the chaotic economic situation generated a cycle of inflation, anti-inflationary policies, strikes, mild repression, and social violence that dominated the political scene for the remainder of the Ibañez presidency.[43]

Neither the coalition that supported the Alessandri regime between 1958 and 1964 nor the policies pursued by that regime allowed the direct participation of the labor movement or promoted the improvement of the lot of the Chilean worker. As Alan Angell points out, "until 1970, government and unions, as if from mutual hostility, kept aloof . . . with very little contact except in the area of industrial conflict where the government was more likely to be seen as an ally of the employer than of the union."[44]

The relations of labor with the employer, meanwhile, were framed within the paternalism of the industrial relations system created in 1924. It allowed extensive employer interference in union affairs and provided no sanctions against those employers who did not obey its provisions. Not surprisingly, several surveys indicate that until the early 1960s, employers were quite happy with the system of labor relations.[45]

There is little doubt that throughout the period the role and actions of the labor movement were determined by the economic conditions of the working force, and especially by the inflationary process. The most pressing problem for the labor leaders was ensuring that wages rose at the same rate as the cost of living, as demonstrated by the fact that 52 percent of all the strikes between 1961 and 1970 were geared to obtain improvements in wages and salaries.[46] Thus, following Recabarren's two-pronged approach, the CUT simultaneously pursued the long-term destruction of the capitalist system through a revolution led by the organized workers. In the short run, the goal was to improve the living standards of the workers, using the working class's voting power.[47]

How successful were the unions in their struggle to improve the economic and living conditions of the Chilean workers? Data on overall distribution of income and variations in real wages and salaries indicate a dismal situation. For instance, average per capita income rose 30 percent between 1940 and 1954, while blue-collar per capita income rose only 9 percent for the same period as compared with 38 percent for white-collar workers and 43 percent for employers.[48] Regarding distribution of income, the data for the same period shows a pronounced inequality. In 1967, the medium income for a blue-collar worker was $100 per month, while the medium income for a white-collar worker was $327 and for an entrepreneur was $744 per month.[49]

The behavior of real wages and salaries did not help to improve the skewed distribution of income. On the contrary, both industrial and agricultural workers experienced a decline in their incomes since the real minimum wage for both declined by eight times between 1955 and 1970. In fact, both blue- and white-collar workers—but more the former than the latter—experienced a constant decline in real income between the early 1950s and 1970.[50] Faced with a divided labor movement, expanding political participation, and a competitive political system, the unions tried to counteract both their declining income and their political exclusion by developing what is best described as a symbiotic relationship with the political parties. The parties, for their part, were eager to co-opt electoral clienteles.

The mutual needs of parties and unions created a relationship that has to be analyzed at two different levels. At the national level, the Marxist-oriented CUT had a close relationship with the Socialist and the Communist parties. The white-collar workers' organizations first developed close ties with the Radical Party and, at a later stage, with the Christian Democratic Party. At a different level each union or specific sector within the working class developed its own relations with a political party or with a specific congressman who acted as broker between the union and the political organization at large. This brokerage function was exercised by politicians of all political colors who made this one of their most important political functions. The end result of the process was the incorporation of segments of the organized urban population in the state, the expansion of the functions and services of the state, and the passage of a mass of particularistic social legislation devoted to the protection of specific groups.

Summary

The enactment of the 1925 Constitution put an end to the political paralysis and socioeconomic chaos that had characterized the early twentieth century. From a political standpoint, it involved the partial incorporation of the urban political forces that had been demanding political rights since the late nineteenth century. From a socioeconomic standpoint it adopted a notion of a state charged with satisfying the growing needs of a fragmented and rapidly urbanizing society. The two most important policy programs of the state were the import substitution policies and the social security legislation.

Because of its multiclass nature, and because of the nature of the policies adopted, what developed in Chile was a form of populism. However, in Chile, populism operated under a democratic regime framed by the 1925 Constitution, which checked and balanced the power of both the Executive and the Congress, and a political party system in which ideological and clientelistic politics combined to give stability to the political regime, but not to the society. Here the populist model incorporated the more articulate sectors of the urban society, forming multiple and changing alliances into which different segments of the industrial bourgeoisie, the middle and the working class were incorporated through the different political parties. The state, in turn, had to provide a multiplicity of benefits and services to the most vocal and/or crucial elements of those coalitions.

In practice, the established elites adapted to the new situation by allowing proven power contenders into the political game as long as they did not seek to unseat established power groups.[51] As a result, the process of political incorporation demanded a constant expansion of the socioeconomic functions of the state.

Several analysts have argued that during this period Chile had an "Estado de Compromiso"[52] in which the inability of any social class to control the state by itself led to the constant incorporation of new social groups and constant transactions among them. I would argue that, although it is true that new groups were constantly incorporated into the system, there was in fact no real "compromise." On the contrary, because of the lack of a societal agreement, each politically mobilized group demanded more and more from the state, and since the economic foundations of the state were weak, this led to a vicious circle characterized by inflation, more socioeconomic demands, and a further expansion of the state functions. The key element in this process was the control of Congress by the political right.

In the final analysis, the 1925 Constitution had extended political and social rights to the middle and working classes, but in practice it had failed to reduce socioeconomic inequalities. On the contrary, inequalities continued and there was an even more pronounced process of social fragmentation. To what extent this fragmentation was augmented by the social security legislation is a fundamental question that I will answer in the following chapters. I will also show the negative impact that social fragmentation had on the overall political system.

The democratic principles of the 1925 Constitution provided new foundations for Chile's social narrative. The democratic ideology sustained by the Constitution and the dominant class highlighted Chile's uniqueness in the Latin American context. Chile, just like the rest of Latin America, had a democratic constitution, but unlike the rest of Latin America the Constitution served to create a stable and organized political regime. However, one must remember the origins of the Constitution to understand its real implications. The Constitution was perceived as a tool of the more enlightened sectors of the elite and the military to avoid the much feared social and political upheaval well described by President Arturo Alessandri. Thus, its purpose was to create a system of limited and segmented incorporation of critical groups. The others—the majority of the blue-collar workers, the peasants, and sectors of the middle class—hoped that sooner or later, they would benefit from the promise of democracy and unity. The electoral process and the political parties served as the channels through which the narrative was propagated. The gap between electoral promises and the capacity of the politicians to deliver them was constantly growing. The partial delivery of the promises had a series of interesting effects on the economy, on the political process, and on the society, fueling a process of social fragmentation and creating expectations that democracy and economic equality were one and the same. What is clear is that the system, just like the narrative, claimed to serve the entire population, but in reality served a minority.

CHAPTER 3

The Social Security System, 1924–1964

The Chilean social security system was both a natural byproduct of the political and economic system described in the previous chapter and a crucial element in the populist-oriented style of statecraft pursued throughout the period. Its development reflected the competitive nature of the political system and the urgent socioeconomic problems that affected the majority of the population. The system mirrored the fragmented nature of the society in general and of the working class in particular. Through clientelistic relationships developed with political parties different groups at different times obtained benefits which, in the long run, created a chaotic, discriminatory, fragmented social security system that protected only the most articulate groups within the urban-oriented coalition. The rest of the society had the hope that those benefits would be given to them in the future.

The conservative approach to social insurance of the 1924 legislature was better suited to the characteristics of the nineteenth century, oligarchic government that existed in Chile at the time of the law's passage than to the populist state of the mid-twentieth century. However, the conservative approach to social insurance was applied in the context of a political framework which stressed the social functions of the state. The resulting contradictions were reflected in the process of expansion of social security coverage, as well as in its inequities, and both were augmented by the import substitution model adopted in the 1930s that fostered the coexistence of a modern urban society with a pre-capitalist system of social relations in the countryside. All factors converged to create an unequal, fragmented social security system.

Here again the gap between rhetoric and reality was enormous. While the social security system was presented as providing benefits to all Chileans, the reality is that it provided very good benefits to those with power and few or none to the rest. However, this narrative was certainly helpful for expressing the image of unity and a state that served all Chileans.

This chapter is divided into four sections. The first takes up the historical threads delineated in chapter one and deals with the incipient social insurance system, the creation of the main funds, and the division between blue- and white-collar workers. The second section deals with the population covered by the system and the urban/rural dichotomy, stressing the overprotection of the urban and mining sectors and the underprotection of the rural sector. The third section deals with the financial structure and the benefits, stressing in both cases the inequities of the social security system, and the final section deals with the administrative structure and the costs of the social security system. It is important to note that the social security system was formed by the pension system (retirement, disability, and survivors), the family allowance system, health and maternity benefits, and workman's compensation. The emphasis in this book is on the evolution and comparison of the three major components of the system: pensions, family allowances, and health benefits.

The Birth and Development of the Modern Social Security System

Before 1925, Chilean social legislation was formed by a few isolated laws that dealt with selected, specific problems of the working class or favored groups, particularly the military. In fact, the first system of pensions was introduced in the 1810s for the widows and orphans of the men who fought in the wars of independence. In 1855, President Montt settled a series of army revolts by granting pensions to the loyal military. In 1858, the civil servants for the first time were granted the right to form a compulsory savings fund. In 1866 sailors obtained pensions and in 1881 the veterans of the War of the Pacific and their survivors became entitled to a pension. President Balmaceda, in 1888, established a system of retirement pensions for civil servants paid by the government.[1]

As shown in chapter two, the twentieth century brought massive social problems and strikes. Among early legislation was a 1911 law that granted retirement pensions to the powerful railroad workers. In 1915 the pension system for the military was enlarged and the first medical care system for the army and the navy was established. In 1916, the Workers' Accidents Law was enacted. This law established for the first time limited employer's liability and the employer's obligation of discharging the burden of proof. Although never fully applied, this law represented a major step in the evolution of the social laws in Chile. The following year, the Ley de Salas Cunas, the Nursery Law, obligated the employer to maintain a nursery in industries employing more than fifty women and to give mothers time off during the day to feed their babies.

The pension system for the railroad workers was expanded in 1918. It is important to note that this pension system was designed on an occupational basis and did not grant benefits to the more militant, and certainly needier, nitrate workers, but to the members of a mutualist society formed according to the civil law and accepted by the state. It provided a number of benefits to the conservative and well-organized railroad workers operating in Santiago.[2] Unlike the nitrate workers, this union stressed cooperation between the workers and the state and not conflict between workers and employers.

Two major bills dealing with the creation of a social insurance system were introduced to the Congress between 1921 and 1924: the liberal bill, part of the Labor Code bill presented by President Alessandri, and a conservative bill, introduced by the deputy and physician Exequiel González Cortés. The liberal bill was drafted entirely by Moisés Poblete, who relied heavily on foreign precedent and experience, particularly the French system.[3] The bill proposed the creation of a national insurance system, applicable to blue- and white-collar workers alike, that provided a full range of benefits for both the disabled and the able-bodied unemployed. The González Cortés bill, on the other hand, had been influenced by the German social insurance system and proposed only the establishment of a pension system for blue-collar workers.

Neither bill was ever discussed by the Joint Congressional Committee on Social Legislation, which had spent the previous three years discussing the union and conciliation sections of the Labor Code bill. Thus, when the young military officers sat in the galleries of the Congress rattling their sabers, the members of the Congress, pressed by the speed of the events, followed their conservative instincts and approved the González Cortés bill.[4] In fact, the clear philosophical differences between the bills certainly facilitated the decision of the Chilean congressmen. The adoption of the liberal bill would have meant the creation of a universal insurance system, whereas the adoption of the conservative bill, organized along occupational lines and with limited state involvement, satisfied the military pressure at the least political and economic cost.

The adoption of the beneficent and paternalistic provisions of the conservative bill was perfectly congruent with the rest of the social legislation approved by Congress on the same night. The new legislation reinforced the divisions within the working class, emphasized state control over the unions and the social security systems, and provided benefits only to selected groups within the working class. The conservative approach was certainly consistent with the autocratic political regime established in the 1830s, but in practice that political system was dying and the new laws were applied in the context of the multiparty system created by the 1925 Constitution.

There is little doubt that the members of the 1924 Congress totally misperceived the extent of military dissatisfaction with the current state of affairs and underestimated the final impact of their actions. What started as a movement geared to obtain prompt payment of the salaries of the military and other public servants developed first into a broad set of socioeconomic demands, and later into the reorganization of the entire political system, as manifested in the 1925 Constitution. In the area of social security, the result of military intervention was the passage of the Law 4054, which established a compulsory blue-collar worker's pension system, administered by the Caja de Seguro Obligatorio. In its original form, the blue-collar fund provided only old age pensions for those sixty-five years or older, disability pensions only in case of total disability, and illness and maternity benefits. The following year, under the temporary military government, four new funds were created: the Civil Servants Fund (Caja de Empleados Públicos), the White-Collar Workers Fund (Caja de Empleados Particulare), the Armed Forces Fund, and the Police Fund.[5]

The Civil Servants Fund was designed to provide pensions based on age and on years of service as well as a number of other benefits, such as health and maternity care, family allowances, and housing loans, just to name the most important. The White-Collar Workers Fund was originally conceived as a savings institution in which pensions, maternity and health benefits, family allowances, and other benefits were provided by the capital accumulated in the savings accounts. Common to the four funds created in 1925 were the notions of combined employer and employee contributions. The funds were administered by a body composed of representatives of the state and the insured and led by a board of directors appointed by the President. Thus, from the very beginning, the laws secured state intervention in the administration of the funds and divided the working class along occupational lines.

The conservative approach to labor legislation and social insurance was to be applied in the context of a multiparty system and not an autocratic state. Given the economic conditions described elsewhere, the result was a process of subdivision of the working class and of the original funds into various units, each seeking to expand the number and quality of the benefits received. The expansion was piecemeal by way of legislative concession of benefits to one small group after another. The central argument here is that the working-class groups tried to overcome political and economic exclusion by becoming the clients of the political parties.

Between 1925 and 1964 subdivision of the funds went well beyond the fourfold division established in 1924 and 1925. A dynamic evolved in which small subgroups separated themselves from the basic funds and secured the creation of special funds. Alternatively, they stayed within the main funds, but obtained special privileges, which amounted to having their own insurance system. The size and power of the group depended entirely on the political circumstances. A group could be as large and important as the copper workers, who belonged to the general Blue-Collar Workers Fund, but enjoyed a whole array of special benefits, or as small as the employees in the Race Track of Antofagasta, who had their own independent fund. This process of fragmentation of the social security system resulted in the creation of about 160 different social insurance funds, and a legal labyrinth of about "1600 laws, decrees, and regulations [which] remained uncompiled and uncoordinated."[6] Each of the different funds provided different benefits. The 160 funds included thirty-one systems of old age retirement, thirty of seniority retirement, thirty of disability, thirty-five of health/maternity, dozens of family allowance and unemployment compensation, and fifty-five of social welfare. In addition there were some 1,150 collective agreements which included clauses on social security. Most of the funds had their own regulations regarding administration, benefits, and financing.[7]

The history of the privileged situation of the copper workers regarding salary, fringe benefits, and social security benefits illustrates some of the characteristics of this process. The origins of the copper workers' trade union organization dates back to 1925, when the blue-collar workers of the largest copper mine, El Teniente, formed their first union. By the early 1950s about 90 percent of the work force in the largest mines was unionized and the unions had developed strong ideological and political ties with the Socialist and the Communist parties. In 1953, new legislation allowed the copper workers to form a *sindicato unido*, a unified blue- and white-collar workers union. According to the new, exceptional, legislation the workers and employees could not only join forces to form a single union, but they could present joint demands.[8] These demands were subjected to a special conciliation process, and workers and employees had the right to strike if the conciliation process failed. Given the critical role of these workers in the national economy it was in the best interest of the country to satisfy their demands. Consequently, workers would demand not only wage increases, but more and better social security benefits and more convenient financial arrangements. In fact, in this case, social security legislation was an integral part of the conciliation process and new benefits were incorporated into the labor contract. Subsequently, these arrangements would be ratified either by law or by decree.

One can justify the existence of a privileged system for the copper workers given the importance that copper mining had in the Chilean economy and the hard working and living conditions. But how can one explain that racetrack workers enjoyed one of the most generous systems? How can one explain that in fact there were at least six different funds for racetrack workers, each with its own pension system and its financial modalities, when the total number of people served by these funds amounted to less than 6,000? Legislation regarding these funds and the special benefits these employers enjoyed was dispersed among at least thirty laws and decrees. Where was the strategic importance of these workers? Or, should all this special legislation be traced back simply to the fact that Chilean legislators were very fond of horse races?[9]

In summary, the fragmentation can be traced to the conservative, paternalistic nature of the social security system which divided the working class along occupational lines; the contradiction between the nature of these policies and the formation of a populist state which operated under the aegis of the competitive political party system based on constantly changing political coalitions that allowed the incorporation of segments of the working class; and the poor economic condition of the working class.[10] In the ensuing pages there is an analysis of some of the most salient characteristics of the system. The reader will have to bear in mind that the extensive number of funds and systems of benefits does not allow a careful examination of the different benefits and modes of financing that existed in each fund. The only document that ever covered the whole was the report produced by the Prat Commission in 1964. The length of that report is 1,600 pages. However, by and large, all the funds provided four standard benefits: old age retirement pensions, disability pensions, maternity and health benefits, and family allowances. The ensuing analysis will focus on the cost and availability of those benefits.

The Population Covered: The Urban-Rural Dichotomy

Central to the expansion of the social security system were two dichotomies: the division between dependent and independent workers, and the urban-rural dichotomy. The Chilean system evolved toward the protection of the dependent, urban worker, while it excluded the independent worker and the rural laborer. Thus, by 1964, 92.4 percent of the wage earners (68.6 percent of the Economic Active Population [EAP]) were covered by the system. The remainder of the EAP, consisting mainly of the self-employed, was practically uncovered—only 2.6 percent of them were protected.[11] By 1970 Chile had a social security system that covered 69.6 percent of the total population and 69.5 percent of the EAP.[12]

Although the extent of the population covered was almost unparalleled in Latin America, the coverage hid a number of fundamental discriminations and inequities. Particularly important was the distribution of coverage among the different sectors of the population. Next to the overprotection of some urban groups such as utility workers and miners stood the underprotection in the agricultural sector in which only half of the population was covered.[13] Both cases are paradigmatic examples of the country's political economy and its social insurance system. As discussed above in the case of the copper workers, overprotection was the result of the combined effect of their organization and the critical importance of their activity for the Chilean economy. With 90 percent of the copper miners unionized and copper amounting to about 80 percent of the nation's foreign currency earnings, it was not hard for the workers to demand and obtain special benefits from the state.

From a geo-economic perspective, the research done by Mesa-Lago confirms the well-established relationship between the degree of industrialization and the extent of social security coverage. The provinces with the highest degree of coverage were the mining provinces of Antofagasta, Atacama, and O'Higgins, while the lowest proportion of population covered was found in the poorest provinces such as Chiloé and Aysen. Thus, the social security system reproduced the existing distribution of wealth along socioeconomic as well as geographical lines.

In Chile, underprotection ran along the clear line of the urban-rural division. By 1966 only 54.8 percent of the rural population was insured and a much lower percentage was actually eligible to obtain benefits from the system. Both were a consequence of a structural socioeconomic phenomenon, the hacienda. This semi-feudal social system was steered by the notions of authority and obedience, which resulted not from personal ties, but from a broad concept of property rights. Those rights had origins in colonial times and were legally consecrated in the Civil Code.[14]

The enactment of the Labor Code in 1931 and the consequent development of a labor law system only partially altered these notions since it reaffirmed the importance of customary traditions in the regulation of agricultural work, legalizing once more the principles of obedience, the lack of an hourly schedule, and seasonal work among others.[15] The Labor Code did regulate sharecropping, perquisite, legal causes for the termination of the contract, wages, and obligations of the peasants.[16] In practice, however, the Labor Code was denied application in the countryside through a number of legislative, administrative, and judicial actions undertaken by the landowners. Loveman argues that "from 1931 to 1964 landowners sought to evade, resist, and modify the limitations imposed on rural proprietorship, and to control the votes of rural labor and thereby maintain control of the national political apparatus on which property in rural land depended."[17]

Between 1920 and 1947 the landowners also resorted to a number of mechanisms to impede strikes in the countryside. They obstructed peasant action individually, at the local level, and at the national level either through their ability to influence local bureaucrats or through the power of their national organization, the Sociedad Nacional de Agricultura. The landowners' problems with peasant unionization were finally resolved in 1947 with the passage of the Law 8811, euphemistically called Peasant Unionization Law, which in fact hindered the legal organization of rural labor for the next twenty years and forbade the right to strike in the countryside.[18]

Another source of discrimination against the rural workers was the judicial system. Although the law allowed the rural workers to make full use of the Labor Courts which had been created to protect the workers' rights, in practice the peasants had little or no access to the system. Here again the reality of life in the Chilean countryside was much more powerful than the laws. Access to the courts required one to go to the city, talk to lawyers, fill out papers, and conduct a series of *tramites*, or bureaucratic procedures, that the peasant could not do. The courts were there, but the peasants could seldom use them.

The law that created the Blue-Collar Workers Fund, like the other labor laws of 1924, did not distinguish between rural and urban workers and made social security compulsory for both. But again, as in other areas of labor legislation, the landowners managed to avoid compliance through a number of schemes that reflected their local and national power. While at the local level they managed to avoid the inspections needed to enforce the application of the law, at the national level they obtained laws favorable to them. Local inspections were essential to ensure the application of the laws. Inspectors were obligated to visit the haciendas and control the enrollment of workers and the payment of contributions. However, an understaffed and underpaid local social security administration could not override the power of the landowners, who stopped them from exercising their functions frequently by bribing them. The most vivid description of this situation is found in a collection of letters written by individual peasants to Chilean presidents between 1939 and 1970 and collected by Brian Loveman. The letters tell of the indifference of inspectors to peasants' complaints and of illegal actions committed by the inspectors and the landowners. Not surprisingly they chronicle a total disregard for the law and peasant claims. As the peasants explicitly say in their letters, they are writing directly to the president as a last recourse.[19]

Even in those cases in which the law was enforced, its application was difficult and cumbersome, given some legal ambiguities never resolved by the legislature. A case in point was the problem of evaluating the perquisites and in-kind payments which were major components of the agricultural wage; another was the evaluation of the land allotment. Finally, the lack of an accounting system on most haciendas made the application of social security laws a titanic undertaking.[20]

Despite Chile's social and political development, the system of socioeconomic relations in the countryside remained frozen within the parameters established by the hacienda system, and inside those boundaries neither social security nor the other labor legislation could be applied. High rates of evasion, the legal assumption of an extremely low wage, extremely low pensions, and general underprotection characterized the social security system in the countryside.[21] In brief, the implementation of the social security system assumed the existence of a capitalist mode of production. To the extent that the hacienda system entailed pre-capitalist social and economic relations, the application of the system in the countryside was very difficult.

Social security administrators tried to palliate some of these problems through detailed regulations regarding the value of the agricultural wages for social security purposes. In fact, these regulations assumed very low wages, allowing the landowners formal compliance with the law at a very low cost for the *hacendado*. The strategy favored the *hacendados*, but undermined the basic goal of the system of providing a sufficient pension to the peasants and undermined the financial stability of the system. In brief, high rates of evasion, the legal assumption of extreme low wages, and general underprotection of the peasants were the basic characteristics of the rural social security system.

In conclusion, the coverage provided by the social security system aimed at protecting all the economically active population, but in practice covered only those urban groups employed in the industrial sector and in the overly developed service and government sectors, while it excluded those workers involved in non-capitalistic forms of production, such as rural workers and artisans.[22]

The Financial Structure

Originally, the Blue-Collar Workers Fund established a general system of contributions from employers, workers, and the state, and a system of employers' and employees' contributions for the Civil Servants Fund and the White-Collar Workers Fund. However, between 1925 and 1964 the two general financial systems degenerated into about fifty financial subsystems, whose skyrocketing costs and constantly growing deficits demanded direct government financing. The government provided funds directly from the fiscal budget or through the establishment of new taxes earmarked for social security.

The financial structure of the system was completely anarchic. In the public sector, employees' contributions ranged between 0 percent and 52 percent of their salaries, while in the private sector they ranged between 28 percent and 49 percent. Insured contributions ranged between 6 percent and 18 percent in the public sector, and from 0 percent to 19.5 percent in the private. State contributions depended on the nature of the role played by the state. In the case of the public servants and the Armed Forces, the state contributed as an employer, while in the case of the blue-collar workers the state was a third contributor to the system and contributed the equivalent of 5.5 percent of the wages.[23]

The expansion of benefits and the lack of adequate resources to finance them led to the establishment of special taxes earmarked to finance social security benefits in a given fund. Through the years the societal contribution to the pension plan of a specific group became quite generalized. The tax might or might not be linked to specific services provided by the recipient of the benefits. An example of the first type was a tax on maritime tickets and cargo directed to the Merchant Marine Workers Fund. Among the second type was a 2 percent tax on all payments due to the municipalities that went into the coffers of the Blue-Collar Workers Fund.[24]

Continual increases in the benefits gained by public employees also constantly augmented the fiscal needs of the social security system and required additional state monies. Thus most pension readjustments for civil servants, the Armed Forces, and the *perseguidora* system, which is discussed in the next section, were financed directly by the state. By 1968, only 11 percent of state contributions to the social security system were related to the state role of employer, and 60 percent were the product of these special commitments taken by the state.[25]

In the final analysis, the most salient characteristics of the system's financial structure were inequality and regressiveness. Financial inequality was the consequence of the large differences in contributions paid by various groups or subgroups, differences not only established by the separate funds, but among groups within the same fund. Inequality was also the result of special taxes which were devoted exclusively to financing a particular benefit within a particular fund. Such inequalities were repeatedly demonstrated by a series of reports and studies.[26] For example, Mesa-Lago concluded that of the four main occupational groups, the Armed Forces contributed least to their own system, followed by blue-collar workers, who contributed 20 percent of their wages; then the white-collar workers (28 percent), and finally the civil servants (42 percent).[27]

Furthermore, those same studies have demonstrated the regressiveness of the system in terms of income distribution. The Prat Report estimated that 41 percent of the social security costs were paid by the uninsured through taxes and through the transference of the employers' contributions into the costs of goods and services, while only 54 percent of the costs were paid by the insured themselves. The same report describes a process of transference of costs among the different insured groups in which the higher income groups, i.e., white-collar workers and civil servants, transferred part of their costs to the lower income groups.[28] The 1968 study prepared by the Superintendencia de Seguridad Social points to a further decline in the insured's contributions to their own system, from 54 percent to 51 percent, and a consequent increase in the contribution of the uninsured from 41 percent to 44 percent.[29] Finally, a study done in 1971 by ODEPLAN, the

National Planning Office, demonstrated the continuation of this trend, showing that only 46 percent of the costs of the system were paid by the insured, while 50 percent was paid by the uninsured. The phenomenon was again reinforced by the transference of money among the different funds. The Blue-Collar Workers Fund with 70 percent of the total insured received only 42 percent of the uninsured contributions, while the other three funds with only 30 percent of the total insured received 58 percent of the uninsured contributions.[30] Furthermore, as Mesa-Lago argues:

> The above mentioned studies have not explored the redistributive effects among sub-groups within major occupational groups. One wonders how much the Armed Forces and those engaged in judicial and legal careers gain from other civil servants, or how much bankers and merchant marines profit from other white-collar workers; or how much racetrack employees and sailors get from other blue collars. It would be interesting to study whether under-privileged sub-groups, such as domestic servants and agricultural workers, are really helped—and if so, to what degree—by other blue collars in SSS [Blue-Collar Workers Fund].[31]

Benefits

The Chilean social security system provided four major types of benefits: pensions, family allowances, health and maternity benefits, and cash benefits. The primary variable determining the nature and quality of benefits received was affiliation to one of the four major funds. Within them, discrimination was the only general rule. To give a detailed description of each of the benefits received by each of the funds is an impossible task; it should be enough to say that the Prat Report identified about 2,200 different systems of benefits.[32]

The Pension System

The social security system provided a wide array of old age and disability pensions to all the occupational groups. Special pensions based on years of service were offered to civil servants and some white-collar workers. By and large, inequalities were manifested in the types of benefits received by the insured, the conditions required to obtain those benefits, and the process of readjustment of pensions.

The major source of inequality in the benefits was found in pension schedules based on years of service, which were applied to the public sector and some groups within the white-collar working force. As usual, the pattern was intimately linked with the divisions and subdivisions operating within the funds and reflected the efforts of certain of these groups to get special benefits as well as the methods used in their computation which determined the size of the pension. Very large inequities were also found in the requirements for a particular benefit and in the methods used to determine the value of the pension. An example of this type of discrimination was found in the Civil Servants Fund, where the pension was calculated as an average of the last thirty-six salaries for most of the affiliates and as the average for the last twelve months for the personnel of the Port Authority (Empresa Portuaria de Chile), while the pension for the top official was based on the last salary alone. Needless to say that in a country with large inflation rates, the shorter the period used to estimate the pension, the larger the value of the pension.

Discriminations appeared to be even stronger if one compared pensions among occupational groups. Here the elements that created the most pronounced discriminations were (a) the period of affiliation which ranged from one to fifteen years; (b) the minimum age required to obtain a retirement pension which ranged from no minimum age required (e.g, civil servants) to sixty-five years for the blue-collar workers; (c) the period of contribution required to obtain a pension based on years of service which ranged from one to thirty-five years; (d) single or multiple conditions required to obtain a pension; (e) lack of uniform rules to obtain a survivor's pension; (f) differences in the concept of disability; (g) anarchy in the system used to calculate the pensions; and (h) the compatibility of pensions either with other pensions or with other forms of income.

Pensions based on years of service and the problem of compatibility of pensions deserve some special attention. The pension for years of service, which was common to a number of Latin American countries, involved the right to obtain a retirement pension upon the completion of a number of years of service. In Chile, the number of years required ranged from twenty to thirty-five years, and it was a benefit enjoyed by the civil servants, the military, and by some groups of white-collar workers.[33] This type of pension is unfair and discriminatory. This modality had originated in the public sector as a way to compensate top civil servants for politically motivated dismissal. Through the years, the expansion of this benefit among different subgroups generated about thirty systems of pensions based on years of service, which only reinforced the existing inequities and constituted a heavy burden for the system.[34] Pensions based on years of service not only created serious financial problems, they were the main source of another fundamental problem in the system, that of compatibility between two pensions or between a pension and a salary. Those who retired at an early age were likely to take another job, eventually becoming eligible for a second or even a third pension, sometimes at ages at which they were still capable of providing for themselves. It is impossible to find a general rule regarding incompatibilities since each of the systems had its own regulations. In general, pensions were incompatible only with affiliation into the same fund, but even this rule had several exceptions.[35]

The problem of the indexing of pensions was extremely complex and closely linked to the problem of the insufficiency of a majority of pensions, especially in the face of the inflation that dominated the Chilean economy throughout this period. The insufficiency, which will be substantiated in the following chapters, was the result of inflation and of the way in which blue-collar workers' pensions were estimated. For about 70 percent of the retirees, the pension was estimated on the basis of an average of the last thirty-six taxable monthly wages, which amounted to about 50 percent of the real wages. Since inflation was at least 30 percent per year, pensions soon became useless. The existing system of readjustment of pensions was totally inadequate to maintain the purchasing value of the pensions and consequently the majority of the pensioners were condemned to poverty.

Related to the discriminatory nature of the system, the ability of certain groups to obtain special benefits, and the general approach to political economy were the *perseguidoras*. The *perseguidoras* (*perseguir* means to chase) were a type of pension which was tied to the salary received by the employee currently performing the job. *Perseguidoras* were created by one of the radical governments to give life-long protection to high-level bureaucrats whose jobs depended "on the confidence of the President," and who were removed with each change of administration. Through the years they were expanded to lower officials in the administration and to members of the Armed Forces and the police. Exhibiting the familiar tendency toward unequal fragmentation seen throughout the rest of the social security system, *perseguidoras* became divided into two groups: *perseguidoras grandes* and *perseguidoras chicas*. *Perseguidoras grandes* were equivalent to the current salary and were the privilege of top officials who had served for at least one year in one of the first five administrative categories; *perseguidoras chicas* were only a proportion of the current salary (75 percent) and were enjoyed by all the civil servants with thirty years of service who were sixty-five years or older.[36]

Perseguidoras became an almost ideal typical example of the way the system at large operated and evolved through the years. They were discriminatory since they were received only by those placed in the higher echelons of the bureaucracy. They were unfair and costly because they were financed from general revenue funds, and they depicted the political power of certain groups to obtain special privileges from the political system under the guise of a social security benefit.

Another interesting phenomenon was the privileged position of very specific groups of workers. These groups could be as important as the copper workers, who had their own separate fund with special benefits, or as unimportant as the race track workers, who also had a separate fund organized around each individual race track that was financed mainly with special taxes on race track betting. Other privileged groups were the employees of the Notaries and Registry of Deeds and the Central and State Bank employees. What prompted the creation of these special funds for no more than a handful of people whose political or economic importance is hard to perceive? It was the clientelistic relations which developed between the workers and the members of congress.

Family Allowances, Health and Maternity Benefits, and Workman's Compensation

A major component of Chile's social security system was the family allowance program. Family allowances are a form of cash benefit that the worker or employee receives along with salary. This allowance is calculated on the number of dependents claimed by the insured. The allowance is found throughout Latin America and also in many Western European countries and its original purpose was to foster and support large families. This program was central to the social security system since it represented 50 percent of total social security expenditures, covered 73.2 percent of the population, and was in general financed by a 22 percent tax paid only by the employer.

Before the 1960s there were at least ten different family allowance programs, each of them granting different types of benefits. Within the family allowance system inequities were mainly the result of the size of the grant, with a blue-collar worker in the general fund receiving a grant that was about one third of that received by a marine merchant officer, and about one half of that received by a white-collar worker or a bank employee.

Although family allowances were dismembered to a lesser degree than pensions they also reinforced the existing distribution of wealth and the existing class distinctions. A central issue in the years to come was the differences in the allowances received by blue- and white-collar workers.

The origins of the protection of health in Chile can be traced back to two laws, Law 4054 of 1925 and Law 6174 of 1938. Law 4054 established that the insured blue-collar worker had the right to receive medical attention in case of illness or maternity, including hospitalization and a subsidy; Law 6174 established a system of preventive medicine. This law, a landmark in Chile's social legislation, established the obligation of all the insurance funds to create preventive medical services geared toward the early discovery of chronic and contagious diseases such as tuberculosis, syphilis, cardiac and kidney ailments, as well as occupational diseases such as silicosis and anthracosis. Simultaneously, the law established the obligation of performing a yearly check-up on all the insured population, and the right of those suffering one of the illnesses covered by the law to obtain 100 percent of their salaries or wages for as long as necessary. The benefits and services provided by the law were financed by a 1 percent wage tax paid by the employer.

The enforcement and application of this law produced a clear improvement in the extremely low health standards of the Chilean population, which were manifested in high infant mortality rates, high death rates, and low life expectancy.[37] But its impact was limited since it protected only the insured and, among them, those who could recuperate from their illness. The Preventive Medicine Law was very consistent with the conservative approach to social legislation and with its own conservative origins. Its author, the conservative politician and public health expert, Dr. Eduardo Cruz-Coke, explained the purpose of the law in the following terms:

> The Preventive Medicine Law and the concept of directed medicine that the law and its regulations and instructions have established aim at a reduction of temporary absenteeism and of its serious repercussions in the economy of the country through the prevention of illness. It also intends to put an end to the medical and social effort involved in the treatment of those who will not recover their health.
>
> Moreover, the law takes into account the fact that in Chile the first machine to be repaired is the man, but not any man. [We have to repair] the worker that is still healthy or the one who is beginning to get sick, since their health is the most important wealth the country has.[38]

The two laws allowed the creation of a number of health systems linked to the pension funds and organized on an occupational basis, making them liable to the same problems that plagued the social security system. On the other hand, these health services had a very large and positive impact on the health of some important groups of the population, especially the blue- and white-collar workers and their families, as reflected in the infant mortality rates which declined from a staggering 21.2 percent in 1930 to 15.3 in 1947, and to only 8.6 percent among the population served by the health system. Death rates also decreased sharply among the population served by the social security system, from 10.2 per thousand in 1941 to 8.4 per thousand in 1947.[39]

In compliance with the law, the five major funds—blue-collar workers, white-collar workers, civil servants, military, and police—created the first services for the treatment of ambulatory patients and later on provided complete medical services, including hospitalization, medicines, etc. Until 1952 blue-collar workers received ambulatory treatment through the Blue-Collar Workers Fund and hospitalization through the Beneficiencia Pública. The limited resources of this organism necessitated its replacement by the National Health Service (SNS), created with the purpose of providing comprehensive, free medical attention to blue-collar workers and indigents, and of performing the public health functions required to maintain the welfare of the whole nation.

Thus only in the area of preventive medicine were the functions of the SNS applied to the entire population, its curative functions were applied only to the blue-collar workers. The SNS was, in other words, the entity charged with providing medical services to the blue-collar workers and the indigent population. Nevertheless, it had a tremendous impact on the health standards of a large segment of the society (roughly 70 percent), bringing under control or eliminating a number of serious contagious diseases and improving most health indicators.[40] The SNS functions were financed both by the Blue-Collar Workers Fund and by the state. The Fund devoted 4.5 percent of its total revenue to the SNS, while the state had to transfer to the SNS the equivalent to 5.5 percent of the revenues of that Fund and those sums earmarked for it in the fiscal budget.

Other institutions also provided medical care. The Servicio Médico Nacional de Empleados (SERMENA) provided care to white-collar workers covered by the general fund and to the civil servants. SERMENA was second only to the SNS in importance and in the impact it had on the population, providing good preventive care but without any form of curative care until 1968. Some of the smaller funds, such as the military and the bank employees, developed their own medical institutions which provided quality attention and a number of special benefits denied to other workers. Among these, the several medical services that served the military ranked among the finest in the country, providing ambulatory and hospital care, medicines, etc.

Finally, regarding workman's compensations, it is important to note that unlike most of the other social programs, these were non-contributory, financed entirely by the employer and administered, not by funds, but by insurance companies. The employer's responsibility was fulfilled by contracting either with a private insurance company or with a public insurance company created specifically for this purpose.

Administration and Costs

By the mid-1960s the administration of the social security system was charged to hundreds of agencies, both in the public and semi-public sector, and was regulated literally by thousands of laws (my own estimate is that there were more than 2,000 laws regulating the system), decrees, and other regulations.

The administration of the social security system involved the participation of nineteen pension funds in the public sector and sixteen in the private sector; twenty health-related institutions in the public sector and fifteen in the private sector; about fifty welfare agencies in the public sector and an undetermined number in the private sector; four public assistance institutions in the public sector and about twenty in the private sector; and one institution charged with workmen's compensations in the public sector and six in the private sector.[41] To the above, we must add those institutions charged with the supervision of the entire system or parts of it. Among them were the Superintendencia de Seguridad Social (henceforth Superintendencia), the General Comptroller Office, the Ministry of Labor and Social Security, the Ministry of Public Health, the Ministry of Finance, and since 1964, the National Planning Office.

To a large extent, the crucial administrative problems of the system were a result of its fragmentation. What has to be stressed is that this dismemberment of the five original funds into hundreds of subsystems was not related to the expansion of coverage that took place through the years. In fact the five original funds had the potential for providing social security protection to all but the independent workers who never received any type of coverage during this period.

The new funds, and the administrative chaos they produced, were conceived as preferential systems that favored organized, vocal, urban groups that already had social security protection but wanted to improve the quality and/or quantity of the benefits that they received.

Internally, each of the different funds was led by a board which was expected to represent the interests of the various parties. These boards and the bureaucracies that administered the funds also became another source of clientelistic pressures, obtaining for themselves benefits such as special housing loans or special medical services that the population insured by the fund did not possess. By 1964 there were 6,700 persons employed in the administration of social security funds.

The atomization of the system into multiple funds, besides destroying the notion of social solidarity, produced a number of financial problems, reflected in the high costs of the social security system. In 1957, administrative costs amounted to 10 percent of social security expenditures, compared with only 3.4 percent in the United States and 1.3 percent in Argentina.[42]

By 1964 the costs of the social security system, as a proportion of the GNP, were among the highest in the world. Social security revenues amounted to 12.2 percent of GNP, while expenditures were equal to 8.2 percent of GNP. These costs, which had increased rapidly during the 1950s and continued to rise during the following years, were comparable only to those of Uruguay in Latin America and to some of the welfare states in Western Europe that had universal insurance systems. Rising social security costs were the result of new benefits granted by the law without adequate financing, rising administrative costs, and the expansion of social security coverage to new groups.[43] The changing active/passive ratio also had a bearing on the costs of the system.

What is even more important than the high costs themselves was the distribution of costs within the system and the insufficiency of the majority of the pensions provided by the system. Regarding the distribution of costs, one cannot fail to notice that the privileges received by small groups, such as those receiving *perseguidoras* and pensions based on years of service, were the most costly items in the system. The insufficiency of the pensions received by the majority of the population was simply the other side of this process. Suffice it to say that the Blue-Collar Workers Fund, which provided insurance coverage to 70 percent of the EAP, received only 22 percent of the funds.[44] In the long run, the sufficiency or insufficiency of a worker's pension was related not only to his or her position in the occupational structure, but to the age of the pension, since the inflationary process constantly eroded the pensions. In this context, the social security system not only reinforced the existing class and income structures, it reinforced the incapacities produced by the life cycle, with the older, less able, and very often sick pensioner receiving a lower pension than the younger and newer retiree.

Finally, the fact that the small funds had resources in excess of their needs reinforced all the previous patterns and increased the costs of the system. In the final analysis, the high costs of the social security system were an integral part of its structure and of the political economy of the country and could not be reduced without a total reform of the system.

Summary

Here once again the narrative and the reality were quite different. No one has summarized that reality better than Jorge Prat, the Chairman of the Commission of Reform. In the letter of presentation of his 1,600 page report to President Jorge Alessandri, Prat stated:

> The present social security system is condemned to its disintegration because it is unfair, because it is oligarchic, because it is discriminatory and because it is ineffective and expensive, both for the working population and the national economy.[45]

A central question emerges from this crude assessment. Why did the social security system have this anarchic, oligarchic, discriminatory, inefficient structure? From our viewpoint, anarchy was to a large extent the result of the contradictions produced by the application of a conservative approach to social and labor policies in the political context provided by the 1925 Constitution. The divisionary and exclusionary nature of the labor legislation of 1925 forced the multiple units that formed the working class to develop clientelistic relations with the political parties. Given the competitive nature of the political system, the parties, in turn, were constantly attempting to capture new political clienteles. Given the weak nature of the economy and the patterns of inequity, parties had to offer something in return for political support. Their access to the state made it possible for them to offer state-granted benefits to compensate workers for the decrease in the standards of living and the structural inequality. As political participation increased and economic conditions worsened or remained the same, the granting of these benefits, and the public policies that granted them, became essential to the existence and continuation of the political system.

Both the political system and the import substitution model adopted in the 1930s involved the inclusion only of the organized urban groups, while it excluded, or partially excluded, the rest of the urban workers and the rural sector. The social security system reproduced within its structures the same pattern of inclusion and exclusion. Chaos and skyrocketing costs were the final consequences of this process.

Between 1924 and 1973 the entire structure of the system depended on the policies made by the 1924 legislators who decided to grant pensions to segments of the working class. The essentially conservative approach had unforeseen consequences.

What the 1924 legislature did not or could not anticipate was that both the labor and the social security laws were going to be applied in the context of a new political regime. Thus the development of the social security system until 1973 was intimately linked to the nature of the political system established in the 1925 Constitution. Chile's unique brand of populism was organized not around a personalistic authoritarian leader as it was in the case of Argentina and Brazil, but around a pluralist political regime and a multiparty system based on unstable political alliances. Those alliances, in turn, permitted the segmental incorporation of the most organized and vocal sectors of the working class. The political parties acted as brokers between the fragmented working class and the state. The most important feature of this arrangement was the clientelistic relationship that existed between the parties and sectors of the working class. However, in the case of Chile there was a contradiction between these clientelistic linkages and the ideological commitment of the political elite. The satisfaction of clientelistic demands certainly interfered with the more global ideological approach. Over the years the contradiction only grew in intensity and strength. This contradiction was central to the inability of both the Christian Democrats and Popular Unity coalition to fulfill their plans. This contradiction was at least partially responsible for the end of Chile's democracy.

The policies reflected both the clientelistic linkages that existed between the political parties and sectors of the working class as well as an elite attempt to reduce some of the major social and economic ills of the society through the expansion of social security benefits. The unstructured, amorphous growth of the system reflected a failed attempt to ameliorate some of the major socioeconomic inequities via social security benefits while also using the benefits to satisfy the needs of specific clienteles and their *patrones*.

Furthermore, the policies themselves began to play an independent political role. This role was twofold. First, policies given to one sector of the working class served as the bases for future demands for other sectors. Second, the very concession of particularistic benefits fragmented the working class even more, creating interest groups formed around the very existence of a given social security benefit. These groups would eventually demand more benefits. The policies then became an active part of this vicious cycle.

The close interaction between the nature of the political and economic systems and the role of the political parties not only contributed to the birth and growth of the system, but obstructed the attempts to reform the system. The same forces that had coalesced to continually approve new social security benefits for small sectors of the population, creating a stratified, unequal, costly, chaotic, and regressive system, coalesced to prevent the establishment of a universal, unified, and more egalitarian system. As we will see in chapter five, opposition to reform the system came from both the rank and file and the political elite. While the opposition of the rank and file can be easily understood as a defense of their rights and privileges, the attitude of the elite is a further indication of their contradictory political role. The structural connections between politics and policies were also reflected in the constant exclusion of the rural sector. Before 1964 peasants were neither political nor economic actors, and consequently they were practically excluded from the social security system.

The analysis of the social security system presented in this chapter appears to be incompatible with the way in which people spoke about this system. The narrative maintained that Chile's system was the best in Latin America since it covered 70 percent of the population and gave generous benefits to all. According to the narrative, the system was a symbol of the concerns of the Chilean state with social equality. It was also presented as symbolic of the functions of a state that tried to bring about unity and harmony in the society. As seen above, social security policies were stratified and unequal just like the other state policies, and just like the society that had generated the system. However, the narrative served an important function: it created the image of a system designed to create equality and protect the poor while it sustained the entire political edifice built on inequality and privileges.

CHAPTER 4

Frei's Revolution in Liberty
The Social and Political Crisis of the 1960s

By the early 1960s Chilean society was again experiencing a crisis produced by the exhaustion of the political and economic model created in the 1930s. The political system based on the inclusion and co-optation of segments of the urban society and the exclusion of the rural sector was for the first time seriously challenged. Simultaneously, serious economic problems such as low rate of economic growth, dependence on exports, and inflation were aggravated by the exhaustion of the import substitution model.

The Christian Democratic program based on the notion of the *Estado Comunitario* (communitarian state) attempted to transform the nature of the Chilean state, the relations between state and society, the functions of the state, and the main forms of articulation of interests. Essential policies included the regime's efforts to integrate the peasantry and the urban poor or "marginals" into the political society, to change the relations between organized labor and the political system, to adapt the import substitution model to contemporary economic conditions, and to expand the social functions of the state. If successful the program planned to narrow socioeconomic differences and the growing gap between Chile's reality and the prevailing social narrative.

This chapter contains an analysis of the general crisis experienced by society and the political system in the early part of the 1960s and the reforms proposed by the Christian Democrats. Special emphasis is placed on their attempts to redefine the state's socioeconomic functions and to integrate previously excluded social groups.

The Political, Economic, and Social Crisis

Only Chile's political facade was stable. Behind it seethed a highly unstable brew of multiple alliances, fragmented parties, and clientelistic relations, all based on the urban coalition formed in the 1930s. Crucial to its top-heavy distribution of wealth and power was the exclusion of the peasantry and the maintenance of the hacienda system.

Prior to 1960, two elements were particularly significant to the internal political instability: governments based on transient multiparty urban alliances that constantly incorporated new fragmented clienteles into the political organization, and the political imbalance between the Executive and the Congress. While the Executive reflected the current distribution of political power, the Congress reflected the distribution of power that existed in the 1920s, since the legislators had refused to change the system of apportionment and to increase the size of Congress in order to make it more reflective of the existing population distribution. It was understood that those reforms would give the major urban centers, and consequently the left, control of Congress and would end the control that the political right and the landowners had of the political system. As a result, the presidents were always faced with the options of "either becoming rightist or dissolving the Constitutional government."[1] One president after another yielded to the political right. Congress, in turn, maintained the privileges and power of the right, and the political price of stability was the acceptance and recognition of the veto power of the land-owning class and the other constituencies of the Conservative and Liberal parties. The veto permitted them to obstruct any substantial social or economic reform.

The other inescapable fact of political life, the fragmented party system, allowed the transient participation and co-optation of the most vocal urban groups into the political regime. Both elements perpetuated the existing social and economic structure, generating a political system that was sustained by a growing set of public policies which, in turn, undermined an already weak economy. This political system was unable to deal with the serious ills of the society and its economy or make any of the required structural changes.[2] By 1964 a number of political and economic factors—of national and international origin—made this crisis very real.

From a political perspective, the inefficiency of the existing system demanded a constitutional reform that would increase the power of the Executive vis-à-vis the Congress and simplify the overly long legislative process which allowed each chamber to revise and amend a bill at least four times. It was clear to all but the most conservative observers that the basic notions, the scaffolding over which the constitutional and legal edifice had been built, were outmoded or completely archaic. President Alessandri, at the end of his term, and Eduardo Frei, at the beginning of his, introduced to Congress constitutional reform bills that increased the power of the Executive, simplified the legislative process, and proposed the establishment of the plebiscite to solve constitutional disputes between the branches of government. In addition, Frei's bill attempted to expand and restructure political participation by creating new forms of worker and peasant organizations.

Some of the perennial problems of the Chilean economy discussed in chapter two reached a critical point by the mid-1960s. Among the most critical economic problems was the decline of the agricultural sector, which in 1964 produced 20 percent less than in 1940, creating balance of payment problems, inflationary pressures, rural-urban migration, and slow rates of economic growth. Also critical were high inflation rates and an unequal distribution of income, which not only meant low living standards for a large percentage of the population, but economic stagnation, thus stimulating monopolies, restricting the market, and perpetuating the low growth–high inflation cycle.[3] Dependence on copper and the relations with the multinational corporations were also reaching critical points, because of both the instability of the copper market and the growing opposition to the presence of Anaconda and Kennecott, the two multinational corporations that exploited Chilean copper. Moreover, the import substitution process, while it had achieved some of its purposes, was showing a number of strains due to the limitations of the national market, the cost of technology, and scarcity of capital.

Many cleavages divided Chilean society; the deepest was the urban-rural dichotomy. But rural society and urban society were themselves divided. Rural society was split between landowners and peasants. The landowners, in turn, were divided into at least two broad categories, the owners of the big pre-capitalist haciendas in the fertile Central Valley, who, by and large, belonged to the Chilean oligarchy, and the smaller landowners of the South, who had joined the ranks of the bourgeoisie. Politically speaking, the oligarchy had maintained its ties with the Conservative Party, while the modern landowners belonged to either the Liberal, Radical, or the Christian Democratic Party. Peasants were divided along occupational lines and according to their relationship with the landowner (*inquilinos* lived permanently on the land and *afuerinos* were temporary workers). Urban society was even more divided. Each of the three basic social classes was, in turn, divided into a multiplicity of groups. Divisions ran along occupation and economic status lines, among others.

Of the many social problems that existed in Chile at the time, two were considered to be crucial by the leaders of the Christian Democratic Party, the persistence of the semi-feudal relations in the countryside and the appearance of the marginals in the urban environment. Both of them were intimately related. The question of marginality will be analyzed in this chapter and the rural problem will be analyzed in chapter five.

The Christian Democratic Party: Philosophy and Policies

From a political standpoint, this period was characterized by the rapid decline of the Radical Party, which since the 1930s had been at the center of both the political spectrum and most of the alliances that typified this period, as well as the rapid growth of the Christian Democratic Party.

In a highly stratified society, where political parties represented either fragments of social classes or occupational groups, the Christian Democratic Party (PDC) was an exceptional organization that gained support from such diverse groups as businessmen, industrialists, small landowners, bureaucrats, professionals, peasants, and marginals. Such a broad multiclass party could be forged only because its leaders replaced the typical class-oriented analysis pursued by the other political parties with a global analysis of the social and economic problems and stressed communitarian principles over clientelistic politics.[4] The party was formed by a group of young ex-conservatives led by Eduardo Frei, Eduardo Castillo Velasco, and Rafael Agustín Gumucio, who found in the writings of Jacques Maritain the philosophical inspiration that nurtured the newly created party. Maritain's philosophy combined the Catholic principles that Frei and the others had acquired in their early political careers with the notion of social equity and individual freedom that had made them leave the Conservative Party.

Fundamental to the ideology of the PDC were Maritain's notions of common good and the organic role of the state, the nature of the relations between state and society, and of the individual's role in the society. Maritain had argued that the best form of government is found in the Communitarian State, one that is communal because it considers the common good superior to the individual will; pluralist in the sense that it is formed by communities inferior in rank to the political state; theist because it recognizes that God is the source of Natural Law; and finally, one that respects the principles of liberty, fraternity, and justice.[5] For Maritain, the political society should ensure the welfare of the whole and, at the same time, enhance individual freedom by liberating men from political, social, and economic bondage. Essential to the freedom and liberation of the individual, and especially important to the liberation of the lower classes, is the respect for natural and civil rights and the respect for the rights of the worker, which include the right to a just wage, the right to unionize, and the right to social security, health protection, and unemployment compensation.

While Maritain provided a theoretical blueprint for the newly formed party, Chilean society provided the critical juncture at which the leaders of the PDC applied this philosophy. According to Maritain, the organic society has to be formally organized along pluralist and democratic lines, while the organic state could not be simply an expression of various societal pressures, as is the liberal state, but an organism charged with performing and achieving common societal goals. In practice, the accomplishment of this task required the existence of a strong executive to lead the society and the state and a congress which complements and rectifies the executive's functions. As Castillo Velasco argues:

> The function of the [communitarian] state is to administer political affairs. The state is neither above society—as is typical of the totalitarian state—nor does it complement the will of the citizens—as is characteristic of the individualist state. The state has meaning

only as a manager of the common good. The state is the largest community within the total community.[6]

The state envisioned by the Christian Democrats had to be created within the political reality of Chile. The first task before the PDC leaders was to transform the populist state created in the 1930s into a communitarian state. This involved a redistribution of power among the branches of government; a transformation of the system of interest aggregation and articulation permitting the incorporation of previously excluded sectors; and structural reforms geared to change the pattern of land ownership and the system of social relations in the countryside to re-orient the country's role in the international economic markets and to obtain a better distribution of the existing resources. In the words of Frei, these policies aimed at the creation of "a truly humanist society."[7]

The Political Economy of the Frei Administration

President Frei's program attempted to deal coherently with the structural problems of the Chilean economy, and also those created by the economic crisis of the 1960s. The principal actor in this program was the state, which, through a new set of policies and a new group of technocrats, would steer the national economy toward a pattern characterized by higher rates of economic growth, increased production and productivity, and control of the inflationary process. The state, as a supreme organ of society, would also deal with the powerful multinational corporations by realigning its relations with them and it would redistribute a portion of the national income.

To pursue this program, Frei needed extensive internal and external support. Internally, Frei planned to capitalize on the unparalleled margin of his electoral victory,[8] and on the future growth of the PDC political base, which he hoped would result from the rapid implementation of socioeconomic programs favorable to large sectors of the population. External support was almost assured by the practical and ideological convergence of his program and that of the Alliance for Progress, the European PDCs, and the Catholic Church.

The economic program required that the rate of GNP growth be tripled, personal income redistributed, and inflation eliminated gradu-

ally. Following the structuralist approach, the Christian Democrats
argued that the main barriers to sustained economic growth were the
low productivity of the agricultural sector, lack of control over copper
production and marketing, the low level of domestic investment, and
the low net national savings rate, which averaged only 1 percent of the
GNP for the period between 1950 and 1964.[9] Thus two policies were
essential to achieve the desired growth rates: the agrarian reform,
which, from an economic perspective, would put an end to the lagging
impact of that sector in the national economy; and the Chilenization
of the copper industry. The latter would allow the state to have direct
control over the sector that provided over 80 percent of the foreign exchange received by the country and would make those funds available
to economic and social programs already targeted by the government.

A second major component of the economic program was a set
of stabilization policies. Needless to say, chronic inflation was linked
to a number of other economic problems such as the low rate of savings and investment. But it was understood that price stability could
only be achieved after other economic goals were reached. In the
words of an analyst, "the stabilization program would advance as fast
as the process of structural reforms would allow it to advance, which,
in turn, would make it possible to obtain simultaneously economic
growth and redistribution of income."[10] Prices would then be gradually controlled and inflation rates would decline to 10 percent in the
third year of the administration. The wage policy, on the other hand,
was designed to permit moderate wage increases in balance with the
increases in prices and productivity gains.

The program also attacked the fiscal crisis of the state and attempted
through a package of reforms to put an end to the traditional system of
deficit spending funded by the Central Bank. It also aimed at obtaining
direct control over the policies of the Central Bank, which was governed
by a body formed by representatives of the public and the private sectors,
and improving the tax collection system. Through the tax reform, fiscal
policies would become a key element of the redistributive program.

Finally, the creation of the Andean Common Market would allow
the deepening of the import substitution process. President Frei and
the members of his economic team were aware that the import substitution model was at a critical juncture. The limited nature of the
national markets and the high cost of capital goods and technology

threatened the entire economic structure devised in the 1930s. For Frei, the solution depended on a process of regional economic integration channeled through a new, smaller organization, the Andean Common Market, which would allow not only the expansion of the national markets, but the establishment of a common approach toward direct foreign investments and technology transfers as well.

Foreign capital and technology were central elements in the development strategy. Both would be controlled by the state and would be used to finance the socioeconomic plans of the administration. Its designers knew that it could not be totally implemented in a six-year period, but would be only initiated by the Frei administration and fully implemented by the next Christian Democratic government.[11] In the final analysis, the entire program depended on how the structural reforms fared in Congress and on the government's ability to attract foreign capital and invest it in those sectors of the economy singled out as crucial to the economic development of the nation.

The government almost immediately initiated those aspects of the program that could be implemented by administrative fiat, but all the structural reforms proposed by the administration required congressional approval, and both the left and the right opposed Frei's reforms. Consequently, any assessment of the Frei administration has to distinguish between those reforms that required congressional approval and those that could be implemented by the Executive.

In the economic policy area the government was quite successful not only in capturing foreign investment, but in directing it to the targeted areas. Stallings, an analyst who is not particularly impressed with the achievements of the Frei administration, admits that "Frei understood the nature of the accumulation process in Chile better than Alessandri did. His advisers realized that the state had to provide the main portion of domestic investment, and they knew how to bring in foreign investment."[12] By 1970 the state controlled 70 percent of total domestic investment.[13]

Attempts to increase the private savings rate were not successful, and the forced savings scheme proposed by the government in 1967 produced a serious political crisis for the administration. In the area of income distribution, some of the government policies had a positive effect. In the rural sector the peasant unionization law produced a significant increase in the real wages of the agricultural workers. Their wages increased over 100 percent between 1965 and 1970.[14] The results of the stabilization program were mixed. Inflation decreased from 46 percent in 1964 to 29 percent in 1965, 23 percent in 1967, and 18 percent in 1967, but the government goal of reaching an inflation rate of 10 percent by 1967 was not met and the inflationary spiral began to climb again, reaching 32 percent in 1969. Finally, economic growth was quite erratic, increasing from 4.6 percent in 1965 to 9.2 percent in 1966, sliding to 0.8 percent the following year, and growing again to 5.1 percent in 1969.[15]

Attempts to Create a Communitarian State and an Integrated Society

No other political party in the history of Chile had been in a better position to attempt a transformation of the political system than the PDC, which between 1965 and 1969 controlled the Executive and enjoyed an absolute majority in the House of Deputies. Despite this majority, and the commitment to reform the system shown by the administration and the Christian Democrats in Congress, their success was partial at best.

Soon after taking office, the government introduced into Congress a constitutional reform bill which detailed a change in the relations between the branches of government. The bill gave the Executive exclusive initiative in those issues dealing with economic and social legislation and those involving public expenditures, while reducing the role of the Congress in the legislative process. It also proposed the creation of normative laws that aimed at producing comprehensive standard norms to deal with specific issues, and the establishment of the plebiscite as a mechanism to solve disputes between the Executive and the Congress. The bill also expanded the constitutional protection of labor rights and the concept of social property.[16]

The bill was defeated in Congress since the right claimed that the increased power of the Executive vis-à-vis Congress would be the end of Chilean democracy. In 1970 the administration introduced another constitutional reform bill which, although it was based on the same principles as the first, was more acceptable to the opposition because it did not alter so drastically the power relations between the branches of government. Thus, the 1925 Constitution was reformed, but only during the last year of the Frei administration. The reform introduced the plebiscite to resolve the conflicts between the Executive and the Congress, expanded the right to vote to illiterates, accelerated the legislative process, and reserved for the Executive the right to initiate laws that involved fiscal expenditures.[17]

The structural reforms desired by the administration required at least two major pieces of legislation, one dealing with the Chilenization of copper and a second with the agrarian reform. Even though both reforms were approved by the Congress in 1967, they had been substantially modified.[18] The Chilenization of copper resulted in joint ownership between the state and the foreign companies, expansion of production, and increases in the quantities of copper refined in Chile. An increase in tax revenues and modifications in the pricing system also resulted from the reform. Despite these gains, many nationalistic and economic needs remained unsatisfied and the left continued demanding full nationalization.[19]

The process of agrarian reform, essential to the transformation of Chilean society, was initiated as soon as Frei came to power. The administration pursued a two-pronged approach: to use a limited agrarian reform law approved during the Alessandri administration, and to introduce into Congress a bill aimed at transforming the structure of rural property and creating a communitarian property system financed and supervised by the state. The agrarian reform approved by Congress in 1967, the product of a compromise with the right, looked very different from the bill introduced by the President. It established the obligation of the government to pay 10 percent of the value of the expropriated land in cash, while the remainder had to be paid in twenty-five and thirty-year bonds. As expected by the right, this financial hurdle slowed down the reform process, and by 1970 the government had expropriated only 18 percent of the country's irrigated land and about 12 percent of the non-irrigated land, while only 28,000 families, out of an expected goal of 100,000, had been resettled; 90 percent of the land assignments were done on a communitarian basis.[20] From another perspective, the introduction of the Agrarian Reform Bill put an end to the support that the Conservative and Liberal parties had lent to Frei.

In conclusion, although the Christian Democratic Party controlled the Executive and had a majority in Congress, it could not obtain from Congress the passage of the laws needed to change the political organization and to carry out the structural reforms. In the case of the political laws, a partial reform was enacted at the end of the administration's constitutional period, the impact of which would be felt during the next election and during the next presidential period. The land reform law, on the other hand, was the result of a compromise with the right, and consequently it imposed serious limitations on the administration's power, restricting its ability to fulfill the promises made to the peasants.

The Grand Design for Social Integration:
The Policies toward the Peasantry and the Marginals

President Frei's commitment to carry out a "Revolution in Liberty" was more than a simple campaign slogan. Frei aimed at, and at least partially achieved, a profound transformation of Chilean society, incorporating, at least temporarily, those living on its periphery, the peasants and the marginals, roughly 55 percent of the population.[21] Moreover he was committed to reorganizing the structure of the labor movement and to transforming the discriminatory social security and health systems into universal efficient welfare programs. The notions of integration, participation, freedom, and equality, central to the communitarian state, were also central to the reforms proposed by Frei.

Within the social program of the Frei government, one can distinguish three major policies: those that favored the peripheral sectors of society, those that dealt with the organization of the working class, and those that reformed the social security system.

The policies encouraging the integration of the peasantry and the marginals were part of Frei's grand design to transform Chile's divided society into a single community, and they reflected better than any others the complexity of the social issues confronted by the administration. Marginality and the exclusion of the rural sector had political, economic, and social causes and consequences and by the 1960s were linked to national and international problems.

Throughout Latin America the import substitution model and the process of state-sponsored capitalist development that followed did not alter the basic rift between the city and the countryside. On the contrary, the process created islands of economic and social development in the urban areas and ignored the rural sector from both a social and an economic perspective. In these dual societies the further deterioration of the countryside relative to the development of the city caused people to migrate from the rural to the already overpopulated urban areas. This process, known in Latin America as "metropolization," produced a number of other socioeconomic phenomena among which marginality was the most important.[22]

Marginality involves large migratory movements from the rural areas to the large cities which, given their own structural limitations, could not absorb them. These immigrants find themselves excluded from the urban society both physically, as most marginals live in the outskirts of the cities, and economically since they joined the already large urban population of unemployed and underemployed. Over a long period, this migratory process led to the formation of large communities living in the outskirts of the cities in a permanent state of isolation and desolation.

In the case of Chile, this phenomenon was particularly serious given the persistence of semi-feudal relations in the countryside and the low productivity of the agricultural sector. Between 1952 and 1960, 75 percent of the population living in the *Poblaciones Callampas*, the Chilean equivalent to Brazilian Favelas,[23] were immigrants from the rural areas. Furthermore, 80 percent of them had come from the central provinces, the area where the hacienda system was prevalent.[24] Prior to the 1960s the living conditions and fate of the marginals had been entirely ignored by the organized elements of the society and by the political system at large. But in an environment of growing political awareness, economic crisis, and regional upheaval spearheaded by the Cuban Revolution, the growth of the marginals represented a threat that could not be ignored.[25]

Father Roger Vekemans, a prolific writer and advisor to President Frei, stressed the double nature of the phenomenon, arguing that the marginals gained neither employment nor social benefits, and that given their internal disorganization they did not and could not have any input in the political process. Vekemans, who influenced the theoretical thinking as well as the policies of the Frei administration, argued that the *callampero* was a man expelled from his own world and never accepted by the modern city. The government planners, following Vekemans, argued that the problem was global and profound, since it affected the totality of the human endeavor and the entire society. Moreover, since the marginals lived in a state of social disintegration and isolation, and since they did not have the capacity to impact the political process, they would not be able to overcome this situation without the help of an external agent or agency. The solution to the problem required global and profound action and demanded a total involvement of the community, led by the state.[26]

President Frei decided to incorporate this sector of the society into the party and the political system before the aftershocks of the Cuban Revolution could reach this excluded, poor, and displaced group. In other words, Frei, like Arturo Alessandri in the 1920s, decided to expand the political system to previously excluded sectors in order to protect the existing political and economic system.

In the policy arena, Vekemans's proposals took the form of the creation of the Consejería de Promoción Popular, a national agency charged with promoting integration of marginals into the urban society and with developing of an internal organization that would transform the marginals into political actors. The dimensions of the task were clearly understood; it attempted to provide organization, social services, housing, and, if possible, productive employment to almost one-fourth of the total population. The role of the state was not only to provide the required services and benefits, but to organize the marginals along territorial and functional lines. These organizations, in turn, would assure the future political incorporation of this class. This task had to be spearheaded by the state, but once the marginals had overcome their incapacity to coalesce, the state was to transfer the control of these organizations to the marginals themselves.[27]

The legal history of the Promoción Popular program points to the recalcitrant nature of the social structure and political organization. Both the right and the left opposed the Promoción Popular Bill; the right because it did not want to have those masses organized, and the left because it expected to obtain political gains from their current condition. Nevertheless, the Consejería carried out its promotional and organizational job through administrative fiat, and by 1970 it had created 19,190 community organizations.[28] However, Congress had effectively deprived the Consejería of a legal structure and certainly its institutional weakness, mainly the lack of a budget, impinged upon its ability to provide the promised services and deprived the government of the expected political benefits.

Among all the lines that divided Chilean society, the division between rural and urban society was the most pervasive and the clearest indicator of the depth of Chile's social dualism. Only a few miles from the elegant boutiques of Providencia Avenue, from fashionable discotheques, luxurious mansions, and internationally famous ski resorts, the hacienda persisted as an anachronistic and exploitative remnant of colonial times, with a semi-feudal social structure, an archaic organization, and an inefficient economy.

In the mid-twentieth century, the hacienda remained a political and economic anachronism which allowed the landowners to maintain their grip on the rural population and parts of the state. The hacienda and its inhabitants were crucial to the perpetuation of the entire socioeconomic organization, providing not only a very inexpensive source of labor for the landowners but also the votes that maintained the political system.

The first fissure in this seigniorial system of domination that had been in place since the eighteenth century appeared in 1958, when an electoral reform proposed by President Ibañez eliminated the control and coercion characteristic of elections in the countryside. But it was not until 1965 that a real transformation of the hacienda took place, a direct result of the election of Eduardo Frei to the presidency. He and his administrative cadres were committed to destroying the hacienda and incorporating the peasantry into the national society. The transformation of the countryside was achieved through a number of legislative and administrative actions, among them the Agrarian Reform Law, the Peasants Unionization Law, and the actions of two bureaucratic organisms, the National Institute for Agricultural Development (INDAP) and the Corporation of Agrarian Reform (CORA).

The legislation on peasant unionization presented to Congress in September 1965 authorized the formation of rural unions and rural federations of unions with power to negotiate collective contracts and established the peasants' right to strike. Opposition from the political right was, as expected, immediate and strong. Once again, by attempting to identify the welfare of the nation with the welfare of the agriculturists, the right obstructed passage for almost two years. *El*

Mercurio, the most articulate organ of the Chilean right, typically edi-
torialized, "The country will not be able to stand the suspension of
agricultural activities. Any initiative that pretends to change the existing regime [of industrial relations] and that could imply a recognition
of the right to strike of the rural laborer, will open a course whose
repercussions we cannot foresee."[29]

Unfortunately for the landowners, the poor performance of the
agricultural sector during the previous thirty years lent scant credibility
to their argument, and the Peasant Unionization Law was approved in
April 1967. At the heart of the newly enacted legislation was the establishment of the right to strike, to organize at the local and the national level, and to negotiate collective contracts. Moreover, the law
protected the union leaders from arbitrary dismissal and protected the
economic solvency and independence of the unions. The importance
of this law cannot be underestimated since it marks a turning point in
the history of Chilean social legislation. The law, approved a few
months before the Land Reform Law, destroyed the personal dependence ties of the hacienda system and, therefore, incorporated about
30 percent of the population into the polity.

The process of unionization that followed the approval of the law
was fast and massive. The formation of those unions was affected by
the actions of the INDAP technocrats under the direction of Jacques
Chonchol, one of the most articulate proponents of the communitarian society and a well-known rural expert. INDAP, which had been
created in 1963 with the purpose of coordinating and implementing
activities related to agricultural production, rural education, and community development, organized and later on mobilized the peasantry
in order to make them capable of assuming the responsibilities involved in their own development and the development of their communities. The promotional labor of INDAP, based on the notion that
the development of the peasantry rested on its mobilization and organization and its access to modern technology and rational systems
of production, was overwhelming and preceded legislative reform.[30]
By December 1965 INDAP had assisted in the formation of 488 local
unions with a total membership of 20,782, and by early 1967 it had
promoted 106 communal unions with a membership of 30,374; it had
created 2,500 committees of small landowners with 90,000 members

and 600 Centros de Madres.[31] INDAP also sponsored courses to edu-
cate the rural population and to form labor leaders. In only one year
over 7,000 peasants participated in those courses.

Both the left and the right were prompt to attack Chonchol and
his cadres of peasant organizers, accusing them of promoting a system
of state syndicalism, which restricted the personal freedom of the
peasants and caused irreversible damage in the countryside. But
Chonchol was able to maintain his program at full speed until mid-
1967, when, as a result of the first economic downturn and the first
political rift within the PDC, his leadership collapsed. Chonchol left
INDAP and later on the party.

In brief, the process of peasant unionization during this period was
to a large extent the result of the actions of a group of young, highly
committed technocrats who acted mostly by administrative fiat. Under
the guidance of strong and influential leaders they were able to change
the functions of the bureaucracies that dealt with rural problems and
remained almost invulnerable to political attacks as long as they had
the undivided support of the President and the party and had the resources necessary to carry out the program. When both began to collapse in mid-1967, the actions of the technocrats began to slow down,
but the peasants were already undergoing a dynamic transformation
that could not be stopped. The government's retreat did not halt the
organizational process; it only left a power vacuum that was filled by
the leftist parties, who had made their political appearance in the
countryside mainly as a result of the PDC's reforms. In turn, a process
of political polarization of the rural society was initiated, which culminated during the Allende government. This process was characterized
by illegal and sometimes violent actions by the peasantry and limited
intervention on the part of the government. According to Loveman:

> The extent of the mobilization of the *campesinos* originally induced
> by the government exceeded in the magnitude and intensity the
> government's ability to control it. The government rejected sys-
> tematic repression, yet it also refused to allow illegality to become
> the institutionalized pattern of agrarian reform. The campesino
> movement magnified the internal contradiction within the govern-
> mental party and left the original dilemma—how to carry out a
> revolution within a viable legal order—more pronounced.[32]

The rural policies affected the relations between the landowners and the political system in at least two different forms. On the one hand, the traditional links between the landowners and the bureaucracy were severed by the technocrats of the PDC, depriving the landowners of their ability to define rural policies. On the other, the rural unionization law allowed the landowners to unionize, giving them the opportunity to develop modern interest associations that enhanced the power of those landowners who were not involved in the politics of the Sociedad Nacional de Agricultura, the landowners' peak association.[33] In fact, the new cadre of rural technocrats had destroyed the traditional pattern of informal influence that the Sociedad Nacional de Agricultura had exercised on those sectors of the bureaucracy responsible for making agricultural policies, depriving it of the power to define the parameters of rural policies and to inhibit the actions of the relevant government agencies.

In pursuit of increased freedom of association, the Rural Unionization Law established the right of the landowners to form local unions, and to represent rural proprietors in the collective bargaining process, creating a union movement among rural proprietors previously nonexistent at the local level. Thus, in the process, the government, by combining the Sociedad Nacional de Agricultura (SNA) and the local unions, forced the landowners to modernize their organization. The traditional power of the SNA over the legislative branch was reinforced by the power that the new unions had at the local level.[34] In brief, the Rural Unionization Law transformed the process and form of interest aggregation and articulation in the countryside both in regard to labor and landowners, becoming probably the only public policy enacted during the Frei administration that fully reflected the concept of the communitarian society envisioned by the PDC. The law effectively transformed relations between state and society and between the factors of production.

Policies toward the Working Class

Basic to the notion of the communitarian state and an integrated society was the role of the intermediate organizations, especially the unions, in the political and economic life of the nation. As envisioned by the party's programs, pluralist, free, and representative unions would become the dynamic agent to transform the enterprise and the society.[35] In practice, however, the transformation of the industrial relations systems and the wage policies pursued by the administration produced a serious rift, both between organized labor and the government and between the government and the party.

From the outset the labor policies of the administration were framed by the ideological position of William Thayer, the influential Minister of Labor. Thayer, traditionally identified with the right wing of the PDC which, in turn, was heavily influenced by the sectors of the industrial bourgeoisie that belonged to the party, argued that unions should be free, uncontrolled entities that instead of concentrating their actions in the defense of the economic interests of the working class should promote the transformation of the economic organization of the country and the capitalist enterprise into communitarian enterprises. Moreover, while this process of transformation took place, unionism was to be brought in line with the country's economic capacity.[36]

A bill transforming the industrial relations systems created in 1924 was proposed by the government in February 1965. The bill eliminated the single compulsory plant union, allowed the formation of unions in the public sector, eliminated the differences between blue- and white-collar workers, and established the right of the workers to participate in the management of the enterprises. As was the case with all the other reform bills presented by the government, this one was unanimously opposed by all sectors of the political arena, as well as by labor leaders of all ideological colors. In this case, however, the opposition included also members of the PDC, something that had not happened with the major reform bills presented at the beginning of the administration.

What was the basis for this unanimous opposition to the modernization of industrial relations? Certainly the major problems with the bill were political and not technical. From a technical point of view, several labor law specialists noted that the bill represented a clear improvement over the existing legislation. The proposed bill complied with most of the International Labor Office (ILO) recommendations regarding freedom of association, expanding unionization to sectors of the society which did not have this basic right, removing most of the numerous mechanisms of state intervention that restricted union power, and finally, eliminating the discriminatory distinction between blue- and white-collar workers.[37] Opposition was, in fact, clearly the result of political problems. The compulsory plant union and the fragmentation of the union system had become the power base of thousands of union leaders who, in turn, had forged the entire brokerage system which mediated between clienteles and political parties. The union leaders had transformed the major weakness of the system into their own personal base of power, a power base that would be destroyed by the proposed legislation. For the unionists, including those belonging to the government party, it was more acceptable to live with the limiting provisions of the Labor Code than with the liberalizing rules of the modern legislation. Moreover, both the left and the right had their own reasons to oppose the law. The right condemned the notions of worker participation in the management of the enterprises, while the left condemned the pluralist principles advocated in the bill, which would allow the formation of parallel syndical organizations at the national level, weakening the hegemony that the Chilean Workers Confederation (CUT), controlled by the left, had over the workers movement. The reform of the industrial relations system was never approved by Congress.

The attempt to reform the unionization structure set up a conflictive pattern of interactions between the government and the organized urban workers, but it was the wage policy pursued by the government that produced the worst confrontations. The most critical of them took place in November 1967, as a result of the Workers Capitalization Fund.

According to the government's program, inflation was going to be gradually contained, assuring the workers a yearly wage increase equal to the increase experienced by the Consumer Price Index. The economic crisis of 1967, and especially the lack of improvement in the national savings rate, forced the government to modify the system of wage readjustment for that year. The administration proposed to give the workers a wage readjustment that was equivalent to the inflation rate of the previous year, but a quarter of the wage increase would go to the formation of the Workers Capitalization Fund, to which the employers had to contribute an equal amount. The fund, according to the government plan, would be managed by representatives of the workers and the state and would be used to accelerate the process of industrial development, creating new industrial enterprises owned by the workers. The bill suspended for one year the rights to strike and to engage in collective bargaining.[38]

The government plan faced first the opposition of the PDC and later that of the entire Congress. At the party level, the plan deepened the already marked differences between the three different factions that had coexisted until then: the "officialists," the "*terceristas*," and the "rebels." The officialists, representing the right wing of the party, supported the plan; the leftist *rebeldes* led by Chonchol opposed it; while the independent *terceristas* led by the president of the PDC, Rafael A. Gumucio, tried to resolve the differences.

Reasserting temporary control of his badly splintered party was the only victory that Frei could claim in relation to the Workers Capitalization Fund, better known in Chile as the "Chiribono affair," a term coined to indicate that this was a bond whose capital would never be paid to the workers, reflecting the total lack of confidence in the government fund. In the final analysis, Frei, after using all his political clout, managed to have the party approve the financial aspects of the plan, but the limitations on the right to strike and to engage in collective bargaining were soundly rejected. However, this temporary victory was followed by a much larger defeat, both for Frei and for the party itself. The plan was defeated in the Congress because of the opposition of the workers and the left who interpreted the entire issue as a government manipulation to place on the back of the working class the costs of the development program. The right, whose votes the government expected to have, opposed the bill on the grounds that it involved an added expense for the employers. For the PDC the Chiribono affair marks the beginning of its political disintegration. In late 1968 the *rebelde* faction left the party and formed MAPU, the Movimiento de Acción Popular Unido.

The congressional defeat was followed by a reorganization of the Cabinet and a political realignment of the PDC, in which the emphasis on total independence, or *camino propio*, and confrontation with interest groups was replaced by a turn toward the right. Consequently, after 1967, most of the programmed reforms did not come through; inflation increased and production fell; the government doors were partially opened to the bourgeoisie, and relations with organized labor, including the labor sector of the party, turned violent, with increasingly frequent strikes and other evidences of social unrest.

The rejection of the communitarian approach left the government with basically only one option, to slow down the process of reform, which in Chile could only be interpreted as a turn to the right. Rafael A. Gumucio, former president of the PDC, said that "rather than an instrument of revolutionary change, we are [now] an instrument of the status quo, administrators of the system, guarantors of the established order."[39]

Summary

As mentioned elsewhere, the basis of Chile's political stability was its capacity to combine the absorption of a limited but always expanding number of interest groups into the political system. Politicians served as brokers, linking these numerous clienteles with the system as a whole. These two elements, coupled with a shared interest of the political elites in the preservation of the system, made the Chilean political system one of the most stable in Latin America.

The advent of the Christian Democratic government represented a break with Chile's most essential political traditions. President Frei not only won the election by an absolute majority, but he did so not as a candidate of a coalition, but of one party, running on a single party program. Moreover, the nature of the party's program was certainly a novelty in Chilean politics. The electorate, accustomed to either the paternalistic politics of the right or the clientelistic politics of the radicals, was faced with a program that stressed issues such as national integration and national interest, which were quite foreign to the political environment. A large part of the electorate, in its search for a solution to its multiple socioeconomic problems, opted for this new alternative.

Carrying this mandate, the Frei government decided to pursue simultaneously a program of social and economic development along with a program of political reform transforming Chile's most resilient socioeconomic structures, creating a profound change in the functions of the state. The government rejected the traditional ways of making politics, *politiquería*, and reasserted the belief that a cadre of well-prepared and highly inspired technocrats could do for Chile what the traditional politicians failed to accomplish in the previous century.

What was not clear was how the PDC could accomplish all this within the parameters of Chilean politics and economy and in the context of a highly divided society. Success was expected to result from the simultaneous implementation of both the political and economic components of the program. One can argue that if the reforms were more superficial and required only the passage of simple legislation, the chances of success would have been much greater, but all of the basic reforms implied constitutional amendments, which inevitably required the support of either the left or the right. This forced the administration to compromise on some of the essential aspects of its program and to delay the initiation of several of them for a couple of years, breaking the coherence of the plan and basically eliminating its chances to succeed.

The result of the delays and compromises in the critical programs were both economic and political. From an economic perspective, they denied the government the means to carry out its ambitious program of structural transformations that would, in turn, improve the living conditions of the majority of the population. Politically, the consequences were at least twofold, since they affected the party's future and the future of the entire social organization.

At the level of the PDC, the formal split of the party and the creation of the Movimiento de Acción Popular Unido (MAPU) was only the culmination of a process initiated in early 1968, during which the *rebeldes* competed with the left in launching the most acerbic attacks on the government, challenging the political road chosen by the administration. At stake was the maintenance of the *camino propio* (independent road) versus an alliance with the left. While Frei and the right wing of the PDC argued for the "independent road" as a still viable alternative, the *rebeldes* argued that pursuing the *camino propio* across the map of Chilean politics had in the past meant acceding to the pressures of the right, as they claimed the government had done since the Chiribono affair. In a position paper presented to the party's convention in 1969, the *rebeldes* argued that

> We ought to liberate ourselves from the myths of the ideology of centrism such as the "camino propio"—the eternal equidistant between the right and the left—[and stop] presenting ourselves as

an alternative to Marxism and Communism . . . all of which, in practice, leads to a divided country, and an alliance with capitalism and neo-capitalism.[40]

The divisions of the party, first in 1969 and later on during the Allende government, put an end to the political ambitions of the PDC and its viability as a centrist force capable of conducting the nation along a unique reformist path. To some extent, it seems that just as the PDC was able to transform the political system, the political system, in turn, transcended the party and transformed it into an institution as fragmented as the rest of the society.

The halfway achievements of the program had several consequences, both for the society and the state. The reforms in the rural sector and the policies toward the marginals released forces that until then had remained excluded from politics. President Frei noted in 1969 that over 20,000 organizations had been created in the marginal area, while over 500 unions and 3,500 committees had been created in the rural sector. But the Chilean congressmen resisted relinquishing their brokerage role and the clientelistic system in which it was rooted. In fact the enormous expansion of the polity rapidly overcame the absorptive capacity of the PDC. Congress in general was deluged under a tidal wave of new demands, which its members tried rather desperately to satisfy, expecting that they would be able to co-opt a sizable part of the forces newly released by the reforms. An excellent example of this phenomenon is found in the 1968 Wage Readjustment Bill to which the congressmen added 2,500 new articles, 1,000 of them dealing with the concession of social security benefits.[41]

Certainly, the PDC program aimed at producing just that expansion of participation, but, according to the Christian Democratic blueprint, the expansion would take place within new, more structured channels and would be complemented by a redistribution of power among the branches of government, which would increase the power of the Executive. The congressional refusal to modify the distribution of power and the channels of communication between the state and the society created a large imbalance between the societal forces and the capacity of the political system to satisfy them. The old politics of accommodation and partial reform became insufficient to deal with the pressing societal problems.

Moreover, the fundamental alterations involved in the reforms proposed by the PDC transformed the legislative process into a zero-sum game in which all participants acted under the belief that their own economic and political survival was at stake. The members of Congress, accustomed to partial and incremental reform, reacted to the sweeping reforms proposed by the PDC by resorting to the use of their favorite tools, political bickering and obstructionism, in a way not altogether different from their counterparts of 1924. Both the left and the right felt threatened by the PDC policies, and their political elites stiffened their position. Simultaneously, polarization was increased by the political decline and later by the division of the Radical Party, the centrist organization around which many of the coalitions of the past had been formed.

Thus, polarization resulted both from the erosion of the traditional center and the parallel appearance of political movements in the extreme right and in the extreme left. The seriousness of the commitment of Patria y Libertad on the right and the Movimiento de Izquierda Revolucionario on the left was fully demonstrated during the Allende government.

The extent of the political problems of 1969 was such that the otherwise reluctant members of Congress agreed to approve a constitutional reform that modified the distribution of power among the branches of government, accepting some of the reforms proposed by the Frei administration in 1964. The erosion of the political system had acquired a life of its own.

Undoubtedly, the administration was prompt to deliver the major bills geared to reform targeted areas, but, given the nature of the political system and the barriers set by the Constitution to its own reform, those major pieces of legislation were either rejected by Congress or subject to substantial changes. Given the interrelationship that existed among the different aspects of the program, the lack of congressional approval of the major reforms endangered the entire program.

The transformation of the role of the state, the creation of new forms of interest articulation, and the incorporation of new sectors into the political society were all attempted and only partially achieved or achieved only at the end of the presidential period. Consequently, the administration was deprived of reaping any benefits from those carefully crafted programs.

One has to conclude that the major goal of the Frei administration, that is, the establishment of a communitarian state and an integrated society, could not be accomplished in the Chilean political environment of the 1960s. As has been discussed above, the existing political organization and the vested interests of the many sectors of the divided Chilean society could only permit incremental change, but could not allow the overhaul of the political system. The reforms pressed by the administration threatened every conceivable sector of the society, because they involved relinquishing rights and prerogatives that had become part of the sociopolitical and economic fabric of the nation. In the words of President Frei.

> My major problem is the implacable fight presented by both the right and the left, which in the final analysis coincide. The first one [fights] because it feels threatened by the social transformations; the second one, because the success of this experience [the process of transformations] conducted in liberty threatens the very basis of their existence.[42]

Frei's attempts demonstrate that there was no room in Chilean society for communitarian solutions. During the Chiribono affair, the influential General Secretary of the Chilean Workers Confederation (CUT) argued, "We are against the chiribonos because more than a project of wage and salary readjustments, this is the expression of a policy that tries to reconcile the social classes."[43] Certainly, neither the organized workers nor the organized landowners, neither the bourgeoisie nor the middle class, neither the right nor the left were interested in pursuing a common goal. In fact, it seems that communitarianism was an anathema that had no place in the Chilean society.

The policies of the communitarian state involved at least a minimum degree of consensus on the existence of a national interest, and this consensus did not exist in Chile. However, compromises either with the right and/or the left allowed the administration to obtain partial reforms that impinged upon the society in the years to come. Reforms in the countryside made the peasants active political participants, while the policies toward the marginals incorporated an entire social class to the realm of politics. Given the incapacity of the PDC to effectively transform their economic status, both groups began to move within the political system in search of better luck.

In brief, the reforms effectively destroyed the basis of the populist state, but they were not able to replace it with a new form. The reforms also set in motion a process of massive political incorporation characterized by the development of intermediate organizations that very shortly ran out of the control of the party and the government. Finally, this process of political mobilization was followed by a process of polarization of the political forces.

The failure of the Frei program reveals the deep and profound differences that existed in Chilean society and the great differences that existed between the narrative and the reality. The program did offer the possibility of creating a society in which the class differences would be somewhat reduced; it offered the possibility of social integration along the lines of the communitarian idea; it offered a set of policies that if implemented would turn some of the promises made by the narrative into a social reality. The left's attitude of opposing the Frei programs in order to maintain the support of its constituents appeared to have succeeded in 1970 with the election of Salvador Allende. However by 1973 the success quickly and violently disappeared among the smoke of bombs and gunfire. The right's attitude of denying Frei the resources required to carry out his program backfired, at least in the short run, since the population opted for a much more radical approach to solve the existing social problems. In the long run, the overthrow of Allende and the policies of the Pinochet regime allowed them to maintain their economic power.

CHAPTER 5

The Politics of Social Security Reform under Frei, 1964–1970

F rei's attempt to reform Chile's social security system, and his partial success, provides an excellent illustration of the complexities of the Chilean political process and the difficulties encountered by any government attempting to carry out structural transformations. The Frei administration pursued the reform of the social security system through administrative and legislative channels, encountering a considerable degree of success in the first and an equivalent defeat in the second. The various reform bills proposed by the administration are described and analyzed in this chapter, as well as the administrative policies carried out by the Frei government. All stress the multiple links that existed between the political organization and the social security system. The attempted policies were an excellent example of Frei's goals, such as the integration of the rural areas into the modern society and the creation of new forms of interest articulation and aggregation that cut across socioeconomic classes.

Commitments to Reform

Since the 1950s every president of Chile had argued for the need to reform the social security system, and each had committed himself to a *Reforma Previsional* or social security reform.

During the presidency of Jorge Alessandri, this commitment materialized in the creation of a special commission charged with the task of studying and proposing the guidelines for reforming the entire system. This commission was known as the Prat Commission, after the name of its chairman, the well-known social security expert and politician, Jorge Prat. Between 1959 and 1964, the commission, formed by top social security administrators and labor law experts, analyzed the existing social security legislation and prepared a reform bill. Its final product was the most thorough study of the social security system ever made in Chile.

In its 1,600 pages the Prat Report analyzed and criticized each of the components of the social security system, emphasizing the anarchical nature of the system, the lack of coverage of large sectors of the society, the inequalities, and the high cost of the system. The Prat Commission called for the creation of a universal, uniform, and sufficient social security system. It recommended a universal system of benefits and financing as well as a universal approach to health care and a universal family allowance system. It recommended a functional administrative approach and suggested that the entire system be administered by four main funds: one for pensions, one for family allowances, one for health benefits, and one for workman's compensation. The reduction in administrative costs and the elimination of privileged pensions would allow, in turn, a reduction of the social security tax.[1]

The Prat recommendations, finished the last year of the Alessandri administration, were never applied. As was traditional in Chilean politics, in the final year of the administration the government was busy attempting to keep the economy from sinking and, at the same time, trying to present the best possible face for the upcoming elections. Certainly this was not the time to propose a social security reform. Nevertheless, the report prepared by the Prat Commission has endured as a titanic accomplishment, and as the most authoritative and complete analysis of the system ever done.

Frei's position favoring a total reform of the system was clearly expressed by the president himself and top government officials, who argued for a complete, organic restructuring of the pension, health, family allowances, and occupational accidents programs.[2] A first manifestation of this commitment to reform was the Constitutional Reform Bill introduced to Congress in December 1964, in which the rights to social security and health were included among the social rights of the citizens.[3]

In May 1965, in his first annual State of the Nation speech in front of the Congress, Frei declared,

> It is the decision of my government to undertake the integral reform of the social security system. The multiplicity, disparity, privileges, omissions and injustices of the present system not only constitute a permanent factor of unrest and disturbances, but they are a paralyzing obstacle to the achievement of the economic development plans and the social reforms that are part of our program.
>
> In this legal proliferation we have reached incredible extremes, legislating in favor of small groups and, many times, in favor of only one person, thwarting all sense of universality on which modern social security is conceived, and confusing its objectives with those of Public Assistance and Welfare.
>
> I must say to the country something which is not new, but that nevertheless is a fact: this system will inevitably lead to the bankruptcy of the social security funds, or the bankruptcy of the country.[4]

In the same speech, President Frei summarized the main deficiencies of the entire system: (a) lack of universal coverage; (b) insufficient benefits for the majority of the population while certain small groups received excessive protection; (c) unequal distribution of revenues among the funds; (d) outmoded conception; (e) costly administration; (f) anarchy in the financial structure; and finally, (g) "irritating discriminations, fruit of a legislature which was concerned with the interests of certain groups and not with the interests of the community as a whole."[5] And he added that his government was working on a new bill that would entirely reform the social security system, adopting the recognized principles of universal, integral coverage and unified administration and eliminating discriminatory privileges and inequalities. Moreover Frei, as a demonstration of his commitment, announced that this process had already been initiated through a number of administrative actions geared toward the same purposes. The most important of those actions was a 100 percent increase in the family allowances received by the blue-collar workers and peasants.

President Frei's promises of social security reform materialized through two distinct mechanisms. Legislatively, bills were introduced to Congress that aimed at reforming the central aspects of the social security system. Administratively, social security coverage and health services were expanded to those sectors of the population that until 1964 had remained excluded from the programs. In addition there were increases in certain benefits to particular sectors of the population.

On the legislative front, the administration did not initiate any major action during 1965 other than the formation of a commission charged with the preparation of three reform bills dealing with family allowances, occupational accidents, and pensions. The commission was formed by top social security experts under the leadership of professors Patricio Novoa and Alvaro Covarrubias and was known as the Novoa Commission. The following sections will analyze the contents and the fate of the reform bills proposed by this commission and the administrative reforms carried out by the Executive.

Family Allowances: Administrative Improvements

On 6 January 1966, William Thayer, the Minister of Labor and Social Security, announced that the Commission had finished the preparation of a bill reforming the system for family allowances. The bill was based on the principles of universality of coverage, uniformity of benefits and obligations, and a unified administration.

It is important to note that the economic and social impact of family allowances was comparable to that of the pension system, and that the bill prepared by the Novoa Commission sought to obtain its entire reform. The bill adopted the well-recognized principle of universality of coverage, to be achieved by expanding the system to the self-employed, providing uniformity of benefits and obligations, and expanding the benefits by adopting a more modern concept of family benefits. Particularly important was the new administrative system which involved the creation of new entities called Compensatory Funds. These funds were organized according to territorial, professional, or economic units. The units were similar to those proposed to administer the occupational accident insurance in both their corporatist structure and their social function. The creation of these new funds would eliminate the differentiation between blue- and white-collar workers. These and other provisions of the law clearly indicated that its overall purpose was to eliminate differences among occupational groups. A new National Fund of Family Benefits was created to centralize the collection of revenues and equalize benefits across the society.

The reform to the family allowances program was not only a keystone in the construction of social security reform, it had an economic and political importance of its own, bearing strongly on the industrial and the redistributive policies pursued by the administration. From an economic perspective, family allowances amounted in 1968 to 4.1 percent of the GNP and 27.7 percent of social security revenues, and, according to some estimates, it represented up to 20 percent or 25 percent of the wage bill.[6] Central to both processes was the establishment of a system of equal and proportional contributions across the board, and the creation of a flat system of equal benefits for blue- and white-collar workers, distributed and controlled by the National Fund. From a sociopolitical perspective, the program's elimination of the differences between blue- and white-collar workers, if approved, would become a landmark in Chile's social legislation. Furthermore, the administrative reform would deprive the existing funds of one of their larger sources of power and revenues.

Perceiving the strong opposition that a bill of this nature would generate, the Executive decided not to request urgency for the bill, and to immediately open the doors to compromise. In the Foreword to the bill, Frei and Minister Thayer explained that the administration was aware that "there would be need for a profound study on the part of Congress in order to introduce the necessary modifications in an environment of open dialogue."[7] But opposition to the project was of such magnitude that the administration decided to abandon the legislation. In the words of Covarrubias, "[T]he bill was opposed by the right and the left, and it was so unanimous that it never went beyond discussion by the Labor Committee of the Chamber of Deputies."[8]

Nevertheless, the administration did not give up in its basic commitment to expand family allowances to certain sectors of the population, nor in its desire to bring more equality to the system. Through amendments inserted in other laws, the government obtained the legislative approval needed to expand the system to all students up to twenty-three years of age, to adopted and stepchildren, and to pregnant women.[9] Equality in the benefits provided by the system was pursued through administrative channels and through insertions in bills that dealt with specific sectors of the working class, but were not related directly to social security (e.g., the Agrarian Reform and the Peasant Unionization Law). These administrative actions were designed to increase the allowances of the lowest income sectors, especially those of the peasants. As a result of these policies, President Frei was able to declare that in 1967 the allowance received by a blue-collar worker was three times larger than in 1964.[10]

In brief, total reform of the family allowances program was not accomplished by President Frei. From a technical point of view, the bill proposed by the administration complied with the ILO recommendations and certainly represented an improvement over the existing system, but it was politically unacceptable since it attacked one of the programs dearest to the most articulated interests. In the face of opposition to a total overhaul of the system, the Executive sought to advance as far as possible through administrative channels, while pursuing at the same time partial, incremental legislative reforms that were wholeheartedly accepted by the members of Congress, regardless of their political affiliation, because they involved only the expansion of certain benefits to specific sectors of the society.

The Reform of the Health System

The health policies of the Frei regime were built on the notions that health is a basic right to which all the inhabitants of the country are entitled and that the state has the obligation to provide medical attention to all who could not afford it themselves. The notions emphasized the need for curative and preventive medicine and from its inception, the administration worked toward an integral solution of the problem of health, beginning with the formulation of the First National Health Program. The program contained a general diagnosis of the health conditions of the Chilean people and a number of programs designed to alleviate the most critical problems.

The most serious critiques of the existing system focused on its organization and the coverage. Regarding the organization, the program criticized the existence of both private and public medicine. The private area satisfied the needs of the upper class and sectors of the middle strata. The public health system provided curative services for the blue- and white-collar workers and the indigents, along with their families, and preventive medicine to the civil servants and sectors of the white-collar population and their families.

Excessive bureaucratization and centralism were part of the problem of the public health sector, but it was recognized that the central issues were the scarcity and skewed distribution of resources.[11] Regarding coverage, the program detected a lack of services available to the rural inhabitants and those living in the marginal urban areas. Since those were also the lowest income groups and had the highest infant and maternal mortality rates, they had to become the subjects of expanded medical attention.[12]

Thus, the National Health Program proposed the reorganization of the public health sector and its expansion, both in terms of the population effectively protected and of the quality and quantity of the services received by the population. In the long run, both problems would only be solved by creating a United Health Service, Servicio Unico de Salud, which would provide medical attention to the entire population. However, given the nature of the existing system and the costs involved in its transformation, the Executive opted for a gradual modification of the health delivery system.[13] The health policies pursued by the government are best studied in an administrative dimension, i.e., the implementation of the Plan Decenal de Salud, and along a legislative dimension through the Ley de Medicina Curativa.

The Plan Decenal de Salud (Ten-Year Health Plan) contains the policies designed and implemented by the administration to improve and expand the public health sector. The program had two basic objectives: to obtain a 2 percent yearly reduction of the mortality rate, and to be able to satisfy, at the end of the ten-year period, the medical demands of the population. Studies showed that only half of those demands were satisfied and that the sectors whose demands for medical attention could not be satisfied were primarily those who did not have social security coverage.[14] By 1964 the general infant and maternal mortality rates, even though they had been constantly declining since the creation of the SNS, were still quite high. Especially alarming were the infant mortality rate (102.9 per thousand live births) and the maternal death rate. Even more alarming were the enormous differences between the average rates and the infant mortality rate in some of the southern provinces where the infant mortality rate was as high as 390 per thousand live births.[15] Accordingly, the ten-year plan implemented through the SNS earmarked increased resources for these two groups, increasing the number of medical hours and the number of beds devoted to children and pregnant women and creating peripheral clinics and emergency centers. By 1968–69 the infant mortality rate had declined to 81.1 per thousand live births, exceeding the government expectations.[16]

The government success in this area resulted not only from the improvement in the medical attention offered to the lowest income sectors, but from a general improvement in the standard of living and educational level of those sectors. These improvements were the consequence of government policies toward the rural sector and the marginals, complemented by the literacy campaign initiated in 1965 and specific sanitary and nutritional policies pursued by the government, such as the distribution of milk, which directly attacked undernourishment, one of the crucial factors in the high infant mortality rate.[17] Aware of the magnitude and impact of malnutrition, the government focused on undernourishment as a key piece in the health program. Between 1964 and 1967 the administration almost doubled the amount of milk distributed free to children under six years of age. The distribution of milk was coordinated with an expansion of pediatric attention and educational programs for the mothers. The programs succeeded in reducing the infant mortality rate.

Despite the persistence of inequalities in the distribution of health and problems such as malnutrition, the reforms carried out by the Frei administration represented an important step toward the improvement in the distribution of health, particularly in the marginal and rural areas and for children and mothers, affecting a dramatic improvement in the health statistics.

Deep in the trunk of the evolutionary tree of health policies in Chile was the original association between the social security system and the health system. This association determined the division of the public health system along occupational lines. Since its inception, the public health area functioned around the SNS, which provided around 90 percent of the public health services, providing medical attention to the blue-collar workers and the indigents and their dependents. The SNS also performed general sanitary, epidemiological, and other functions that dealt with the entire population.

The remainder of the public health sector was formed by the health services for the military who enjoyed high-quality and complete medical attention, and by preventive medical services and limited curative attention available to the civil servants and the white-collar workers through the Servicio Médico Nacional de Empleados (SERMENA).[18] The absence of a system of curative medicine for the civil servants and the white-collar workers was one of the major deficiencies of the entire public health area. In other words, through SERMENA, the 250,000 persons affiliated with the white-collar workers fund, the 186,000 people affiliated with the civil servants fund, the retirees of both funds, and the dependents of both active and retired white-collar workers and civil servants only had access to preventive medical attention, and to curative attention only in cases involving cardiovascular, neurological, and pulmonary diseases. These groups amounted to 1,400,000 people, or almost 10 percent of the population.[19]

Partially following the conceptual basis delineated in the Health Plan, the government decided to deal with the issue of curative medicine for the white-collar workers and the civil servants, not through a new bill, but by modifying a bill introduced by the Alessandri administration. These modifications presented in 1965 sought to create a system in which the targeted groups could choose between obtaining medical attention through the SNS, or privately, through registered physicians who would receive the equivalent of the SNS fee.[20] From the point of view of the government planners, this system would serve as an initial step in the process of unification of the public health sector, through the voluntary incorporation of sectors of the middle class into the system. The financial structure, based on a contribution equal to 1.5 percent of the salaries paid by the employers and the employees, was perceived to be in line with the redistributional policies of the government.

The project fell immediately under the heavy fire of several groups: the Colegio Médico, the Chilean Medical Association, SERMENA, the civil servants, and groups of public health specialists. While some opposed the bill because it would bring even more people to the doors of the already overcrowded SNS, others opposed it because, by providing the option between private and public medicine, it would introduce yet more discrimination to an already stratified system.[21] The heavy criticism suffered by the government bill, and especially the criticism of the Colegio Médico, had an impact on the members of the Congress, who decided to name a subcommittee to draft a new bill.[22]

After over a year of discussions the subcommittee accepted the formula proposed by the Colegio Médico, the Sistema de Libre Elección (Free Choice System), which involved the right of the white-collar workers to obtain subsidized private ambulatory attention and either subsidized private hospitalization or hospitalization in the SNS. Administratively, it involved the participation of the Colegio Médico, SERMENA, and the SNS for the hospitalization services. SERMENA was also charged with the administration of a medical assistance fund, the financial backbone of the system, that was formed by contributions paid by the employees (1 percent of the salary), the retirees (1 percent of the pension), and a 2 percent contribution paid by the White Collar Workers and Civil Servants funds. The fund subsidized up to 50 percent of the price of the medical visit of the higher income groups, and up to 70 percent of the price of the visit in the case of the lower income groups. The value of the different services rendered by the physicians would be periodically fixed by the Minister of Health.[23]

This law, approved unanimously by Congress in May 1968, is a paradigmatic example of the nature of the process of social legislation in Chile, and, as such, deserves some attention. First, it reflects the preeminence of Congress over the Executive in the legislative process. In this case, even though the Executive had a congressional majority, the members of the legislature were much more inclined to respond to pressure from below than to the ideological commands from above, and consequently changed the entire nature of the law. Second, it is clear that Congress was not geared to take bold initiatives, but once the Executive had taken those initiatives, all the political parties sought to profit from them for clientelistic purposes. Third, the prolonged congressional discussion centered around the nature of the system that was going to be created, the relations between the private and the public sectors, and the role of the different interest groups.

And the Colegio Médico, SERMENA, and the Civil Servants and White-Collar Workers funds determined the administrative form taken by the system and the relations between the public health sector and private medicine at large.

The position taken by the Colegio Médico in opposition to the provision of ambulatory services through the SNS on the basis that the overcrowded SNS could not provide those services adequately was certainly well grounded. However, behind the administration's bill was the assumption that the SNS would receive a massive infusion of money from the social security funds and the state, which would allow it to expand its operation and provide the required services. Moreover, as was argued by the Minister of Health, the SNS was already providing attention to a large group of lower income white-collar workers who did not have the means of obtaining private attention without receiving any compensation for those services.[24]

Physicians' opposition to the government bill was grounded basically on economic reasons. In the context of a system of public and private medicine in which 99 percent of the physicians were employed by the SNS at much lower salaries than other professionals in the public administration and of a poor society that did not have enough resources to spend on health, the administration's proposition spelled economic disaster for the physicians.[25] In fact, it would have forced them to expand the number of hours served in the low-paying public medicine sector, and it would have meant the disappearance of a sizable number of new patients from their private offices.

From the point of view of SERMENA, the government's bill represented the beginning of a process of merger with the SNS, and it was understood as a maneuver on the part of the government to shore up the dwindling SNS finances with the funds provided by the White-Collar Workers and Civil Servants funds, at the expense of SERMENA. For them the best policy involved the provision of ambulatory attention, directly or indirectly, through SERMENA, leaving hospital care in the hands of the SNS. Reflecting traditional class differences, the representatives of both the Civil Servants and the White-Collar Workers funds opposed the government bill. Their views coincided with those of SERMENA, arguing for an expansion of the system around the existing institution. Neither from a social nor from a financial standpoint were they ready to merge with the blue-collar workers.

In the final analysis, the law reflected the position of the white-collar workers, the civil servants, and the Colegio Médico. The Sistema de Libre Elección advocated by the Colegio Medico involved an expansion of the private over the public sector, giving the Colegio control over the physicians registered in the program. But the physicians lost control of what turned out to be the most crucial piece of the program, the determination of the fees paid to the physicians, which remained an exclusive governmental decision. SERMENA secured an important part in the system, since it retained the administration of the fund created to finance the system controlling the payments made both to the physicians and to the SNS, which was charged with providing hospital care.

Why did an administration that had an absolute majority in the Congress accept this hybrid system, which, from their own perspective, served to introduce more discrimination into the health system and did not represent a step toward the unification of medical services? Analysis of the congressional debates clearly indicates that the Executive was well aware of the nature of the program being approved by the legislature and its contradictions with the government policies in that area, but, given the multiple foci of opposition generated by the bill and the financial strains produced by the deteriorating economic situation, the Executive seems to have accepted this as a temporary solution, as a step toward the increase in medical protection.

The Ley de Medicina Curativa provided effective and integral medical care to a half million people, but the system had a negative impact on the blue-collar workers since the facilities of the SNS were never expanded in the proportion required to absorb the white-collar population, creating permanent conflicts over the utilization of the SNS physical plant.[26] From a financial perspective, the fund created by the law proved to be insufficient to satisfy the costs of the program, and SERMENA, a financially solid institution until the creation of the system, developed a large debt to the SNS, increasing the financial strains of that organism.[27] From the physicians' point of view, the system did not render the benefits that they had anticipated. In fact, the Executive retained control over the fees paid by SERMENA to the physicians, and succeeding administrations were extremely reluctant to increase them. As many physicians argued, the expansion of the curative medicine to the white-collar workers was effectively accomplished on their backs.

The Reform of the Pension System

The Frei administration pursued the reform of the pension system on two different levels, using two different mechanisms: it sought to expand it into the rural sector by fully implementing the existing legislation, and it tried, unsuccessfully, to reform the entire pension system through legislative means.

The Expansion of Coverage

As has been repeatedly shown, the capacity of a given social group to obtain social security protection was linked to its capacity to articulate political demands. In this context, the lack of social security protection of about 50 percent of the rural population and the lower benefits received by those in the system were simply a result of the exclusion of this sector from the coalitions that dominated Chilean politics during the mid-twentieth century. This process had already led to the existence of two parallel societies ruled, in practice, by different principles and laws. Those laws and practices had traditionally restricted the rights of the peasant to organize and therefore to have an impact on the state and its policies.

As discussed in chapter four, the administration's attitude toward the rural sector resulted from the preeminent position that rural problems had in the development program, as well as the political decline of the right during the first years of the administration. This new attitude called for the elimination of the archaic system of socioeconomic relations in the countryside and the reduction of the power of the landowners, in particular, and the right, in general, who were depicted as archaic social elements, or *momios*.

Thus, the expansion of social security coverage and the enforcement of the labor law system were the result of both the temporary political decline of the right and the appearance of new administrative cadres committed to the enforcement of those policies. Among those cadres, the bureaucrats involved in INDAP, Institute for Agricultural Development, and CORA, the Corporation of Agrarian Reform, were particularly committed to the process of rural reform.

In the social security field this administrative zeal was reflected in the creation by the Labor Department of Special Committees of Rural Control (CEFA), which was charged with the task of enforcing the existing labor laws in the rural areas.[28] The effective implementation of the laws required the control of about 75,000 agricultural units. With a staff of about 255 inspectors this task was unattainable. Given the administrative limitations the Labor Department decided to initiate an experimental plan that combined the resources of the Department with those of the Superintendencia de Seguridad Social to form teams of inspectors that would sweep a given area. The inspectors had the authority to investigate working and living conditions for compliance with laws and to impose heavy fines on the landowners if they did not comply. The success and effectiveness of the program produced its expansion to the rest of the country. As one peasant put it, "[F]or the first time in the history of Chile . . . justice is being done and the law is being applied to those accustomed to evading it."[29]

Two major problems characterized the application of social security laws in the countryside, lack of coverage and low pensions. If the lack of social security coverage in the rural areas had been the result of the power of the landowners to evade the social security laws, the lower pensions there were the result of discriminations in the wage legislation which had traditionally established a minimum agricultural wage much lower than that received by urban workers. By 1964 the average daily agricultural wage was 13.9 percent of the average wage paid to an industrial worker and 33.9 percent of the average wage received by a petroleum worker.[30] Laws concerning rural minimum wages had existed since the early 1950s, but were openly discriminatory, despite the fact that they had been theoretically passed to protect the rural worker. Some improvement in the situation of the peasant took place after the enactment of Law 15020 (1962) which established a minimum agricultural wage, created a system of re-adjustability, and determined the cash component of the wages. This last point concerning the cash component was one of two issues addressed by the law which were necessary for the application of social security provisions in the countryside; the other concerned the problem of family allowances.

The persistence of pre-capitalist relations in the countryside was evidenced in the fact that only part of the wages were paid in cash (25 percent in 1953), the remainder was represented by the housing provided by the landowner, the land the peasant was allowed to cultivate for himself, and other customary arrangements. The lack of regulations regarding the proportion of the wages that had to be paid in cash had without any doubt facilitated the exploitation of the peasants and served as another source of evasion of the social security laws. By establishing first, a minimum wage, and second, that at least 50 percent of the wage had to be paid in cash, the law facilitated the application of social security provisions.

Regarding family allowances, it had become customary among the landowners to retain the payment of them openly, violating the labor laws and committing a crime tacitly accepted by the authorities. A government memorandum records that

> there is a 'black legend' about what was called the robbery of the family allowances of the peasants, produced by the unscrupulous actions of patrones who cheated their workers.[31]

Law 15020 created an efficient procedure to file and resolve complaints about such violations.

The Frei administration sought first to reduce wage discriminations. Law 16250 (1965) made the minimum agricultural wage equal to the minimum industrial wage and established that at least 75 percent of the wage had to be paid in cash. Moreover, the law also defined the exact content of the non-monetary part of the wage and limited the working day to eight hours, making compulsory the payment of overtime, a regulation that already existed and had been applied in the urban sector since 1925. These provisions were followed by the Peasant Unionization Law and the Agrarian Reform Law, which effectively ended the pre-capitalist system of agricultural exploitation and made possible the full application of social security legislation in the countryside. Finally, the government, through its health program, improved the health delivery system in the rural areas, making available to the peasants services that had previously been inaccessible.

The Comprehensive Reform of the Pension System

After President Frei eloquently defended the need for a social security reform, expectations grew that a reform was imminent. By August 1966 it was unofficially known that the Novoa Commission had finished drafting a complete reform of the pension program and that the bill would soon be introduced to Congress. By October the administration still had not initiated the legislative process, but public controversy about the nature and extent of the reform had already begun.[32] Thus the reform of the pension program was being opposed prior to its public announcement on the basis that the reform would damage the interests of the workers. The government reacted by offering to open up a dialogue with all the forces that opposed the reform, recognizing that as long as the contemporary political regime remained, it would be impossible to change any part of the pension system without at least the partial support of the interest groups. The reform bill was, in fact, already in the hands of the Undersecretary, who was waiting for the political opportunity to introduce it to Congress.

The bill prepared by Patricio Novoa, known as Anteproyecto de Reforma de la Seguridad Social, contained a total reform of the existing social insurance system. It established a national social security system which provided integral coverage and similar benefits and obligations to all dependent and independent workers and students, and a universal welfare system. It created a system of old age, disability, and survivor pensions, as well as a number of medical benefits for the workers and their families, unemployment compensation, and maternity benefits. The bill eliminated all existing differences between blue- and white-collar workers.

The proposed funds could be established by employers' or workers' associations, representing either a territorial or professional unit or a specific economic activity. The funds would be administered by a body formed by representatives of the employers and employees. Employer's contributions to the fund amounted to 20.5 percent of the wages or salaries, workers' contributions amounted to 6.5 percent, while the state contribution was 14.5 percent for all the insured population except for civil servants and military personnel. The general reduction in the size of the contributions was the result of the elimination of two of the most expensive items in the social security bill, the pensions based on years of service and the *perseguidoras*.[33]

The administrative structure created by the bill applied the principles of unified administration by the beneficiaries. From this perspective the most salutory aspects of the bill were to reduce the number of funds to no more than twenty and to eliminate the differences in coverage created by occupational divisions. The bill increased the power of the Executive, who was given the authority to create funds and to determine the population covered, depriving Congress of those powers.

Novoa and the other members of the commission went beyond a simple modification of the system, seeking to integrate the social security system into the national economy and to break ground for the future foundation of a welfare state. For instance, the Anteproyecto created a compulsory savings plan whose funds would be steered into the housing sector and established a rational system of pension readjustments that would protect the retirees against inflation. The creation of a universal program of social assistance and a system of unemployment insurance, in addition to the emphasis on issues such as preventive medicine, rehabilitation, and professional retraining, made the proposed legislation among the most advanced social laws in Latin America, transforming the particularistic, stratified social security system into a universal, integral income maintenance and welfare program.

Despite the fact that the reform bill was ready to be sent to the Congress by late 1966, the government opted not to initiate the legislative phase of the reform at that time, since both the Executive and the PDC were already involved in the legislative fight for the Agrarian Reform and the Copper Agreements, two key issues that had already become entangled in the legislative thicket. In fact, since the administration had already been forced to compromise on the extent of the Agrarian Reform in order to get approval of the Copper Agreements that modified the status of the American-owned multinational corporations involved in the exploitation of copper, it seemed politically unwise to send the social security bill at this time. Sending this bill to Congress would only make those two projects and the social security bill more liable to the pressures of the opposition. Political wisdom led the PDC leaders to keep the social security bill out of congressional hands until the other two issues were resolved.[34] Legislation on the Agrarian Reform and the Copper Agreements was not passed until mid-1967, but again, political and economic considerations postponed the decision to send the reform bill to the Congress. The previously mentioned economic crisis and the subsequent political crisis made the prospects of steering the bill through Congress very bleak.

The year 1968 looked propitious for obtaining the passage of the bill, since the president had not only regained control of his splintered party, but he had brought under control the labor sector of the PDC, which would have certainly opposed the legislation. Furthermore, at the ministerial level, the replacement of Thayer by a low-key, but efficient technocrat, Eduardo León, was also a positive sign. It had become increasingly clear that the social security reform would not be enacted if the administration retained Thayer,[35] whose problems with labor had deprived him of the necessary credibility and leadership with both workers and members of the Congress inside or outside his own party. León, with a fresh and more open attitude toward labor, looked like the person to negotiate the passage of the law. Finally, at the congressional level, the passage of the Agrarian Reform, the Peasant Unionization Law, and the Copper Agreements had cleared the way for a debate on a new structural reform. Since 1968 was not an election year, it was believed that the members of Congress would have enough room to legislate.

Once more the mere prospect of having the Reforma Previsional discussed by Congress created enormous uproar, with the advantage that by now everybody knew the nature of the proposed reform, giving the affected groups the opportunity to express their views. The instant opposition to the reform forced the Executive to delay again the introduction of the bill to Congress.

The bill never was introduced to the Congress nor was it officially discussed by any of the political parties or labor organizations. The political risks posed by the Reforma Previsional were without doubt too large to be faced by a government that was becoming increasingly isolated from its own supporters, by a party whose internal divisions were more profound than the commitment of its founders and leaders to solve them, and by a political system whose own polarization was depriving its participants of the ability to see when their particularistic interests had to be put aside in favor of the national interest. According to *El Mercurio,*

> When the parties abandon their political mission of searching for serious solutions [to the national problems] and they devote their actions to the adulation of the electorate, it is natural that they become subject to the pressures of the verbal extremists, and of those mentalities incapable of building a real *política.* Internal quarrels, personalistic attitudes and precipitated actions are the fruit of the political climate in which the collective interests are lost, and the low passions proliferate.[36]

The seeds of the future destruction of Chile's political system were already implanted.

In August 1968 the government opted for a different course of action. Instead of sending the Anteproyecto prepared by Novoa, the Executive decided to send to Congress a much shorter social security reform bill that partially modified the pension and the family allowance programs. This bill was appended to the 1969 Fiscal Budget Bill as a means of forcing a speedy passage through the Congress.[37] The main elements found in the twenty-one articles of the bill were: (a) elimination of *perseguidoras* and pensions based on years of service only for those persons that had worked less than ten years and for those that became affiliated after 31 December 1968; (b) establishment of uniform requirements for old age and invalidity pensions; (c) creation of the Cajas de Compensación de Asignación Familiar, and authorization for the government to transfer the surpluses of the Family Allowance Funds; and (d) concession of an authorization to the Executive to modify the system of incompatible pensions and the structure of contributions within the next three years.

The new bill certainly failed to reform the system as the administration had hoped, but at least it would set the basis for the elimination of its major vices. The bill clearly avoided dealing with the "vested rights" of those who had been affiliated for over ten years and tried to deal mostly with the younger generation of workers and with the future. The bill also sought to rationalize the use of the Family Allowances funds, a proposal which would easily improve the benefits received by the majority of the workers without substantially harming the rights of the privileged minorities.

The administration, this time through the Minister of Finance, reaffirmed its commitment to social security reform and asked for a patriotic action on the part of the members of Congress and those groups affected by the reforms, "in order to avoid transferring to future governments a problem that is acquiring enormous proportions."[38] But this appeal was heard neither by the members of the Congress nor by the interest groups; instead, the bill generated instant opposition.

The PDC set up a committee to study the bill, but this divisive issue served only to bring to the fore old tensions, which had become more acute anyway as the 1969 parliamentary elections neared under the shadow of decreasing party popularity. At the same time the government, trying to smooth over differences with the organized blue-collar workers and hoping that they would understand that a reform could only favor the majority of them, initiated discussions with members of the CUT Directorate. After almost a year of discussions during which CUT consistently opposed the reform, the conversations broke down. The government did not pursue the passage of the modified reform through Congress, since it was certain of its defeat.

The letter with which CUT put an end to the negotiations with the government and which marks the end of the Frei administration's attempt to reform the system expresses the uncompromising attitude of the organized workers, and, to some extent, it reflects the way in which the entire political system operated. "The workers have unanimously opposed the social security reform bill introduced into Congress in mid-1968 because it lessens the conquests obtained [by the workers] through long years of fights."[39] The president of CUT then added that, in agreement with the decisions taken by the Fifth National Congress, the CUT demanded that a social security reform should be based on the following notions: (a) maintenance of each one of the social security benefits obtained by each of the sectors of the working class; (b) direct and effective participation of the authentic representatives of the working class in the administration of the funds; (c) rejection of the fusion of funds at the will of the President; (d) estimation of all social security benefits in re-adjustable units;

(e) immediate equalization of the family allowances received by peasants, blue-collar, and white-collar workers; (f) uniform requirements for old age pensions at sixty years of age for males and fifty-five for females, or after thirty and twenty-five years of work respectively; (g) establishment of an unemployment subsidy, equal to the average wages of the last six months; (h) establishment of a maximum pension equal to eight minimum wages; (i) expansion of the system to the uncovered population; and (j) creation of a new financial structure based on a tax paid only by the employer and by a progressive new tax to be paid by those in the upper income brackets.

There is little question that most of the demands presented by CUT were unattainable. It was unrealistic to propose a reform that would maintain each of the rights and privileges of each sector of the working class, while expanding the population covered, increasing the benefits, and reducing the contribution of labor. Furthermore, the insistence on an increase in the social security tax paid by the employer was both politically unattainable and economically catastrophic.

Should the letter then be interpreted as demagoguery, seeking only to obstruct the PDC policies? To some extent one can interpret the letter as a purely political document which reflected the political opposition of the communist-controlled CUT to the Frei administration. But the letter also reveals the realities of Chile's political economy as well as the economic deprivation of Chile's working class, whose economic situation had not drastically changed despite the government emphasis on improving the standard of living of the working class.[40]

In fact, the CUT letter explains the role that social security had acquired in Chile, a role which had nothing to do with the recognized universal principles of social security, but was the result of the declining real income of the working class. In this context, the benefits provided by the social security system were considered not as income maintenance in duress or retirement, but as necessary supplements to a perennially insufficient wage. This, in turn, explains the virulent opposition to relinquishing any of their rights and privileges and the constant fighting for new benefits. Furthermore, this income provided by the state had been a direct consequence of the political power of labor, which, limited by law and practice in its ability to improve its contractual arrangement, had resorted to using its political influence to supplement its income. In other words, the income that could not be obtained by the contractual labor relation had to be obtained from the state through the clientelistic relations that sectors of the working class developed with the political parties. As the CUT directorate argues in another section of the letter:

> These benefits, scarce as they are, have been the product of hard battles and constitute essential and primary mechanisms for the defense of the interests of the working class, always threatened by the oppression of the employers and the reactionary governments which result in unemployment, political persecution and low wages.[41]

However, this strategy of the workers certainly backfired. As it has been shown the workers had the ability to extract new benefits from the politicians and the political system, but these unfunded benefits generated budget deficits and inflationary pressures that only worsened the workers' situation. Because of inflation those benefits soon became insufficient, generating new pressures for more partial benefits.

Summary

The social security policies pursued by the Frei administration have to be analyzed in the context of the existing political system and in the context of the other structural reforms proposed by the President.

The distribution of power in the vast machinery of the Chilean state allowed President Frei to carry out those reforms that could be enacted by administrative fiat, without the intervention of the Congress. Committed to reform, the Christian Democratic cadres acted as the instruments of a process which, by and large, involved application of the existing legislation or of principles adopted in the early 1920s, such as expansion of coverage to the rural sector or a redistribution of fiscal resources such as in the expansion of health services. In these areas the administration moved rapidly and with a clear concept of the goals it aimed to achieve.

The existing distribution of power, on the other hand, made it impossible for the Executive to effect a complete legislative reform of the system. The universality of the opposition generated by the social security reform leads to the conclusion that the issue was deeper than a conflict of political ideologies or party lines; it was an issue rooted in the very substance of the political and economic system, and, as such, its resolution required the prior reform of the entire political structure. At one level both the right and the left agreed on the need to reform the system, the right because it was costly and inefficient, the left because it was discriminatory and stratified. At another level everybody, regardless of their political color, rejected the reform because it hurt the interests of their party's clients. For example, while the government was initiating the reform process, the right was proposing to decrease the retirement age for blue-collar workers.[42] This bill and the hundreds of other bills that increased social security benefits to small groups and individuals indicate that members of Congress, regardless of their political disposition, always supported the expansion of the system. Clearly, this process was a consequence of the clientelistic-competitive nature of the political system and the divided nature of the society. In the words of President Frei:

> I am aware that such an important undertaking [the social security reform] is going to create even greater opposition than the one produced by the Land Reform. In matters related to social security, all agree in considering unjust and inconvenient the present rules, but when the moment arrives for people to lose their privileges, they show violent rebellion and bring all sorts of pressures to bear.[43]

A reform of the social security system such as the one proposed by the administration would undoubtedly damage the interest of the core constituencies of the political parties prompting those parties to reject any reform proposal. Consequently, social security reform first required a reduction of the role of the political parties in the policy-making process in addition to a transformation in the relations between the branches of government. More importantly, it required a transformation in the basic understanding of the functions of the state.

In fact, one can argue that the social security system had become such an intrinsic part of the entire political apparatus that it could not be reformed unless the entire political system was also reformed. As the thousands of social security laws indicate, social insurance had become one of the key mechanisms by which the system maintained and reproduced itself. It is very likely that if the constitutional reform proposed by Frei in 1965 had been approved or, in other words, if the power of the Congress and the interest groups had been curbed, the reform would have been possible, but without it the social security reform could not become a reality.

In conclusion, what the administrative success and the legislative failure demonstrates is that, in the context of the political system that existed in Chile in the 1960s, a powerful leader, followed by dedicated cadres who believed in a new role for the state, could accomplish some tasks by simply putting the bureaucratic machinery to work in the service of those interests. And that the most vigorous program could not move in the legislative area unless a formal redistribution of power between the branches of the government preceded it, a redistribution that would enhance the power of the Executive vis-à-vis the Congress.

The failure of the Frei administration to reform the system shows once more that in Chile, in the 1960s, the different political forces did not have any capacity to compromise and that there was no real interest in approximating mythical unity. In fact, the chances of reaching that mythical unity were disappearing very quickly.

CHAPTER 6

The Failed Road
to a Socialist State

Politics and Social Security Policies
during the Allende Regime, 1970–1973

D uring the three years of the Allende administration, Chile
underwent a number of political transformations that had
begun long before Allende came to power but which were
accentuated by the policies pursued by that administration. Political
processes whose roots are intertwined with the origins and evolution
of the populist state were intrinsic to the crisis of the Allende administration. They came to the fore as a result of the policies pursued by
the government of Eduardo Frei and became critical issues during the
years of Unidad Popular (UP) coalition. Thus, despite the different
nature of the policies followed by the Frei and Allende regimes, there
is, from our viewpoint, a continuity of political effect between the administrations so that they constitute one analytical unit.

This chapter attempts to highlight the most salient elements of
the socioeconomic model proposed by the Unidad Popular coalition,
as well as some of the most important political phenomena, particularly the decline of the system of checks and balances established by
the 1925 Constitution, the changes in the forms of interest representation and aggregation, and the changes in the role of the state.
All these factors impinged upon the ensuing governmental crisis, contributing to the destabilization of the political system and to Allende's
downfall.[1]

As in the past, social security policies were an integral part of the regime's approach to the economy and society. Although social security policy making was not at the center of the political discussion, it was effectively used by both the government and the opposition to strengthen their electoral forces, having an indirect effect in the structural transformations attempted by Allende. Those policies involved an expansion of the system to new pressure groups and an attempt to restructure the health delivery system.

There is no doubt that the traditional political elite had lost a great deal of power during the 1960s, but the communitarian state envisioned by Frei was not created and Chile's society continued to be unequal and stratified. Frei's reforms clearly intended to solidify the capitalist system under more modern arrangements and like President Alessandri in the 1920s he encountered almost universal opposition. Just like in the 1920s the political paralysis and economic crisis was to be resolved through military intervention. However, the intervention of 1973 was to be premised not on ideas of inclusion but on the exclusion of large sectors of the society.

There is a great deal of continuity between the policies of the Frei and the Allende administrations. Both attempted to transform the basic distribution of political and economic power and both attempted to create a more equitable and unified society. However, the political right was not interested in the implementation of the official narrative. Narratives are effective systems of social control; they are precisely premised on the idea that they will sustain an existing socioeconomic system without posing a threat to the interest of those who developed the narrative. As the Allende policies began to threaten those interests, the policies of the elite had to shift from loyal to disloyal opposition.

On the other hand, the political environment of the 1960s and early 1970s contributed to the radicalization of important sectors of the society. The Cuban Revolution and the revolutionary movements inspired by Castro and Guevara, the war in Vietnam, and the events in Europe and elsewhere in 1968 contributed to the creation of a new belief in the power of the people versus the government. In Chile these events would contribute not only to the election of Salvador Allende, but to a generalized radicalization of the political environment in which the power of the traditional elite was undermined. The elite's response was fully felt in 1973.

The Chilean Road to Socialism

Fundamental to understanding both Allende's candidacy and presidency was his backing by a loosely formed coalition of parties that ranged from the centrist radicals to the anti-system socialists. In this coalition Allende was at best a catalyst. His prestige and popularity, which went beyond that of the political parties of the left, made him the best candidate, but his political views represented neither all the positions comprised by the coalition nor the views of important sectors of his own Socialist Party.

As a former student leader, physician, founder of the Socialist Party, Minister of Health, Senator, and President of the Chilean Senate, Allende's political career could be matched only by the career of his political enemy, but personal friend Eduardo Frei. Allende belonged to a now extinct brand of Latin American politician who were capable of combining a clear ideological base and a deep knowledge of their country with a broad appeal to the masses. In the case of Allende, both his friends and enemies alike recognized the respect he had always shown for political institutions and his ability to maneuver within their limits.[2]

Through the years the differences between the socialists and the communists, as outlined in chapter two, had increased, becoming critical after the 1964 election. In fact, after Allende's defeat in 1964, the socialist and the communist political lines became totally divergent. The communists reiterated their belief in the use of the democratic system to gain power, arguing that the defeat in the 1964 election had been the product of the inability of the Socialist and Communist parties to expand their popular base. The socialists, on the other hand, resolved in their 1967 convention to reject once more the electoral road,[3] but in line with their previous ambivalence, the rejection did not mean a refusal to participate in the elections. By 1969 the Socialist Party was clearly divided into two camps: the majority faction led by the rebellious senator Carlos Altamirano that had opted for the revolutionary line, arguing that "revolutionary violence provided the only means to reach power,"[4] and the minority faction led by Salvador Allende that supported the formation of a multiclass, multiparty coalition to win power through the electoral process. This was also the approach followed by the Communist Party. The coalition would include not only the popular parties, but those representing the advanced sectors of the middle class, such as the leftist sector of the Radical Party and the two groups that had recently abandoned the Christian Democratic Party, the MAPU and the Izquierda Cristiana.

To the ideological and strategic differences among the parties of the left were added the traditional rivalries that were focused on the control of the labor movement and the representation of the working class, as well as deep personal conflicts such as those existing between Allende and Altamirano. In the final analysis the conflicts that plagued the Allende administration were the result of both the profound differences—ideological, pragmatic, and personal—that existed among its heterogeneous membership and the unrelenting opposition of the Christian Democratic and National parties, as well as the policies of the U.S. government. The internal political conflicts and the U.S. policies are analyzed below.

As the Chilean electorate went to the polls in September 1970 it was faced with three options: a right-wing coalition supporting former President Jorge Alessandri that stressed conservative economic management, honesty, and the personal economic and political experience of the candidate; a Christian Democratic candidate, Radomiro Tomic, who stressed the need for a *camino propio*, an independent Christian Democratic government, and a program of fairly radical reforms including nationalization of copper and land reform; and Salvador Allende's Popular Unity coalition. What is interesting here are two contradictory processes. On the one hand, Alessandri obtained a larger percentage of the vote in 1970 than in 1958 (in 1958 he obtained 31.6 percent and in 1970 he obtained 35.2 percent); on the other hand, Allende's vote in 1964 was higher than in 1970 (38.9 percent in 1964 versus 36.6 percent in 1970). Finally, the combined vote of Allende and the 28.1 percent of the vote obtained by Tomic clearly indicates that the society was supportive of major socioeconomic reforms.[5]

The Program

The program of the Unidad Popular combined a number of structural reforms, such as a new land reform and a complete nationalization of copper, with redistributive measures, e.g., wage policies and taxes, and with welfare state–type policies, such as the creation of a universal social security system and a universal health system.[6]

Having diagnosed a profound crisis in the entire political and economic organization, the UP argued that the crisis could only be solved by transforming the existing system of dependent, underdeveloped capitalism into a socialist system. The role of the UP was to initiate the process of transformation of the state and the society.[7] As Sergio Bitar, former Minister of Mines, notes, the UP program was the result of the combination of four different principles: (a) the socialist notion of nationalization of the means of production, a policy that was expected to initiate the key economic and political transformations; (b) the Dependencia-theory rejection of the developmentalist approach and the emphasis on changing the country's articulation with the international economic system, reflected in the policy of nationalization of copper and decreased reliance on external finances; (c) the adoption of the ECLA (United Nations Economic Commission for Latin America) notion of an economic development strategy based on the consumer goods industry; and (d) the Keynesian emphasis on the role of the fiscal policy as a key element in the reactivation of demand.[8]

It is important to place in proper perspective the revolutionary nature of the program, which "aimed at transforming the socioeconomic basis of power and creating a new correlation of forces that would allow them to control the state, and to generate a new hegemonic ideology."[9] According to Allende, this two-pronged approach—transformation of the economic base and transformation of the role of the state within the existing institutional framework—constituted *la via chilena al socialismo*, the Chilean Road to Socialism. In the words of Allende,

> We want to utilize bourgeois institutionality, to make possible the changes that this country needs, and it is claiming, in the political sphere, in the economic sphere, and in the social sphere in order to arrive to socialism. In the Chilean case the use of this institutionality is possible because it [the institutionality] is spacious and open to these changes.[10]

Essential to Allende's strategy was the notion that the existing constitutional structure would allow the beginning of changes in the economic role of the state, which, in turn, would be able to transform the basic economic structures of the society. Once the original transformations had taken place, the dialectic process originated by them would allow the transformation of the legal structure, changing the political configuration of the state. In other words, from Allende's standpoint the entire transformation of the state depended on the success of the economic program and its capacity to change the distribution of economic power within the society.

In practical terms, according to Allende, given the nature of the Chilean political system and the minority position of the government, the Executive should pursue policies that would allow the administration to increase its popular base of support. Once a majority had been achieved, the state would begin the process of transforming legal structures through constitutional mechanisms. Two policies would spearhead the process, the creation of the "social property area" and the income redistribution policy.

The creation of the social property area involved the socialization of the economic mainstays: banks, large industries, utilities, and the large distribution companies. This process was expected to have a political as well as economic impact.[11] Politically, the process of socialization would erode the power base of large sectors of the bourgeoisie while increasing popular support for the administration by delivering to the workers one of the basic campaign promises, namely, worker control of the means of production.[12] From an economic point of view, the fiscal control over those key sectors of the economy would allow the state to capture the surplus produced by those enterprises, surplus which would be channeled toward the redistributive policies pursued by the government. This would also positively affect the political support for the UP.

Redistribution of income also had a political and an economic component, serving concurrently to increase the UP's popular support and to spur a process of increased production, which, during the first stage, would not require any increase of investment but would be carried out by using the idle industrial capacity. Moreover, increased demand for consumer goods would reorient industrial production toward the consumer goods industry, which was basic to the economic strategy of the government. In the ensuing years the costs of the process would be absorbed by the economic resources generated by the nationalization of copper and the socialization of the major industrial concerns.[13]

In summary, income redistribution would generate a process of demand-led economic growth, changes in the composition of demand, and a change in the productive structure which would move industry toward mass production of consumer goods and away from the production of intermediate goods. One expected effect of all this would be a positive shift in the balance of payments. Politically, the redistributive policies implemented through a combined system of wage increases and price controls would expand the UP's popularity and its congressional power in the coming elections. Once this congressional majority was achieved, the UP would focus on the transformation of the political structures.

The entire strategy was based on the assumption that the transition to socialism would proceed in stages and that it would evolve from the use of the electoral system to increase the support for the government and its program.[14] As a result, the program contained a well-balanced set of policies geared to win an electoral majority formed by the middle and working classes, the peasantry, and the marginals. The key piece in this strategy was the success of the economic policies, which was expected to render enough surplus which, in turn, would be distributed among the low-income groups that comprised the majority of the population.

The Popular Unity in Power

The last two years of the Frei administration were characterized by a generalized economic and political crisis. Inflation, always a good indicator of Chile's political and economic health, began to increase in 1968, after a four-year decline, and reached 34.9 percent in 1970. Public expenditures in housing and public works decreased, affecting the rate of unemployment which began to climb and reached 7.0 percent in 1970. Moreover, Allende's electoral triumph produced a large capital flight, which, in turn, put pressure on the currency and produced a drop in private investment.

As soon as the new administration came into power it sought to apply, simultaneously, its economic and political strategy using redistributive policies as the basis for both. At the same time, the government initiated its program of structural transformations that involved an accelerated and full application of the Agrarian Reform Law, passed during the Frei administration; the passage of a constitutional reform that made possible the nationalization of the assets of the two copper multinationals; and the nationalization of banks and large industrial and commercial concerns.

In the short term, redistributive policies based on wage and price controls were quite successful. They generated a sizable increase in the workers' share of the national income, which grew from 52.8 percent in 1970 to 61.7 percent in 1971.[15] GNP increased by 7.7 percent and unemployment decreased to 3.8 percent. The major problem created by implementing the UP economic model was a burgeoning fiscal deficit, which, for 1971, was equivalent to 36 percent of the total budget. In spite of their short-term success, in the long run these policies created enormous pressures on the economy, generating an inflationary spiral of unprecedented proportions.

The attempt to simultaneously carry out structural transformations and short-term redistributive policies was unique to the Chilean experience and it illustrates the difficulties involved in any attempt to transform an underdeveloped capitalist economy into a socialist one. Two other elements contributed to the failure of the process: the dependent nature of the economy and the fact that the entire political system operated under the aegis of a balanced distribution of power between the Executive and Congress. This two-pronged process produced economic and financial tensions which were rapidly propagated by the structural transformations taking place. The international political and economic environment, especially the policies pursued by the Nixon administration to strangle the Allende government and undermine its political and economic base, the hostile reaction of Chilean capitalists who did not trust the government and consequently refused to invest, and the rapid increase in workers' demands above and beyond the political and economic means of the government exacerbated tensions and fostered the ensuing economic crisis. By mid-1973 the inflation rate reached 323 percent per year, while industrial output had decreased 10.7 percent and deficit spending was equal to 50 percent of the budget. To satisfy the conflicting political pressures and the lack of external financial resources, the administration resorted to expanding the money supply, which, during 1973, increased 3,400 percent.[16]

From a political perspective, the short-term redistributive policies produced beneficial effects. In the municipal elections held in March 1971, the UP vote increased to 49.75 percent, and in several by-elections that year the regime received similar demonstrations of popular support across the nation. Nevertheless, the electoral victories did not change the two basic weaknesses of the regime: the Allende regime was still a minority government which controlled the Executive branch and around 40 percent of the Legislature and it was a conflictive, coalitional government. Allende, as head of the regime: and at least nominally head of the coalition, had to deal with both of these issues.

Allende expected to be able to override the limitations imposed by the minority nature of his government by increasing its popular base of support, both within the working class and also within the middle class. Expansion into the middle class and co-optation of middle-class groups into the coalition were fundamental strategies of both Allende and the Communist Party, and they were designed not only to increase the electoral forces of the coalition, but to patch the battered legitimacy of the regime. In the long run, these policies were expected to generate a parliamentary majority that would allow the UP to change the constitutional structure and the very nature of the state.

Although Allende was able to design a strategy that would permit him in the future to alter the basic structure of power, he could never design a strategy to deal with the distribution of power within the coalition. Conflicts among the parties were both practical and ideological. Practical conflicts arose when the UP decided to run the state apparatus through a quota system, allowing each party a proportion of the civil service jobs, and also allowing them to proselytize and dispense political patronage from the government bureaucracy, just as all their predecessors had done. This division of jobs brought conflict, incoherence, and inefficiency to the government and deprived the administration of the effective use of the bureaucracy. The bureaucracies and the bureaucrats were nothing but a tool of either the party or the party factions that controlled them and they were used to advance particularistic interests.

Ideologically, the conflict was centered around the divergent socialist and communist strategies. The communist strategy proclaimed the need to "consolidate first, advance later" (*consolidar para avanzar*), while the socialists argued for the need to do just the opposite: advance first, consolidate later.[17] Since the bureaucracy had been divided among the coalition parties, the end result was a chaotic administration and contradictory policies which impaired Allende's effectiveness and forced him to act as an arbitrator among competing political interests instead of acting as a leader. Consequently the stalemate continued and the coalition could never adopt a unified strategy.

The different ideological stands held by socialists and communists became vital to the survival of the government as they tried to decide policies regarding three critical areas: the problem of political violence and *espontaneismo* or spontaneity, the government's position vis-à-vis the existing political institutions, and the definition of the economic sectors. These three areas also constituted the foci of the conflict not only within the coalition, but between the UP and the opposition.

Espontaneismo is a term developed during this period and used to describe the processes of land seizures, the occupation of industries, commercial establishments, government agencies, etc., as a result of a direct action of the masses, geared to produce the rapid solution of real or fictitious labor-management conflicts. It is necessary to add that the degree to which those actions were spontaneous is highly questionable, since most of them were directed and organized either by the Socialist Party or by the Leftist Revolutionary Movement (MIR). Although Allende and the Communist Party consistently opposed these tactics, in practice the government did not dare to use force against those participating in the *tomas*, or takeovers. These actions became part of the daily political scene and had considerable economic impact—for instance, in the first eighteen months of the administration, peasants permanently occupied 1,700 rural properties.[18] From a political standpoint, these actions wrested legitimacy from the administration and the President's actions.

Political violence resulted from the actions of various groups in the right and the left that had opted for a rejection of the peaceful, electoral road to solve their socioeconomic and political grievances. In the left, the most important of these groups was the Movimiento de Izquierda Revolucionaria (MIR)—the Leftist Revolutionary Movement—that had appeared in the late 1960s under the leadership of combative middle-class students and was supported by the revolutionary sector of the Socialist Party. In the right, the most vocal group was the Movimiento Patria y Libertad—the Movement Fatherland and Liberty—which was prepared to create the conditions needed for a military intervention against Allende.

At least three different forms of "violent" political organization developed within the left, the *focos* or rural guerrilla movements, the *campamentos* formed by shantytown dwellers, and the *cordones* formed by industrial workers. All of them operated under the control of the MIR or the Socialist Party and were supported by prominent socialists.

Both the takeovers and the environment of political violence impinged upon the relations between the government and the opposition and among the parties in the Popular Unity. Despite Allende's verbal condemnation, political violence and *espontaneismo* continued contributing to a chaotic social environment, impressing upon the people the notion that they were governed by an inefficient president and an anarchic administration. They also created the impression that the administration, or sectors within the administration and the governing coalition, carried out and condoned actions and policies that were unconstitutional. The environment of political violence and the takeovers not only undermined the legitimacy of the administration, but also created an image of inefficiency and anarchy that was central to the downfall of President Allende.

Above all, the issue of defining the economic sectors fully institutionalized the conflict among the members of the coalition and between the branches of government, prompting the final polarization of the political system. The definition of the economic sectors involved the legal determination of which industrial and commercial enterprises would be included in the Social Property Area, an area crucial to the entire program. Since its inception the administration had been discussing the mechanisms it would use to establish the state sector of the economy as well as the size of that sector, but the lack of agreement among the members of the coalition regarding both questions thwarted the drafting of the required legislation. In lieu of that legislation a not-very-legal system of requisitions was initiated based on the Decree Law 520 of 1932, which allowed the government to requisition or expropriate any industrial enterprise that failed to comply with the law that regulated prices and stocks or that refused to use its full capacity. Under the leadership of the socialist Minister of Economics,

Pedro Vuscovic, who openly argued for a rapid and total nationalization of the economy in order to destroy the economic base of the bourgeoisie and its imperialist allies, a total of 328 enterprises were transferred to the state in a two-year period, using this decree.[19] In this case the lack of agreement within the coalition and the lack of legislation resulted in a short-term victory for the socialists, who had argued for a massive nationalization policy. In the long run it substantiated the claims of illegality and impaired the ability of the government to negotiate with the opposition.

However, the consequences of Vuscovic's rapid nationalization drive were not only political. This policy also had serious economic consequences given the poor economic management of these enterprises and the speed with which the process of nationalization took place. The nationalized enterprises and the enterprises that had been the object of *tomas* were placed in the hands of *interventores* or government-appointed managers, named not because of their technical expertise, but because of patronage. To illustrate the consequences of this process it is enough to point out that by the end of 1972 the losses of these corporations were estimated as 50 billion escudos.[20] On the other hand, given the lack of both foreign and domestic investment the government could not adequately support the companies that were in the hands of the state. Thus to the poor management was added the lack of investment and technical assistance that the newly nationalized sector required to produce efficiently.

A similar phenomenon happened in the agricultural sector where the Minister of Agriculture, Jacques Chonchol, used the land reform law enacted during the Frei administration to expropriate agricultural properties while supporting the forceful takeovers carried out either by MIR or MAPU followers. The deepening of the land reform process involved the expropriation of about one million hectares in a two-year period. Chaos reigned everywhere in the countryside: in the land reformed during the Frei administration, because the government was not supporting the creation of a communitarian form of property and, consequently, was not supporting the peasants that had received land under Frei; in the non-expropriated area because of the mounting fear of expropriation or *tomas* and the little interest of landowners to invest in the land; and in the newly expropriated land because of administrative and technical problems. The end result was a decline in agricultural production estimated at about 4 percent for 1972 and 16 percent for 1973.

What is important to note here is that the *tomas,* the requisitions, and expropriations of industrial and agricultural properties involved a de facto transformation and expansion of the economic functions of the state. The process of political violence, on the other hand, points to the erosion of the political system.

The Christian Democrats, meanwhile, anticipating the importance of the definition of the property areas and its political and economic impact, introduced to Congress a constitutional reform bill which proposed the creation of three different forms of property—private, mixed, and public—placing rigorous limitations on the Executive's power to transfer industries from the private to the public sector and on the state control of those industries. Although the amendment was unacceptable to the Socialist Party, conversations about this issue between the government and the opposition, and discussion among the parties of the UP, began shortly after the bill was introduced and continued until a few days before the coup. Although the moderates in both camps were close to an agreement, not once but several times, the extremists in the PDC as well as in the UP did not perceive the need to compromise.

In fact, what happened during this period is a process of political polarization characterized by the weakening of the political center. This process of erosion of the political center that began in the final years of the 1960s continued rapidly through 1970 and 1971, with its complete demise in 1972. This erosion was characterized by the weakening of the PDC, the division of the radical party, and the rebirth of the traditional right, which became the second most powerful political force. In the UP the extremists seemed to have the reins of the nation.

The tenuous political agreement between Allende and the PDC, the Estatuto de Garantías Constitucionales, that allowed the socialist leader to take power lasted only until July 1971, when the PDC introduced to Congress the constitutional amendment on the property areas. The short honeymoon was then succeeded by a transitional period in which the PDC acted as leader of the legal opposition, trying to make possible a compromise with the administration that would allow them to solve the contingent issues. However conversations between the PDC leadership, in the hands of the moderate Senator

Renán Fuentealba, and sectors of the UP, especially the communists and the radicals, were always obstructed by the right wing of the PDC, led by Frei and by the socialists, who were constantly and publicly threatening the Executive with their departure from the coalition if the administration compromised the program in any way.

The process of political polarization produced by the divergences between government and opposition concerning the future form of the socioeconomic organization was reinforced by some of the institutional changes resulting from the Constitutional Reform of 1970, which had changed the balance of power between the Congress and the Executive, reducing the power of the Legislature. In the words of Arturo Valenzuela:

> The Christian Democrats who had supported such a reduction [of the power of the Congress] had hoped they would still be in the presidency. Ironically, they were now the largest single party in a Legislature whose only powers were negative ones. It could reject or approve, but no longer could bargain and compromise.[21]

The Constitutional Reform had increased the powers of the President and the Executive's ability to carry out structural transformations, but it had reduced the congressional arena, constraining the ability and power of the members of Congress to maneuver and compromise. Moreover, Allende could not take advantage of the increases in the power of the Executive branch because of the profound divisions within the coalition that, in turn, divided the bureaucracy. Who, then, had political power? It seems that only those at the extremes of the political spectrum had at least enough power to obstruct agreements among the contending forces, while pressure groups took to the streets to try to grab as much power as they could.

The political center disappeared in 1972 with the formation of a new coalition, the Confederación Democrática, formed by the National Party and the PDC. The formation of the Confederación Democrática marked the end of the Chilean multiparty system. The multiparty system which had functioned and sustained itself on the basis of a flexible system of alliances was replaced by a polarized two-party system with each alliance located at the extreme of the political spectrum. That the new system lasted only a year was only one of the many fatal consequences of its formation.

Concomitant to the weakening of the political center and the traditional forms of political conciliation and accommodation was the emergence of a number of pressure groups. These groups, known as *gremios,* acted independently from the political parties and sought to pursue a direct defense of their socioeconomic interests. *Gremios* were formed by professionals, businessmen, landowners, etc., who had previously acted through the political party system, but now perceived the party's inability to influence the political process. In response, they moved, just as the rest of the society was moving, from institutionalized pressure to direct action. These actions were epitomized by the truckers' strike of 1972, which brought the entire country to a standstill. For pluralism, *gremios* substituted polarization, institutionalized in the formation of the Comando de Acción Gremial (Unified Command of Gremial Action)[22] comprising a variety of business and professional organizations. As Julio Durán, the president of the Colegio de Abogados (Chilean Lawyers Association) and former senator and presidential candidate argued, the Comando was a "wartime organization created to fight the anti-Marxist war."[23]

The disappearance of the political center and the identification of each of the branches of government with two irreconcilable political camps, had in fact destroyed the basic fabric that held together the Chilean political system. President Allende, aware of the seriousness of the situation, called the military into the Cabinet to enhance the Executive's legitimacy and tilt the political balance in his favor. However, the military had also become politicized and polarized, and Allende's decision to invite them to join his administration only deepened that process. Two distinguishable groups had already appeared within the military: the constitutionalists, led by the Commander-in-Chief of the Armed Forces, General Carlos Prats, who argued that the first duty of the Chilean military was to defend the government of the constitutionally elected president; and the institutionalists, who argued that the policies of some sectors of the government were endangering the military institution and that under those circumstances the primary duty of the military officers was to protect the unity and survival of their institution. By mid-1973 these two positions became irreconcilable.

Thus a divided military was called in to bridge the differences between the two branches of government. The new Cabinet, led by General Prats, was determined to find a solution to the institutional dispute between the Executive and Congress, at least regarding the economic program, and to create the social conditions required to allow the political forces to establish a truce. The military would also guarantee that the parliamentary elections of March 1973 would take place in an environment of political freedom. As soon as a degree of social peace was reestablished, all the political actors began to focus on the elections and the ensuing campaign polarized the political forces even more, consolidating the anti-Allende forces under the banner of the Confederación Democrática.

In practice, the March parliamentary elections involved not the renewal of the Congress but the survival of the entire regime. Thus, while the opposition was attempting to obtain two thirds of the votes in order to be able to impeach the President and put an end to the UP government, the UP sought to obtain the parliamentary majority needed to get the passage of its program. Both fell short of their goals since the opposition got 54.2 percent of the vote, and the UP only 43.9 percent. The election, instead of resolving the political crisis, only confirmed the extent and the degree of the existing polarization and the depth of the political division.

The electoral results, the inability of the political system to resolve the critical problems of the nation, and Allende's decision to call the military into the government, all reaffirmed the belief that the political system had reached the point of being neither operative nor viable. As a result, the masses who observed an unwritten armistice during the electoral period took to the streets again with renewed violence. The paramilitary groups of the right and left who had been proclaiming all along the futility of the electoral exercise were the only short-term winners. It was clear that the political stalemate, the *empate político*, was not going to be resolved by any political mechanism, but by force.

In the meantime the political stalemate continued. Frei continued to push for a definition of the economic areas, the Socialists continued threatening Allende to leave the coalition if any compromise with the PDC was worked out, and Allende either personally or through the more moderate elements in the coalition continued to search for a solution. And the military, the newest political actor, made it clear to the President that they would continue in the Cabinet only if Allende promulgated the Property Areas amendment, if the military could disarm the paramilitary groups, if the government tried to solve the problems with the United States, and if there was an attempt to create a more orderly administration. Although Allende wanted the military to stay, he could not satisfy these conditions without risking a breakdown in the coalition. The military left the Cabinet at the end of March much more divided than before, leaving the state and the society also more divided than ever before.

The departure of the military was followed by an intensification of the mobilization and polarization processes and of political violence, while political compromise was rendered impossible by the growing number of extremists on both sides. In order to solve the question of the economic property areas, the opposition was now demanding a plebiscite. Allende continued to search for political solutions, while refusing to deal with the leftist extremists. And the military began to rattle their sabers. The first coup attempt took place on 23 June 1973.

As the situation continued to deteriorate Allende turned again to the military for support and legitimacy. On 9 August 1973 a new Cabinet headed by General Prats was formed, which, as Prats correctly wrote in his diary, was Chile's last chance. But a growing number of military men and civilians deeply resented this action, and the decision of General Prats to support the constitutionally elected President deepened the rift within the military. On 22 August the Council of Generals voted to condemn Prats's decision and Prats had to resign. The same day the Chamber of Deputies passed a resolution declaring the illegality of the Allende administration. A second military Cabinet was formed on 28 August, but this one did not include any of the Commanders-in-Chief. General Prats was replaced by General Augusto Pinochet.

Although the analysis of Chile's international political and economic relations do not fall within the scope of this book, it is impossible to deal with the downfall of the Allende government without at least mentioning the impact of the United States' policies. The central issue here is Allende's commitment to transform Chile into a fully independent country through the nationalization of copper. The damage inflicted to U.S. investors and the Cold War environment determined the nature and extent of the U.S. policies.

It is now a matter of public knowledge that CIA operations geared to undermine Allende's power began during the presidential campaign and were intensified after election day with the formation of the Forty Committee which in September 1970 authorized a campaign that would create a climate of political and economic crises in Chile.[24] The U.S. government's goal was to induce the collapse of the economy and create political chaos. The Nixon administration and the executives of the large multinational corporations with investments in Chile wanted to topple the Allende government through covert operations. The confrontation between Allende and the Nixon administration was prompted by Allende's decision not to compensate Kennecott and Anaconda for the nationalization of the mines and the "intervention" of I.T.T. The nationalization itself was implemented through a constitutional amendment passed unanimously by the Chilean Congress in July 1971 and it was up to Chile's Controller General to determine the compensation given to the copper companies by the government. In October of that year the Controller General announced that because the companies had taken over $700 million in excess profits the government would not pay any compensation. At about the same time the government "intervened" the Chilean Telephone Company, a subsidiary of I.T.T., and I.T.T. began to pressure Washington to place an embargo on Chilean copper and to cut off loans to Chile.

In September 1971 the Forty Committee approved the expenditure of $700,000 by the CIA in support of *El Mercurio*, followed by $815,000 to support the opposition parties and another $965,000 for *El Mercurio* in April 1972.[25] According to former ambassador Nathaniel Davis, the U.S. government spent a little over $6 million for covert actions during Allende's three years in power.[26] The U.S. money certainly strengthened the opposition, particularly those groups that resisted compromise and a political solution to Chile's problems and reduced the economic strength of the government and its ability to deal with all the social and economic problems, but the covert operations themselves did not bring down the Allende government.

As this chapter tries to demonstrate, by 1973 the entire political and economic system of Chile was in a state of crisis. U.S. actions certainly contributed greatly to the crisis, but from my perspective the roots of the problem had to be found in Chile's socioeconomic and political evolution during the mid-twentieth century. Furthermore, President Allende and the other moderate political leaders failed to understand the impact that his policies would have on both the traditional political elite and the military. Maybe, in the final analysis, Allende and the leaders of the moderate left—as well as its base—were the only true believers in the democratic myth. From the standpoint of the political right the official narrative was beginning to lose its objective. The creation of a unified society was to remain as a myth, not a reality.

The Social Security and Health Policies of the Allende Government

Social Security: Expansion of Benefits

Both the UP program and its Appendix, the forty basic measures that the government would implement upon coming to power, showed the firm intention of expanding the social security system and health services to the entire population. *Previsión para todos* (social security for everybody) and *Salud para todos* (medical attention for everybody) were old favorite slogans of the left. Allende, as a physician and former Minister of Health during the Popular Front period, had shown a special interest in social programs throughout his political career.

The main objectives of the government in the area of social security were defined in the administration's economic plan and in the agreement signed between the CUT and the government in December 1970. In the area of social security the five-year economic plan enacted in 1971 called for expansion of coverage, uniformity of benefits, increasing the lower pensions to make them equivalent to the minimum wage, establishment of unemployment insurance, an effective welfare system, reform of the financial structure, the replacement of the tripartite contributory system with a system of direct taxes, decentralization of the administration, and elimination of the differences between blue- and white-collar workers.[27] Clearly, the implementation of these measures would have involved a total transformation of the social security system and the creation of a welfare state, but very few of them were actually implemented. The government only achieved an expansion of coverage and the improvement of the minimum pensions.[28]

On the other hand, the agreement signed between the government and the CUT after Allende's election involved the restructuring of the relations between the state and the labor movement. The document contained a number of governmental commitments geared to benefit the working class in labor relations, social security, and labor participation in the social and mixed property areas. In the area of social security the agreement called for a 100 percent increase of pensions across the board, the establishment of uniform family allowances, benefits for the blue- and white-collar workers, and the representation of workers on the boards of the social security funds. In the area of labor relations, CUT asked for a reform of the Books Three and Four of the Labor Code, dealing with the union system and the labor tribunals, the legal recognition of CUT, an across-the-board salary increase, and measures geared to protect employment and to reduce the unemployment rate. Finally, the workers requested direct participation in the administration of all the nationalized enterprises and those jointly owned with the private sector.[29]

The expansion of social security coverage that took place during the Allende regime operated according to traditional patterns—the creation of a new social security fund. The Caja de los Comerciantes Minoristas (the Retailers Fund) provided social security benefits to several groups of independent workers such as small businessmen, artisans, merchants, small landowners, independent miners, and priests and nuns, as well as to the largest previously unprotected group, the independent workers, who amounted to about 900,000 persons. The creation of this new fund increased the percentage of population covered to 76 percent of the Economic Active Population. These groups were incorporated in SERMENA for health protection.[30]

The government moved very quickly to improve the livelihood of both the retirees and the workers by granting increases in the minimum wage, augmenting the minimum pensions, and also increasing the value of some of the lowest pensions as well as the value of the pensions received by the military and the police. The administration also created the Fondo Unico de Nivelación de la Asignaciones Familiares (Centralized Fund for the Leveling of Family Allowances) which was expected to increase the value of the allowances and to eliminate the differences between the family allowances received by blue- and white-collar workers by 1973.

It is especially important to analyze these policies in the context of the 1970 Constitutional Reform, which gave the Executive the exclusive right to initiate social security legislation, and in the context of Allende's need to create a multiclass alliance that would constitute a solid political base for his regime. It is noteworthy that Allende expanded the social security system not to new sectors of the working class, but to middle-class groups that could be crucial to the political survival of the regime, and he did it by using the preferred mechanism of the middle class, the creation of a new social security fund.

Probably the most important accomplishment of the administration in the area of social security was to increase the blue-collar workers' pensions. The situation of the blue-collar worker retirees was extremely critical. Over the years the value of their pensions had been eroded by inflation. Repeated demands to obtain substantial improvements in the pensions had been denied both by the Alessandri and the Frei administrations due to the lack of a system that would allow the government to fund the indexing of pensions. The attitude of the Allende administration was entirely different. By administrative fiat, the administration improved those pensions substantially. According to Galvarino Melo, the Director of the Blue-Collar Workers Fund, between November 1970 and November 1972 pensions increased on an average of 520 percent.[31] The government also ended the practice of not paying pension increases mandated by law, which had become customary in the past. For the first time in many years, the retirees received the pension readjustments on time. In the words of the president of the Association of Retirees, Raimundo Doorman, "[W]e used to live without a cent; sometimes we did not even have money for food, and suddenly in 1971 they began to pay us money they had owed us for years and years. For many old people it was the first time we had one million pesos in our hands."[32] In the words of a pensioner, "I think that we are recuperating our human condition. Before it was a crime to be old. Now the Fund [Blue Collar Workers] is doing its best to give us the benefits that we could never obtain in the past."[33] The administration also simplified the traditionally long and tedious bureaucratic processes required to obtain social security benefits.

Family allowances also had a priority. In December 1970 the Minister of Finance, Américo Zorrilla, announced a 100 percent increase in the family allowances of the blue-collar workers, a measure that affected 1,600,000 people. Family allowances for the members of the military and the police increased by 110 percent, affecting about 118,500 people and the family allowances for those affiliated with the Civil Service Fund were augmented by about 90 percent. By mid-1973 family allowances had been raised by 200 percent. The goal here was to equalize all family allowances by 1976.[34]

Just as presidential actions in the area of social security can be interpreted as a mechanism used by Allende to capture the support of large sectors of the middle class, presidential inaction served the administration to consolidate the support from the working-class organizations. Consequently, Allende did not attempt to deal with any of the social security problems which, in the past, he had constantly condemned. Allende knew that any thorough reform of the system would hurt the "acquired rights" of the workers and would be vehemently opposed. Allende did not have either the political will nor the political power to carry out any major reform of the system.

Furthermore, Allende not only accepted the status quo, but actually reinforced the stratified and discriminatory nature of the social security system. For instance, when the government was in the process of nationalizing the copper mines, among the conditions placed by the copper workers to support the nationalization process was a constitutional guarantee that their social security rights would be maintained and that their pension system would not be assimilated with those of the other public servants.[35] A similar phenomenon occurred during the nationalization of the banks. In this case the government had to give assurance to the bank employees that their fund and their privileged system of benefits would be maintained.

In brief, the social security policies of the Allende regime were not geared toward the transformation of the system. The partial reforms implemented during this period expanded the system to some of the groups that lacked protection and improved the benefits received by those sectors of the population considered critical to the survival of the regime, such as the working and middle class, the military, and the police. At the same time, the administration guaranteed the maintenance of the privileged systems of those organized workers and employees whose support the government required in order to carry out some of the structural reforms. What one sees is that, as a result of the Constitutional Reform, the President had finally obtained better control of the policies and that he could use them for the benefit of the administration. In this respect the Constitutional Reform of 1970 effectively moved the center of social security patronage from the Congress to the Executive branch

Health for All: Salud para todos

Few in Chile knew as much about the problems and deficiencies of the health care system as Salvador Allende, and few were as determined as he was to improve the health of Chilean lower classes. The administration's plans included the establishment of a unified health system in order to eliminate the legal and practical differences between blue- and white-collar workers, the democratization of the administration of health services, and the expansion of medical services to the entire population. The access to health services was considered to be a basic right to which all of the inhabitants of the country were entitled and the government's approach to health also incorporated the notions of integral attention and emphasis on preventive medical care. In order to satisfy those goals the administration designed a six-year health plan that divided the goals of the program according to age groups. The overall goals of the plan were to satisfy the health needs of the society, to expand attention, to improve the quality of medical care, and to reduce the cost. Just like the Frei administration, Allende's plan emphasized primary care and support for the newborn as well as massive vaccination campaigns and milk distribution.[36] As Allende argued in 1971, there were 600,000 children in Chile with diminished intellectual capacity due to malnutrition.

Organizationally, the administration showed a strong commitment to the creation of the Unified Health Service (Servicio Unico de Salud). The creation of a unified system would not only eliminate the large differences between the health care provided by the SNS (National Health Service) and SERMENA (Servicio Médico Nacional de Empleados), but also reduce the costs. As a first step, the government modified the relationships between the SNS and SERMENA, allowing the SNS to capture a sizable part of SERMENA's resources. The plan encountered the massive opposition of both the Colegio Médico and the white-collar workers. While the physicians feared that the new system would reduce the scope of private medicine and consequently their economic well-being, the white-collar workers foresaw an imminent deterioration of their benefits. The government implemented its program through administrative fiat.[37]

The administration expected to generate a major increase in the demand for health services as a result of the changes in income distribution, the democratization in the administration of health, and the government public campaigns. Special emphasis was placed on popular participation as a mechanism by which the health needs and demands of the population could be expressed and satisfied. The democratization of the health system entailed the creation of the Local Health Boards (Consejos Locales y Paritarios de Salud) which incorporated beneficiaries into the local health administration.[38] The politicization of health was important because it raised a new awareness in the population about their health rights and about the obligation of the state to satisfy those rights. The democratization was also seen as a key element in the process of transformation of the Servicio Nacional de Salud since, according to the government, "the participation of the workers in the power structure of the health system will guarantee the decentralization of the administration and will emphasize the notion that the health system should benefit the majority of the population."[39]

Public awareness of health rights was reflected in the growth of demand for ambulatory medical attention, which increased 15.3 percent between 1970 and 1971, and of emergency attention, which grew 32.3 percent during the same period.[40] The Allende government continued to increase the number of outpatient clinics and emergency services, a program initiated by the previous government, and just as in the past, the administration found that the most serious problem was the lack of qualified medical personnel and their uneven distribution.[41] Targeted groups were again children and pregnant women.

The program of milk distribution was critical to the elimination of malnutrition and its consequences. By November 1972 the SNS could decisively say "that the daily half a liter of milk offered to every child was a reality." The evaluation of the programs accomplished by the SNS by November 1972 indicated that 84.4 percent of the children were getting milk. The program was considered to be particularly effective among school-age children since milk was distributed directly in the schools.[42]

The positive impact of the policies on the health of the society is clearly reflected in the decline of the general mortality and mother and infant mortality rates. Between 1970 and 1973 the general mortality rate decreased at a rate of 1.5 percent per year. Infant mortality was reduced from 31.3 per thousand to 26.9 per thousand in 1973 while the maternal death rate declined from 1.7 to 1.3 per thousand during the same period.[43] Furthermore, there was a clear reduction of infant death produced by infectious diseases and a reduction in malnutrition. It is interesting to note that these improvements were not the result of increased expenditures, but simply the reallocation of resources toward the most vulnerable groups. Most likely, reductions in the illiteracy rate and improvements in the distribution of income contributed to these results. It is also important to add that these policies were the result of administrative decisions and that they did not require congressional approval.

Parallel Crises: The Social Security and the Political Systems

The Social Security System in Crisis

By the early 1970s the social security system was in a deep crisis. Several dimensions of the crisis deserve further analysis: the inequities of the system, the insufficiency of pensions, and the financial crisis.

The system was highly discriminatory regarding the conditions needed to get a benefit, the nature of the benefits, and the financing. The conditions to obtain a pension could vary from zero to fifteen years of affiliation; the age required to obtain a pension ranged between fifty-five and sixty-five years of age; and the number of years of service required to obtain a pension could be as little as fifteen years in the case of the members of Congress, twenty-five years for the racetrack employees, and thirty-five for the white-collar workers. There were about twenty different systems to compute a pension (with or without indexing). There were several different systems of family allowances (the value of the highest family allowance was five times larger than the value of the lowest), and some groups had a number of additional benefits. Finally, workers' and employees' contributions ranged from 7.5 percent to 19.5 percent, while employers' contributions ranged from 6 percent to 52.33 percent.[44]

The question of the insufficiency of pensions for the majority of the blue-collar workers resulted from the combined effect of inflation and the system used to compute the pensions. Year after year the Association of Retirees would attempt to get either an increase in the total value of the pension or a better system of indexing of pensions. As Ivan Ljubetic documents in his history of the Association, the blue-collar retirees encountered all sorts of political problems. In a letter published in 1942, the Association argued that "95 percent of the retirees from the blue collar workers fund had to beg in the streets"; by the 1960s the situation had not improved. In 1965 the Association reported that the pensions did not even allow the retirees to eat, let alone pay rent or buy clothes.[45]

 Since the establishment of the social security system, especially after the mid-1950s, the Congress had been creating an enormous body of social security legislation through legislative riders, or, as the process was called in Chile, through *la via de las indicaciones parlamentarias*. The amendments constantly imposed new obligations on existing institutions or created new ones with total disregard for the financial consequences of their policies. According to Carlos Briones, former Superintendente of Social Security, "the entire social security system has been seriously affected by the obligations which different laws have imposed on it, without creating the adequate resources; and by the disjointed growth of the functions that each of the institutions has to perform."[46] Since a compilation of social security legislation was never made, it is impossible to know the full extent of the privileges and exemptions built around the core social security systems. What we do know is that by the late 1960s, as a consequence of these policies, the entire system was close to bankruptcy, its administration was expensive and inefficient, and that the benefits received by the majority of the retirees were totally insufficient. We also know that these privileges and exemptions revolved around three basic areas: the concession of pensions through special laws to individuals who did not have the legal requisites to receive them; recognition of years not worked or years during which the individual did not make contributions to the system; and concession of pension readjustments to various groups or individuals without adequate financing. By and large, all these laws were approved by Congress without adequate funding, or without funding at all.[47]

Another reason for the financial crisis of the system was the multiplicity of exemptions given by Congress to the entrepreneurs, which depended on two practices, the under-assessment of taxable wages, and the condoning of social security debts. Briones estimated that in 1965 the average taxable wage for social security purposes was around 57 percent of the real wages.[48] By 1973 it had declined to 40 percent of the real wages. This system of legal evasion resulted in a significant subsidy for the employer. This constant reduction of taxable wages, coupled with constant inflation, accounts for the progressive reduction in the real value of pensions. Legal condoning of overdue social security taxes was also a de facto benefit Congress constantly provided to entrepreneurs. It also destroyed the financial solvency of social security institutions and eroded their authority to collect social security taxes.

A final component of the financial crisis was the state's constantly growing debt to the Cajas, especially to the Civil Service Fund. Instead of making regular contributions as employers were supposed to, the state adopted a policy of paying lump sums, usually when the civil servant retired, or when the Caja's coffers were almost depleted. After the second half of the Alessandri administration, this situation improved, and the lump sums at least came with predictable regularity. But the expansion of the bureaucracy that took place during the Frei administration increased state obligations to the system to such a proportion that it endangered its survival.

In brief, the financial crisis of the social security system was not simply a product of the expansion of the system, nor a result of the demographic changes which altered the relations between active and passive population, nor a result of the process of expansion of benefits alone. In Chile, the process of expanding benefits, described by Mesa-Lago, was followed by an expansion of exemptions which became as relevant for the financial solvency of the system as the benefits themselves. Thus, while the expanding benefits reflected the power that labor could exercise over the state, the expanding exemptions reflected the power that the other members of the populist coalition, the entrepreneurs, could exercise over the political organization. The expansion of political participation and the unwillingness of the politicians to carry out political reforms created tensions and a massive economic crisis. In the final analysis, the different societal forces that formed the populist coalition pushed social security to the brink. Whereas the Frei administration tried to check those forces, the Allende regime only fed them.

The End of Politics

In 1972 President Allende and General Lanusse, the Argentine President, met in the Argentine city of Salta. During the reception ceremonies, General Lanusse mistakenly stood at the left of his Chilean colleague, when according to the protocol he should have stood at his right. Upon noting his error, Lanusse said to Allende: "Mr. President, excuse me, I am on your left," to which Allende replied, "Mr. President, be careful, to my left lies chaos."[49] The anecdote suggests the tenor of Allende's political beliefs which, in turn, determined his tactics. For Allende, his government and program could only be conceived within the parameters of the existing institutional order, which he believed was flexible enough to permit the structural transformations and the achievement of the socioeconomic goals proposed in his program.[50] Those goals did not involve, as many have wrongly argued, the creation of a Marxist-Leninist regime. As Allende argued time and time again, he was attempting to initiate the process of structural transformation that would put Chile on the road to socialism.

In the environment of the 1970s President Allende could not impose his political realism on his partners, and his negotiating abilities were limited both by the nature of the Popular Unity and the transformation of the political system. His *muñeca* was not enough to solve the mounting internal conflicts. As Peter Winn has clearly demonstrated in his study of the *toma* of the Yarur mill, President Allende was aware that the actions of the Yarur workers revealed that his leadership was questioned and that it was unclear who was determining the pace and direction of the revolutionary process and who was deciding its strategies and tactics. Within the Popular Unity coalition and government, autonomous yet overlapping centers of authority appeared to coexist uneasily, competing for ascendancy. The *toma* underscored the tension between revolution from below and revolution from above, the contest between workers and politicians, the clash between leaders and masses and their differing visions of the revolutionary process. It was a tension that was never resolved, and in the end it proved fatal to the Chilean revolution.[51]

To a large extent, the failure of the Allende government, both in its economic and political aspects, was rooted in the disunity of the UP and in the polarization of the political system which created an opposition resolved to combat the government, not through the democratic channels used in the past, but through the use of force. To what extent could the Popular Unity have formed a broad coalition that would have allowed the President to obtain legislative support for his policies? In order to form that coalition the Popular Unity would have to make serious changes to the program and most of the leadership was not ready to do that. Probably the only window of opportunity for negotiations existed between September and November 1970 and at that time the leadership was still savoring their electoral victory and had no sense of the extent of their future political problems.

The structural changes produced by the 1970 Constitutional Reform lead one to believe that a unified Executive branch could have accomplished a great deal, even if it did not have a congressional majority. But this assumes the existence of a coherent administration and a coherent political movement capable of transforming amorphous political support into real electoral support. The divisiveness of the UP factions, the political ambitions of several of its leaders, and the lack of a consensus to work within the existing system produced the total destruction of the system and its leaders. On 9 September 2000, twenty-seven years after the coup, the president of the Socialist Party, Ricardo Nuñez declared that "if [my] party would have been more judicious and prudent we would have not had to live through the rupture of the institutional system. If the different political sectors would have listened to the message of Cardinal Silva Henriquez and of President Allende, if we would have not found ourselves in entirely conflictive positions, we would have been able to avoid it."[52]

Finally, Allende, in spite of his political expertise, entirely misperceived the reactions of both the U.S. and the U.S.S.R. to his policies. In the context of the Cold War, the U.S. was ready to protect both U.S. investments in Chile and to maintain its area of influence. As for the Soviets, the Chilean experiment was not very attractive. By 1970 the Soviet leaders were fully involved in their détente policy and enjoying the benefits of the relaxation of tensions with the U.S. Chile was placed deep in the U.S. area of influence, far away from Soviet territory, and it did not offer any clear economic or political advantages to the U.S.S.R. Furthermore, the Soviet leadership was never convinced of the likelihood of success of the Chilean model. Why, then, risk endangering détente? During his trip to the U.S.S.R. in December 1972, Allende was told that the Soviet Union would not provide any significant aid to Chile and was advised to seek an accommodation with the U.S.[53]

The ferocity of the economic and political war launched by the Nixon administration is just beginning to be disclosed and understood. Although President Clinton ordered the declassification of information related to the operations in Chile, important information still remains classified and the secret files are being held by the CIA, the Defense Intelligence Agency, the Pentagon, the National Security Council, the National Archives, the presidential libraries of Gerald Ford and Jimmy Carter, and other government agencies. What we know today is what role the U.S. played in trying to stop the election of Allende, and some of the policies pursued between 1970 and 1973. Thomas Karamessines, a chief of CIA covert operations at the time, told Senate investigators that the efforts to overthrow President Allende never really ended.[54]

The belief in democracy distorted reality once more. President Allende and many of the coalition leaders underestimated the possibility of a military coup despite the deteriorating political situation and the calls for military intervention made by many social actors. Because, according to the myth, Chile appeared as an idealized place in which all conflicts were to be resolved peacefully, as in a unified family, the possibility of military intervention was never seriously considered. Carlos Morales Abarzúa, the president of the Popular Unity coalition at the time of the coup, said that the leadership did not discuss such an action. When the military asked him to report to the Ministry of Defense the day after the coup he thought he was asked to attend a political meeting. Dressed in an elegant silk suit, he parked his car in front of the Ministry of Defense and arrived promptly at the meeting. Little did he know that, still in his silk suit, he was going to be sent, together with many other politicians, to Dawson Island, a prison/concentration camp in the southernmost part of the continent.[55]

Chileans believed that Chile was so different from the rest of the world that the recent experiences with military intervention in other South American countries were not likely. Fernando Alegría, among others, reports that on Sunday, 9 September, two days before the coup, Allende ate lunch with some of his ministers and friends and discussed the failed conversations with the Christian Democrats and the speech he was going to give on Tuesday, 11 September, announcing a plebiscite to resolve the conflicts with Congress and other pressing political issues. During lunch the President received information regarding the movement of troops from Los Andes to Santiago. The President called General Brady, a member of the Army's High Command, who assured him that everything was normal. Allende did not appear to have any reason to doubt the words of a top general. The issue was dismissed despite the insistence of Rene Largo Farías, one of his aides, who had direct information from people who had seen the military trucks going toward Santiago.[56]

It is also important to note that while some of the socioeconomic policies pursued by Allende were successful in terms of generating new sources of support for the regime, the de facto expansion of the functions of the state through the takeovers, requisitions, and interventions were detrimental to the interests of the Allende regime. To the extent that some of these actions were barely legitimate they increased the already profound divisions with the UP, and between the UP and the opposition. They also fueled the opposition's accusations of abuse of power undermining the regime's support among middle-class groups.

La Moneda, Chile's presidential palace, was bombed by the Chilean military on 11 September 1973. As Alegría writes, "Nobody would have ever believed that the Moneda would be bombed and set on fire like in a 'malón' of the Spanish Conquest. But it happened. Allende did not want to choose between fiction and history. He kept both."[57] Both the fiction and the history ended with Allende's life.

CHAPTER 7

Authoritarianism
and Neo-liberalism
The Making of a Capitalist Society

Allende's road was a very dangerous road. The policies endangered the interests of the political and economic elite as well as the interest of foreign capital and the United States. On 11 September 1973 the military acted to avert those threats and to save their own institutions. The bombs that fell on the Moneda Palace destroyed not only the center of Chilean politics, but also the policies that had been associated with the system since 1924.

The destruction of what remained of Chile's democratic political regime was consummated in the bloody coup. In the debacle, not only did President Allende lose his life, but with him died those institutions that had come to be the trademark of the Chilean sociopolitical organization. The Congress was closed; the political parties and the unions were banned and their leaders were killed, tortured, arrested, or exiled. Ironically, even some of those organizations that had proclaimed the need for a military takeover were suppressed.

From the beginning the military government faced two fundamental tasks, the destruction and silencing of the remnants of the previous political order and the reorganization of the society along new lines. As to the former, the expansion of the previous system, the representative nature of the political parties, the deep interactions between the unions and the parties, and the explosion of mobilization of the last years all formed a tightly interconnected political body that required the use of massive repression and violence to dismember. The Pinochet government pursued a most violent campaign against all those who in any way represented the deposed order.

An examination of the Pinochet regime's performance on the second task, the reorganization of the society along new lines, constitutes the core of this chapter. That reorganization involved a total transformation of the political and economic role of the Chilean state. Four features characterized the new political organization: the establishment of an authoritarian government in which civil and political liberties were drastically reduced or eliminated; the existence of a highly personalistic political regime controlled by General Pinochet; the massive use of repression; and the application of neo-liberal economic policies. These policies reduced the social functions of the state, provided the bases for the economic reorganization of the society, and set the parameters for a new development strategy. In the final analysis the combination of the market approach with an authoritarian, personalistic, political regime based on the widespread use of repression led to the atomization of society and the strengthening of the state.

The new regime was determined to change more than just the institutional aspects of Chile's political system. One of its essential tasks was to change the country's dominant narrative. According to the ideologues of the regime, the old narrative that stressed democracy and socioeconomic equality had to be replaced by one based on the market ideology. The regime succeeded in presenting an image that equated democracy with chaos, abuse, economic instability, scarcities, and other social problems. Accordingly, the old narrative had created a misplaced belief in equality that inexorably led the country into such a state. To the extent that the old narrative was associated with Marxist-oriented ideas of equality and redistribution of income, it was defined as dangerous and had to be replaced by a new set of beliefs. According to the new story, Chile's unity and harmony would be attained through the combination of a market economic ideology and authoritarian political system. The combined effect of both would eliminate the social and political divisions generated by the politicians and the political parties. The market, according to its proponents, would generate true freedom and equality.

The Background to the Coup

In Chile the appeals to the military came not only from important societal groups, but also from the Legislative and the Judiciary branches of the government. Throughout 1973 the Supreme Court repeatedly condemned the illegality of President Allende's actions, and in August 1973, the Chamber of Deputies called for the military to stop supporting the Allende regime, declaring that "the Armed Forces and the Police are and should be, by their own nature, a guarantee to all Chileans and not only for a sector of the nation or for a political alliance. Therefore, their presence in the government should be geared to the re-establishment of the full application of the constitution and the laws."[1] The call for military intervention made by the Chamber voiced the feelings held by much of the middle and upper class.

The middle class was fearful of the economic chaos and the increasingly mobilized and demanding lower class. Those fears permeated the military, a middle-class institution. Moreover, specific policies of the Socialist Party and the Leftist Revolutionary Movement (MIR) directly affected the military institution. Among those policies, the call for an open rebellion of the lower military ranks and the formation of a popular army made by the leadership of the Socialist Party and the MIR certainly menaced the survival of democracy, as well as the survival of the military. Finally, the mounting societal conflict and the threat to the military institutions gave the military leadership the reason, or the excuse, to mend the internal rift that had existed since the inception of the Allende regime.

Since the election of Allende, the military had been divided into two camps: the constitutionalists led first by the Commander-in-Chief of the Army, General René Schneider, then after he was assassinated by General Carlos Prats, who believed in the need to protect the government of the constitutionally elected President; and the institutionalists, who placed institutional survival above the protection of the elected government.[2] The role of the constitutionalist Commander-in-Chief of the Army was crucial to maintain the army's support for the President. That very support, however, and the participation of the Commander-in-Chief and other military leaders in the Allende government only deepened the rift within the military.

Increased threats to the institutional survival of the army shifted the internal balance of power. In August 1973, the Council of Generals, in an unprecedented move, demanded the resignation of Prats and of all the generals that were holding Cabinet positions. As Prats wrote in his diary on 23 August, "my ousting is the prelude to a coup."[3] The coup took place eighteen days later.

Patrimonialism: General Pinochet and the Military Ideology

Although there are strong similarities in the origins of the military regimes in the Southern Cone, once in power the Chilean regime began to develop along some unique lines. A central premise of this chapter is that in Chile one does not see the appearance of a bureaucratic-authoritarian regime as in Brazil or Argentina. Instead, power was grasped by a personalistic-authoritarian regime controlled by a ruler who acted not only as an independent player, but who in fact controlled all the strings of power.

Although a full analysis of General Pinochet's personality is outside the scope of this book, it is important to note that to the extent that he, single-handedly, fashioned the political regime, the entire system bears the imprint of his personality. Pinochet has repeatedly expressed his admiration for Napoleon, the Roman emperors, Fidel Castro, and Mao because of the strength of their leadership, their principles, and especially their nationalism.[4] Studies of Pinochet's personality indicate that the country was not ruled by a politician, but by a warrior leading a military campaign.[5] They also show that Pinochet did not trust anybody, not even his closest advisors. In practice, he was the only one who had all the information. His collaborators received only partial information. The objective was to prevent others from making autonomous decisions.[6] Repeatedly, Pinochet argued that the country was at war and that he was going to win that war with the help of Divine Providence. General Pinochet's beliefs and principles were clearly summarized when he declared that during World War II he supported the Germans. He also argued that he never looked at the ideology, only the war, and that Hitler's main defect was that he lost the war.[7]

General Pinochet led a sort of patrimonial system in which the authority of the ruler was uncontested and where the ruler assumed that he had a mandate of Divine Providence. What is interesting about the divine mandate, as seen by Pinochet, is that one gains the favor of Divine Providence through force and purity. For Pinochet, controlling sociopolitical events depended on the will to win, and it is this will that created the conditions which allowed him to reach his goals and to get the favor of Divine Providence. Talking about the actions of 11 September 1973 he stated that "Divine Providence, with her mysterious hand gave the Armed Forces the order and fluidity to carry out the fast and prompt, pacifying action . . . that allowed the Chileans to break the chains."[8] According to General Pinochet, the presence of God was felt not only the day of the coup, but all throughout his regime. The presence of God was also felt by the general in 1986, when he saw the image of the Virgin Mary on the car window, protecting him from his would-be assassins.[9]

His views of the people and the society are equally autocratic and patrimonial. Repeatedly, he argued that the majority of the people were weak because they had a passive attitude toward life. Easily dominated, most of the people forget and forgive very quickly and are easily swayed by the *cantos de sirena* of the politicians. Consequently, the strength of the Marxist ideology was not the result of a clear commitment of a large sector of the population, but simply the result of the weakness of the majority, a weakness characteristic of all democratic governments.[10] The connection between the interests and goals of the ruler and the interest of the country, typical of patrimonial regimes, appears in a number of statements. His concerns about power and strength, his vision of leading the country as if it were a regiment, all point to a definition of power that gave him total and absolute control. General Leigh, the former Commander-in-Chief of the Air Force, declared that when on the day of the coup General Pinochet began to issue *bandos*, or orders, he as well as the other Junta members were really surprised since they had never been consulted. Soon enough the Junta was dissolved.[11]

There is no doubt that the origins of the political ideas of General Pinochet are to be found in the ideology of the Chilean military, which in turn was largely influenced by the German military. The military always saw itself as a separate caste, as a sector of the society separated from the rest, with its own laws, norms, privileges, mentality, ideas. They constituted a subculture based on rigidity and hierarchy, and as they imposed their thinking on the entire nation they created a dictatorial system based on those principles.[12] Moreover, the military culture was based on a myth of invincibility. They had saved the fatherland many times, but their accomplishments had not been recognized. What I am suggesting here is that while the dominant social narrative stressed democracy and equality, the military narrative stressed obedience, hierarchy, force, invincibility, and other Hispanic and Prussian values that sustained a separate military myth. There was a large degree of frustration and righteousness, and the combination of frustration and righteousness only reaffirmed their sacrificial and salvational role.[13]

The military's myth of power as well as their glorious past created a chauvinistic culture based on obedience, distrust, and secrecy. According to General Horacio Toro, member of the Army's High Command, "[M]ilitarism, an illness of the military system, means the imposition of habits, styles and military interests on the government and the society." He adds, "We visualized the creation of a durable state which would inhibit the rebirth of the left and of Marxism, which were considered the great evils of the process. . . . And with this system we regressed to the schemes proposed by the Nazi and the fascist ideologies . . . we built a state geared to avoid the rebirth and the expression of the Marxist ideas. And, for that state to be effective, it could be nothing but a Chilean version of a fascist state."[14] In regard to Marxism, the military spoke about an "implacable attack of the international Marxist system against the most sacred values of the Fatherland and the nation. Thus, the Army, loyal to its most profound and intrinsic doctrine would never stop applying the measures required . . . to struggle against this philosophy."[15] Finally, the military established a linkage between national security and economic development. The economic expansion of Chile was seen as proof of the capacity of the entrepreneurs supported by the military. In the words of a military officer, "there is total dependence between economic development and national security. Accordingly, we must devote an important part of the national budget to the national security system in order to continue the economic progress of the nation."[16]

The religious aspect of the military mission was clearly reflected in the actions of General Pinochet and the zeal with which he implemented the repressive policies. Father Florencio Infante Diaz, Brigadier and Chief of the Army's Religious Services, accurately described the connection between the military and the religious dimensions of the army.

> The military hero is formed through the silent study, the permanent prayers, the dedication to serve others, the serious and firm commitment to accept one's pain in order to prevent the pain of others. There is a secret union between sanctity and heroism. The saint looks at Christ, he imitates his life, thinks about his brothers and lives to love. The soldier looks at the flag, looks all through the Fatherland, loves and lives for it. Happy are those who can combine in one thrust of the spear the two great loves: God and Fatherland. They are the only ones that can liberate themselves from all forms of selfishness and aim at the growth of the Fatherland under the eye of God.[17]

The statements of Father Infante clearly explain General Pinochet's belief in the sacred nature of his mission. He certainly combines the dedication and commitment that Father Infante speaks about. Consequently, General Pinochet concluded that he had a divine mandate to rule and to kill, to torture and to exile. In Pinochet's words, "When confronted with communist penetration [that] represents the destruction of the basic moral foundations from which the Western and Christian civilizations derive . . . society is under the obligation of drastic self-defense." Brian Loveman explains that "when the opponents are heretics, witches, or subversives . . . repression becomes a virtue, torture a means of salvation (for the victim as well as the torturer) and murder a way of extirpating cancerous cells from threatened social organisms. When the body politic is allegedly in mortal danger from savage enemies, no countermeasures are too drastic, no defense unimaginable."[18]

In the 1960s and 1970s the definition of the enemy of the Fatherland came from internal and external sources and both defined that enemy in terms of a foreign ideology which was attacking the nation. The duty of the military, as taught both by local traditions and by the U.S.-sponsored National Security Doctrine, gave the military the justification to come to power. Thus one sees the creation throughout the region of a new type of military regime which had the support of broad sectors of the society and the United States. The salvational role of the military, a recurrent theme in Latin America, took the form of an anti-Marxist crusade of unprecedented cruelty, supported by the United States.[19] A recently released State Department document dated 16 November 1973 not only confirms that the United States had full knowledge of what was happening in Chile but it explains the summary executions carried out by the military as a result, at least in part, of "puritanical, crusading spirit—a determination to cleanse and rejuvenate Chile."[20]

During Pinochet's first three years the destruction of the previous system was the central mission. It is a matter of public knowledge that in order to achieve that destruction the government carried out political assassinations, torture, and imprisonment of political, labor, and student leaders, and of militants of the Socialist and Communist parties and the leftist movements.[21] From an institutional perspective, the destruction of the old political system involved the "suspension" of the activities of the Congress, political parties, and unions. In the new regime, power was concentrated in the Junta de Gobierno formed by the Commanders-in-Chief of the Army, Navy, and Air Force, and the General Director of the National Police, and repression served as the basic channel of communication between the authoritarian regime and a subjugated society.

From another perspective, the elimination of politics involved the replacement of the politicians as conductors of the nation's business by technocrats, who, according to government rhetoric, would act not in response to narrow partisan or class interests, like politicians, but would apply "scientific" knowledge in the best interest of the entire nation. The importance of this should not be underestimated. As Pinochet constantly reminded the people, before his advent, almost everything had been tried and everything had failed due to the ineptitude of the politicians, who acted not in the best interest of the nation as a whole, but in their own best interest and that of their constituencies. The apolitical-scientific approach of the new bureaucrats, he claimed, would put an end to that state of affairs.

The elimination of politics entailed the destruction and replacement of the existing dominant narrative. Destroying Chileans' understanding of democracy was accomplished through the use of repression and propaganda. Within the next three years the government would also develop a new social narrative, based on the ideas of modernity, individualism, and competitiveness.

The Creation of a Personalist-Authoritarian State: Institutions and Repression

Initially, the military Junta found sufficient legitimacy in the state of internal war, the national security doctrine, and the necessary counter-revolutionary role of the government. The military intervention was justified in terms of the illegitimate actions committed by the Allende government and the calls for intervention made by the Chamber of Deputies, the Supreme Court, and important sectors of the society. The military leaders argued initially that they were going to rebuild the central elements of *chilenidad,* meaning the traditional political system, destroyed by the foreign ideology (Marxism-Leninism).[22] However, by December 1973 it had become clear that the regime was not going to permit a quick return to democracy. The government had already dissolved the political parties that formed the Popular Unity, suspended the activities of all the other parties, nullified the electoral rolls, taken control of the universities, and suspended all trade unions. By January 1974 the Junta had all the power.

Throughout 1974 and 1975 the Junta produced a series of formal documents, such as the Declaración de Principios, that were aimed at creating a semblance of legitimacy.[23] Meanwhile General Pinochet was solidifying his power. That process led to the exclusion of the other members of the Junta and the establishment of a personalistic system. By January 1975 Pinochet's title had changed to President and the distance between him and the other members of the Junta had grown dramatically.

In June 1974, faced with the massive increase in repressive activities and the growing fragmentation of those activities carried out by the intelligence services of the different branches of the military, the Junta created DINA (National Directorate of Intelligence), essentially under the control of General Pinochet. The new organization, which depended directly on the Junta, allowed General Pinochet to centralize all repressive operations under one institution, simultaneously eliminating the power of the other branches of the military. DINA was the legal and institutional manifestation of the victory of the army's security apparatus, but most importantly it was the manifestation of General Pinochet's victory over the other members of the Junta. The creation of DINA was undoubtedly the most critical political decision of this early period, since it gave General Pinochet absolute control over the most central political feature of the regime, the war against Marxist subversion. Colonel Manuel Contreras, a close associate of Pinochet and head of military operations in the port of San Antonio, was named head of what Constable and Valenzuela aptly call the Chilean Gestapo. The agency's mission was to infiltrate Marxist parties, eliminate their leaders, and most importantly eliminate leftist ideas from Chilean society. To achieve these goals the DINA personnel was expected to spy, kidnap, torture, and kill.[24]

What needs to be emphasized here is the political nature of this decision. To the extent that the regime defined its mission in terms of the elimination of Marxist thinking, DINA became the most central entity of the government since it was the institution directly in charge of fulfilling the most sacred goal of the administration. The sacred, mythical mission of the organization is clearly defined in its secret motto, "We will fight in the shadows so our children can live in the sunlight." In fact, what Pinochet tried to create through DINA was not a society full of sunlight, but a passive, fearful society, a society deprived of any means of expression and of all political ideas. In the next couple of years, General Pinochet realized that the most effective way of extirpating the Marxist cancer was through a radical operation: the elimination of all forms of politics from the society, or the creation of an apolitical society and apolitical individuals.

Repression was used throughout the military rule, but the purpose of the repressive actions and policies changed over the years. The initial purpose, the capture and destruction of the internal enemy, namely, the Leftist Revolutionary Movement (MIR), was effectively carried out by DINA throughout 1974 and 1975. Once the MIR was destroyed, the organization turned its actions against the leaders and members of the Socialist and the Communist parties as well as labor and student leaders.

In its fight against politicians, students, labor leaders, and anyone suspected of left-wing political activities and/or having valuable political information leading to political activities, DINA used dozens of secret detention centers, a vast network of informants, and about

4,000 agents under the leadership of General Contreras, who reported only to General Pinochet. The agency killed, 'disappeared', and tortured by the thousands. "For Contreras, the crusade against Marxism justified all actions, twisting his military virtues into snarling fanaticism. . . . With time the combination of power and immersion in a seamy underworld also corroded military norms within DINA. Contreras's aides became personal lackeys; call girls were recruited for undercover work and late-night revelry. . . . While his men tortured prisoners in distant cells, Contreras was ensconced among European antiques, chatting on his hot line to the president."[25] The violence, cruelty, and inhumanity of DINA have been vividly described by those who were tortured and by a few of its members and informants. The religious zeal of Contreras and his disciples transformed DINA into a secret brotherhood.

The parallels between Pinochet's Chile and Nazi Germany are not limited to DINA and the Gestapo. Just as in Nazi Germany, Chile had concentration camps in the northern part of the country and in Isla Dawson, and like in Germany the military leaders became jealous of the close relationship between the head of the security services and the leader of the country. But the relationship between Pinochet and Contreras only became deeper, more committed, and more enmeshed in a policy of abuse predicated on the bases of a religious/political mandate with a dash of illegal business deals carried out by DINA. Did Contreras and DINA represent the psychotic edge of a society whose democratic values had collapsed, as Constable and Valenzuela argue, or, was this process simply the application of the military ideology to the society and the ability of the military to define the situation in terms of a permanent war against the enemies of the fatherland? From our standpoint DINA was clearly the most important expression of General Pinochet's power and his idealogy.

DINA's ever increasing pattern of abuse, killing, and corruption forced General Pinochet in 1977 to dissolve the organization, replacing it with the new, although not too different CNI, or National Information Center. General Contreras, who was operating as a cogovernor and had developed a symbiotic relationship with General Pinochet, was awarded a promotion and immunity through the 1978 Amnesty Law. The downfall of DINA was the result of Contreras's international activities pursued under the name of Operation Condor.

These operations included the assassinations of General Prats and Bernardo Leighton, a prominent member of the Christian Democratic party in Buenos Aires, and of Orlando Letelier and Ronni Moffit in Washington. Under pressure from Washington and from military leaders, Pinochet had to dissolve the institution, yet he preserved its policies and maintained his friendship with Contreras.

The CNI-defined mission was to protect the society against its enemies using tactics very similar to those used by DINA. In 1980 the regime launched a new campaign, justified by the need to control a new surge of terrorist activities, presumably carried out by leftists. Surprisingly, it was later revealed that many of the terrorist acts had been committed not by leftist groups, but by COVEMA which was formed by ex-members of the CNI and the civil police. Rivalries between the security agencies would continue throughout the period.

The widespread use of torture and the policy of killing and disappearances were not the only tools of the regime. From the very beginning and through the next seventeen years the army tried to locate leftist and other enemies through what they called "search and destroy missions," which were directed toward the inhabitants of the poorest neighborhoods. Typically, the search and destroy missions would take place in the early hours of the morning, when all males over fifteen years old were searched and some detained. The media reported widely on those operations, stressing that their goal was to clean up the area (*operación de limpieza*) of terrorists. These operations had the purpose of instilling fear in the population, sustaining the notion of the permanent Marxist threat and the need for a state of war and legitimizing periodically the raison d'être of the regime.

There is no doubt that the repression succeeded in destroying political organizations and eliminating any viable opposition to the regime. The short-term effects were fear and paralysis. In turn, fear and paralysis produced the atomization of the society and facilitated the concentration of power in the hands of General Pinochet. While the regime was successfully destroying the political opposition, the Catholic Church emerged as the only force capable and willing to challenge these actions. The remarkable behavior of the Chilean Church during the dictatorship and its solid commitment to defend the abused and try to stop the abuses are particularly interesting, especially when they are compared with the indifferent, or even supportive, policies of the Church elsewhere in South America or Nazi Germany. What Pamela Lowden has called the "moral opposition" to the regime had in fact moral, political, and religious dimensions.[26] The work of the Church's Vicaría de Solidaridad (Vicariate of Solidarity) in defense of human rights in Chile was critical not only because it provided support to those who had been tortured and killed and their families, but because it provided the foundations for the development of human rights organizations and later on a political coalition that would oppose the regime in the 1988 referendum. The role of Archbishop of Santiago Cardinal Silva Henríquez was also remarkable. Cardinal Silva not only created the Vicaría and gave its members a clear mandate regarding the protection of human rights in Chile, he openly criticized the regime. Most importantly Cardinal Silva's role needs to be seen in terms of a powerful moral force speaking on behalf not only of a set of Christian principles, but of the poor and the repressed.[27] In spite of the protection offered by the Church and of General Pinochet's beliefs, the members of the Vicariate also suffered in the hands of the repressors. Its staff was harassed, often detained for no clear reason, and ultimately José Manuel Parada, a controversial and outspoken sociologist working for the Vicaría, was killed by the police in 1985.[28]

Although according to General Pinochet, Marxism was a permanent source of aggression, the administration had to find some legal, formal sources of legitimacy. Several constitutional acts dictated throughout 1976 produced the de facto elimination of the 1925 Constitution. However, the government could not fashion a new political system given the intense struggle between the corporatists, led by Generals Leigh and Díaz, and the emerging power of the neo-liberals. This struggle paralyzed the system both in terms of decisions regarding the political future of the country as well as specific policy decisions, such as social security. The ideological division could be seen in the answers to two basic questions: how soon should the regime be institutionalized and what form should the new set of institutions have. For the corporatists the answer was simple: prompt institutionalization along lines that continued Chile's traditional political history. In the words of General Leigh, "[W]e have to take into account those concepts that are rooted in our idiosyncrasy; the new institutions can neither be disconnected from reality, nor from the essential ways in which Chileans live or think."[29] The traditional principles that the corporatists wanted to respect included political participation, division of power between the branches of government, depersonalized leadership, and respect for individual rights. The solution suggested by prominent members of this group such as the Minister of Labor Air Force General Nicanor Díaz and Pablo Rodríguez, the former leader of the Patria y Libertad Movement, pointed to the establishment of a corporatist set of organizations that would provide a participatory, non-partisan form of representation. However, they could not find a model of representation that would simultaneously contain the principles outlined by Leigh and also impair the rebirth of the Marxist parties. The approach was never clearly spelled out by General Leigh and soon the pendulum began to swing in favor of a group of neo-liberal economists known as the Chicago Boys.

For the neo-liberals the main concern of the government was not to legitimize and institutionalize the regime, but to create the basic political framework required to apply fully the monetarist economic principles. In their view, the consolidation of the market society would bring rapid economic growth which, in turn, would produce the required political support to allow for a peaceful transition from an authoritarian regime to a protected democracy. Therefore, the economic team argued for the maintenance of the authoritarian regime led by Pinochet, the initiation of a set of structural reforms that would provide the framework for the creation of a capitalist society, and the creation of a long-term timetable linking the political opening of the regime to the expected success of the market economy. Sergio de Castro, former Minister of Finance and dean of the Chicago Boys, argued that "the country can only continue advancing along successful lines if the efficient political conduction of the present regime continues and the people can secure the results of our successful policies. [This in turn would] spontaneously generate the forces that would defend the regime, while giving us the time to complete those great tasks not yet achieved."[30]

By July 1977 the struggle between the two groups had ended and General Pinochet made it very clear that his regime would not allow a return to the past. In the Chacarillas speech, the most important political speech since the inception of the regime, General Pinochet argued that "September 11 did not mean only the overthrow of an illegitimate government, but the end of an exhausted political-institutional regime, and consequently the beginning of a new one." The new system was defined in terms of an authoritarian and protected democracy, meaning that the old liberal and naïve political system of the past would be replaced by a new one that would be constructed according to the ideas established in the Declaración de Principios. The new institutionality would create new forms of participation, eliminating the political parties, and it would establish a new legal-juridical order based on the principle of subsidiarity of the state, which was going to be the foundational rock for the new economic system. Finally, the speech contained an outline for a gradual evolution of the system, without specific deadlines.[31]

While the Chacarillas speech contained some basic ideas that would reappear in the future, in the short run, it did not provide the basis for the new institutionality. That would not happen until 1980 with the enactment of the new constitution. In the meantime, General Pinochet was moving to consolidate his personal power. Invoking external aggression and a conspiracy against the Fatherland, General Pinochet, despite the opposition of the other members of the Junta, called upon the people of Chile to show their support for the government in a plebiscite. The plebiscite took place in January 1978. The overwhelming, although questionable, support obtained by Pinochet was then used to legitimize his undisputed leadership.[32] With this victory, he could argue that his leadership was rooted in the will of the people. The full extent of his power was demonstrated on 24 July 1978 when General Leigh was removed from the Junta and from the Air Force.

The 1980 Constitution

The 1980 Constitution represented the culmination of the process of statecraft initiated in 1975. While the plebiscite was geared to render legitimacy to the leadership of General Pinochet, the 1980 Constitution was geared to shape the new sociopolitical and economic organization along the lines set by authoritarian political principles and neo-liberal economics. Leigh's dismissal, followed by the removal of the eighteen top Air Force generals who supported Leigh's position regarding a prompt return to a more institutionalized political system, consolidated Pinochet's power for the years to come. In fact, Leigh's declarations to the Italian newspaper *Il Corriere della Sera,* which ostensibly provoked his downfall, did not contain anything that Leigh had not previously stated, except that on this occasion Leigh appeared to have the full support of the Air Force High Command.[33] Nevertheless, Pinochet proved strong enough to eliminate the intragovernmental opposition. The replacement of Leigh by General Fernando Matthei, a close associate of Pinochet, allowed the President to effectively eliminate the Junta from the conduct of the government. Thus the plebiscite was conceived as a source of both internal and external legitimacy. The plebiscite came at a time when, due to the massive human rights abuses, the external image of the regime was at its lowest point and when the regime was afraid of border conflicts, particularly with Argentina and Peru. Internally, it marks the transformation from a collective to a personalistic leadership and it "legalized" and legitimized Pinochet's right to rule.

From the end of 1978 until the end of 1979, the political debate within the government focused around the constitutional process, and specifically around the Constitutional Commission's report. Given the ideological affinity between the members of the Commission, handpicked by General Pinochet, and the government, the debate was not centered around the future nature of the political regime, which continued to be authoritarian, and personalistic, but around how to institutionalize the personalistic leadership and set guidelines for its future transformation, basically the same two issues that the government had been trying to resolve since 1976.[34] Pinochet, faced with the culmination of the constitutional process set in motion by himself, with a polarization of the internal debate, with the growing decomposition of his security apparatus, and with his personal reluctance to institutionalize the regime, resolved the problem by secretly elaborating, with only the help of his personal advisors, a new constitutional bill. And he effectively eliminated the possibility of any thorough analysis or debate of the bill by simultaneously announcing it to the public and setting the date for a plebiscite in which the population would approve or reject the little-known Constitution.

The drafting of the Constitution, then, took the process of legitimization and institutionalization one step further. Given Chile's legalist tradition, the lack of a constitutional structure was a major weakness. The Constitution, by setting in place a number of political structures, set the parameters of the political discussion within the government coalition as well as future political discussion. Finally, although the Constitution did not represent the freely expressed will of the people, it gave the regime formal legitimacy, which Pinochet constantly used to justify his mandate.

In relation to the newly created political model, the Constitution represented a compromise between the more moderate elements within the government, who argued for a clear limitation of the military regime's life and for the creation of political institutions that would replace them, and the preferences of Pinochet and a few advisors who strongly opposed those moves and wanted to maintain the existing regime. The problem was solved through the establishment of two different political models, to be applied in two different periods: the transitional model, to be applied between 1981 and 1989 (with the possibility of its extension until 1997); and the so-called democratic model which, in fact, was an authoritarian model, that followed the transitional period.

Within the government the discussion was centered on the length of the so-called transitional period. Pinochet's preference was for a sixteen-year period, but this period was considered to be too long to provide any kind of serious internal or external legitimacy. The Minister of Interior Sergio Fernández then devised the two eight-year periods, arguing that given the success of the 1978 plebiscite there was no major risk in establishing a plebiscite for 1988, and that the referendum would renew the legitimacy of the regime.[35] The transitional period was designed to achieve the institutionalization of the existing regime, maintaining and even increasing the personalist, repressive nature of the government. According to former Minister of Justice Mónica Madariaga, the goal was always to establish two consecutive eight-year presidential periods for Pinochet. The first one was going to be devoted to the creation of the new political structures, the normalization of the society, and the consolidation of the economic model, while the second would provide the time needed to apply the new norms in a "normalized" society. A normalized society according to Madariaga was an apolitical society.[36]

The second model, which the Constitution called "democratic," but which rather resembled an authoritarian regime, had a very strong Executive; a Congress that had been deprived of its most basic functions;

a Judiciary dependent on the Executive for its nomination and deprived of its role during the "State of Siege"; and a military empowered to supervise the political system. Moreover, in its original form the Constitution rejected even the most basic notions of ideological pluralism, and left to the Constitutional Court, a body dependent on the President, the determination of future political rights, the functions of the political parties, and the nature of the other intermediate groups that would be created in the second period.[37]

Regarding the protection of individual rights, the Constitution reveals a number of contradictions, produced in part by the government's need to reach a compromise between the authoritarian model proposed by Pinochet and the more democratic formulas proposed by the moderates. Thus, all personal and political rights, although protected in the body of the Constitution, were dependent upon the transitory Article 24, drafted by the Minister of Interior, Sergio Fernández, which established that during the period 1981–1989 the President could arrest, restrict the freedom of the press and information, restrict the right to hold meetings, prohibit the entrance of people into the country, and send people into internal exile whenever there was a threat to the peace of the nation or whenever acts against the public order had been committed. The uninterrupted use of this prerogative on the part of Pinochet between 1981 and 1989 provided the constitutional framework for the continued violation of all basic rights. Basic political and human rights were just as unprotected as they were before the approval of the Constitution.

From an economic standpoint the Constitution formalized the notion of the subsidiary state. Arguing that the interventionist state of the past was, to a large extent, responsible for the economic problems of Chile and the economic crisis of the early 1970s, the Pinochet administration declared:

> The state should only assume direct responsibility for those functions which the intermediate or minor social groups are unable to deal with adequately either because they are beyond their possibilities, as in the case of national security, police work or foreign relations, or because, due to their importance to the community, it is inadvisable to hand them over to limited private groups, as in the case of services or enterprises of strategic or prime importance to the nation.[38]

Moreover, the subsidiary state was to make possible a truly free society.

> The greater the State interference in the society, the less is its true
> liberty, regardless of how widespread may be the exercise of political
> rights. The fountainhead through which liberty offers personal
> and creative effort a margin of alternatives of sufficient variety is
> to be found in a private life and in those activities which are inde-
> pendent from the State, and only subject to its control for the
> common good. Statism, on the other hand, produced a society
> that is gray, uniform, submissive, and without horizons.[39]

Statism, according to the ideologues of the Pinochet administration, had suffocated and repressed the individual, and, as a result, the
full development of the society. Furthermore, statism had changed the
nature of the relations between the individual and society, subordi-
nating the former to the latter. The new ideology would reverse this
situation. According to this ideology the society and the state are acci-
dental relationships and the only substantial element is man, and
consequently both the state and the society have to be subordinated to
the individual. It argues also that the common good will be obtained
only through the achievement of individual welfare and that the law is
the instrument that will allow the fulfillment of individual satisfaction.

The 1980 Constitution went beyond the institutionalization of the
existing political reality; it also gave constitutional backing and structure to the new political and economic model. The Constitution
aimed at the reduction of the socioeconomic functions of the state
and the atomization of the society. The reduction of the socioeconomic functions was obtained by transferring many of these functions
to the private sector. In the words of one of the government's ideologues, "we have to make the state inefficient in order to enhance individual power."[40] At the same time, the Constitution did not provide
the channels for the society to organize itself; on the contrary, it aimed
at the atomization of society through the enhancement of the market
as the central regulator and organizer of social activity. From an economic standpoint, the neo-liberal economic model is now part of the
constitutional make-up of the country. But the influence of the economic team was not limited to the inclusion of the economic model in
the constitutional framework, the entire Constitution bears their

imprint, and especially the influence of the then Minister of Finance, Sergio de Castro. As Pinochet and de Castro repeatedly argued, the economic strategy and the political system "are indivisible parts of the social fabric, and both of them have served as the source that inspires the new institutionality."[41] Nowhere does the conjunction of the political and economic systems become more evident than in the establishment of the eight-year length of the transitional period, which served the needs of both.

From an economic perspective, according to the projections of de Castro, by 1989, after ten years of high rates of economic growth, the shape and nature of the Chilean economy would be totally transformed. According to its proponents, the market economy would transform every Chilean into a property-owner, eliminating poverty from the face of Chile. In turn, the success of capitalism would eliminate forever the threat of Marxism. In the words of de Castro, "this, and none other, is the motive behind the eight-year transitional period."[42] Or as the former Minister of Labor José Piñera argued, "[B]y 1990 . . . Chile will be a developed country. In other words, by the end of the President's period the military government and the Chilean people would have transformed a destroyed Chile into a developed country."[43]

The forecast of the regime was that by 1990 the Chilean population would have acquired such a large stake in the economic system that it would naturally reject the calls of the Marxist parties, eliminating forever the Marxist threat and achieving simultaneously economic and political stability, economic and political maturity, and economic and political development. Consequently, Minister Fernández could safely set a plebiscite for 1989 and be confident that Pinochet's mandate would be renewed and relegitimized.

In conclusion, what Pinochet created was a personalistic-authoritarian regime centered on his personal power. The foundation of the regime was the permanent war against Marxism, the elimination of the old democracy, its institutions, and its narrative. Instead, the new democracy was to be authoritarian and protected, or in other words, it would be a democracy only in name. What the regime did was not to protect democracy, but to protect itself from the will of the people, to protect the political institutions from being really democratic. In the final analysis, what the regime wanted was to eliminate politics altogether, which, despite the brutal repression, still proved to be impossible.

The Neo-liberal Model and the Market Ideology

Origins and Ideology

During its first two years the military government attempted to deal only with the most pressing economic issues such as inflation and the balance of payments deficit. The ad hoc policies pursued during this period could in no way handle the reorganization of the economy. The process of reorganization began at the end of 1974 when the government announced the replacement of the import substitution model of economic development by the outward-oriented model and the replacement of the Keynesian fiscal policies by those designed by the monetarist school of Chicago.[44] The old policies had been attacked by both the right and the left and they had been blamed for all the economic ills of the country such as permanent inflation, stagnation, uneven development, and inequality. Nevertheless, the import substitution model of development and the social and economic policies associated with the model were intrinsic elements of Chilean society since at least the 1930s. Their replacement entailed the abandonment of policies that served to sustain the political edifice upon which the social structure was built as well as the social narrative that served as the foundation for that edifice.

The neo-liberal model and the theories of the monetarist school were presented to the military by a group of well-known academics in the School of Economics of the Catholic University as a coherent body of thought with clear and relatively simple explanations and prescriptions. It seems that the notions of globality, simplicity, and coherence that were attributed to the model captivated the military and made them accept the neo-liberal model.[45] Moreover, the new policy, according to its proponents, would assure that past problems would not reappear, that the country would move onto the path of economic growth and low inflation rates which the import substitution model had been unable to accomplish in over thirty years of application, and that the replacement of politicians with technocrats would allow the application of the benefits to the entire society.[46]

Few things were more foreign to Chilean society than the market ideology and the notions of individualism, competition, and consumption that the ideology involves. Its introduction into the Chilean environment was a result of the influence that the advocates of the neo-liberal model began to acquire within the government and was implemented through a well-orchestrated government campaign in which the old values and ideologies were depicted as being not only outmoded but also conducive to the kind of economic and political chaos experienced by the society in the early 1970s. In the rhetoric of this campaign, a modern rational attitude called for the replacement of those values by the "new ideology," the ideology of the market.

The history of the Chicago Boys in Chile dates from an exchange agreement signed in 1956 between the Catholic University of Chile and the University of Chicago. The agreement, financed by the United States Agency for International Development, allowed the best and the brightest of the students at the Catholic University to get special training at Chicago, while professors from Chicago could teach their doctrines in Chile. There were many interesting elements in this agreement, including the provision of technical assistance generated by the Cold War dynamics, the training of local elites, and the reinforcement of dependent economic linkages between the United States and Latin America. The University of Chicago obtained an audience and a market for its ideas regarding development and modernization which rejected Keynesian economics and the development notions proposed by the Economic Commission for Latin America. The Catholic University, in turn, gained prestige and reputation within Chile.[47]

The Chicago Boys were the product of this successful exchange program. Two individuals became central to the process, Arnold Haberger from Chicago and Sergio de Castro from Chile. Haberger, the leader of the Chile project in Chicago, traveled often to Chile, married a Chilean, and guided his disciples once they obtained positions of power. De Castro, who was one of the first students and became the 'dean' of the group, led the process of transformation in the Chilean economy and society in the late 1970s. The Chicago-trained economists were entirely marginal to the Chilean economic discussion until 1972, when a group of ten economists led by de Castro began to formulate an alternative economic plan. The program, which was financed by the CIA, was in the hands of the military by May 1973, and its goal was to formulate a global economic plan to be used in the event of the overthrow of the Allende.[48]

The period between 1978 and 1980 was crucial both for Pinochet and for the economists trained in Chicago since they all managed to consolidate their power. While Pinochet was affirming his power through the plebiscite and the 1980 Constitution, the Chicago Boys, or 'economic team' as it was called in Chile, obtained full control of economic and social policymaking. The economic team and Pinochet shared a set of views about politics and society that complemented each other.

Like Pinochet, the Chicago School had developed a religious attitude toward economic policies "based on the notion that they represent the true economists, with great faith in the salvational role of the market."[49] The economic principles developed by the monetarist school are considered to be basic for the maintenance of a free society and, according to their proponents, their importance is such that it is virtually immoral to oppose them. These economic principles were essentially religious principles and the economist was defined as the priest with the exclusive access to the sacred principles that regulate social action.[50] Thus it appears that in the late 1970s and early 1980s Chile was ruled by a general and a group of economists who shared a belief in their religious/political/military *and* economic role. They were all crusaders, pursuing the transformation of a heretical system. The Chicago Boys' approach to economics mirrors General Pinochet's fanatical approach to politics.

Following Frederick Von Hayek, the Chilean neo-liberals argued that the market is the only social arrangement capable of regulating human interaction without coercion, guaranteeing at the same time a rationally based behavior and freedom.[51] In the long run, according to the proponents of the neo-liberal model, the market would be able to replace the state as the regulator of economic activity. In the interim, the market ideology would enable the government to legitimize both the economic system and the entire structure of domination through improvements in the standard of living, and it would serve to justify the already accomplished elimination of politics and politicians. "The market serves to hide domination behind the notion of 'técnicos' and technocracy. In a political situation in which the principle of popular sovereignty has been cornered, it is fundamental to legitimize the wise man and the experts charged with the conduction of the authoritarian and technocratic democracy."[52]

In brief, there was a very strong complementarity between the ideological, the political, and the economic models. The principle of subsidiarity of the state dwarfed the socioeconomic role of the state and justified the transference of those functions to the private sphere. In turn, the creation of a perfect market required the atomization of the society, and the political side of that process of atomization involved the disarticulation of interest groups. The market appears as the mechanism charged with the distribution of wealth, but in order to achieve the desired distribution, the "invisible hand" requires the actions of the very visible hand of the state, particularly in order to create a free labor market. The disarticulation of interest groups and the destruction of the political institutions that served as channels of representation of those groups were essential elements in the creation of the perfect market society, and in the establishment of the authoritarian, personalistic political system established by General Pinochet. Furthermore, since economic policy was made and conducted by the leading private economic actors there was a great deal of complementarity at the policy-making level. Between 1978 and 1983 the most important policymakers were associated with the most powerful economic groups.

Finally, the market ideology provided the new social narrative. While the official story of the past stressed the importance of democracy, pluralism, participation, and equality, the new story stressed order, intolerance, technocracy, individualism, and consumption. Now the society would be told a different story, a story based on the promise that the market would create a better society, a society in which everyone would get what he or she deserved. This "new story," however, resembled the "stories" of the past. Just as in the nineteenth century, the story was presented in an authoritarian context in which the society could not question either its content or its implications. In the 1980s, the religious aspect of both the authoritarian leadership and the economic policies and policymakers would deprive the society of any choice. Paraphrasing Milton Friedman, in Chile the society was not free to choose. It had to obey the orders of the political and economic priests.[53]

The Goals

The Chilean neo-liberals articulated a model that was inspired by the economic theories of Milton Friedman. Based on the notion of market freedom, the new model would open the entire economy to the external market and allow domestic economic sectors to compete among themselves, producing high rates of economic growth unachievable in the past. At the same time, the model would allow Chile to overcome her external dependence and bring inflation under control, providing a healthy financial basis for the model. Both the economic development model and the anti-inflationary policies converged at the level of the state, which, despite the neo-liberal rhetoric to the contrary, had a leading role in the entire program. The actions of the state, geared to transform the entire economic structure of the nation, are at the core of this analysis.

In regard to inflation, the government initiated in April 1975 a recovery program designed to normalize the economy and to drastically reduce inflation through "the reduction of fiscal expenditures and the increase of public revenues."[54] In other words, the normalization of the economy would be achieved through a large reduction of the money supply, adjustments in the exchange rate, and the establishment of a new system of tariffs to liberalize foreign trade. These policies would, in turn, reorient the productive structure toward those sectors that were in a position to compete in the international market, displace economic resources to the more competitive sectors of the economy, and finally and most importantly change the role and the size of the state.

The key to this "shock policy," as well as to the economic development model, was the reduction in the size and functions of the state. Thus, the new reduced subsidiary role of the state served not only as a crucial element of the stabilization program, but as the core of the new economic development model and of the political model adopted by the Pinochet regime. In the economic arena, the state would perform only those activities that could not be performed by the private sector, either because they impinged upon the security of the country or because they involved an effort beyond the capability of the private entrepreneur. Following this principle, the government proceeded to disengage itself from a large number of economic activities, especially in its role as entrepreneur and regulator of the economy.[55]

The drastic reorientation of the role of the state involved returning to the private sector 455 of 479 enterprises that were under the control of the public sector and extricating itself from the promotional and regulatory economic activities of both internal and external economic agents. This process was followed by a large reduction of the social and economic sectors of the government civil bureaucracy, which decreased by 5 percent per year between 1974 and 1979.[56] The new role of the state also implied a new role for private economic agents, who had to take command of the development process. The deregulation of the activities of those agents and the creation of a "competitive market" were the next steps taken by the state, and they are known as the "modernizations." The modernizations were achieved through policies that transformed almost every aspect of the society from education to labor unions, from capital markets to the health system.

Strict control of the money supply was the essential mechanism used to effectively eliminate the inflationary disease from the Chilean economy and to initiate a new era characterized by high rates of economic growth, stability, and independence. The orthodoxy with which those policies had been applied prompted the Director of the Central Bank to say that "we are so monetarist that we have reached a point in which the Central Bank does not need to control the amount of money in circulation, this is controlled by itself."[57]

Both the control of inflation and the new development model were based on the elimination of the protectionist system created in the 1930s. This policy of *apertura* or opening of the economy to the external market had a trade and a financial dimension. In its trade aspects *apertura* involved the gradual elimination of tariffs; in its financial aspect it aimed at the creation of capital markets, formed basically with international capital that would provide the necessary financial resources to develop the entire economy.[58] According to the neo-liberal discourse, the liberalization of international trade and finance was going to revitalize the productive structure and to guarantee consumers access to goods and services at reasonable prices while correcting distortions in the price structure. Furthermore, the creation of a strong capital market and the decontrol of interest rates would increase the savings rate and allow a better allocation of those savings.

One of the least-known aspects of the neo-liberal model as it was presented in Chile, and one that certainly should have had an impact on the military, was the claim that the model was the only alternative to overcome Chile's external dependence. This could be achieved by increasing the currency reserves and by diversifying exports.[59] The

Chilean neo-liberals had no difficulty demonstrating both to the military and the entire nation that thirty-five years of import substitution policies had not lessened the ties of dependence.

A final element of the economic program was the stress that its proponents placed on the universality of the neo-liberal policies. The neo-liberal discourse argued that the market benefits the entire society and that consequently is the only truly democratic mechanism. This would make the new policies entirely different from the import substitution model, which gave priority to the industrial sector and neglected the development of the agricultural sector, and different from the Popular Unity program that favored one social class. Following Friedman and Hayek, their Chilean disciples argued that state involvement in the economy had for the past thirty years impaired and limited economic and personal freedom and established a discriminatory, constrained economic system. In the neo-liberal framework, universality, freedom, and equality are automatically guaranteed by the market, which assures each individual the achievement of all his potentialities. The state would not only reduce its economic activities, but it would perform the functions that it retains, in a neutral and impersonal manner, according to the "scientific laws of the economy," and isolated from political or social pressures. The functions and decisions of this "neutral agent" are performed taking into account the interest of the entire nation, and not the interest of one specific class or group.[60]

The New Labor System and the "Modernizations"

As Karl Polanyi has so brilliantly demonstrated, the establishment of a market system is a process that requires the transformation by the state of the existing economic and societal structures, which in turn creates the conditions for the operation of the market system.[61] In Chile, the laws that carried out those changes are known as *modernizaciones*. Thus, "modernizations" are the bodies of laws aimed at restructuring the labor, land, and capital markets and laws that had the purpose of transforming the education, health, and the social security system.

A thorough review of the "modernizations," or public policies aimed at replacing the "old statist system" by the "new market model," lies beyond the scope of this work. Nevertheless, there is no doubt that as former minister Piñera argued, they set the basis for a silent revolution changing the nature and role of the state, setting new parameters for the relations between the public and private sectors, not only destroying contemporary foci of opposition, such as labor, but also reorienting future generations toward the "new belief." Through these policies the government totally transformed the structure of rural property, the organization and principles that guided the educational system, the organization and power of the municipalities, the labor laws, and the laws that regulated the professional associations.

Particularly important both from the standpoint of state-society relations and because of their impact on social security are the changes in the labor law system. Here we can distinguish three periods: the intensively repressive period of the first three years; the "corporatist period" of the years 1976 through 1978; and the neo-liberal period which began in 1979.

After the first three "destructive years" in which the government relentlessly persecuted the entire blue-collar labor leadership which, as we know, was closely associated with the outlawed Marxist parties, there was an attempt on the part of some within the administration to initiate a controlled reorganization of the union movement. Leading the attempt was the Minister of Labor, Air Force General Nicanor Díaz, a close ally of General Leigh. The backbone of this new system was the Labor Code Bill prepared by Díaz advisors. It established a regional system of unions organized according to economic activities, a process of negotiations through tripartite committees, and a restricted right to strike. At the same time, Díaz produced a limited and controlled reactivation of union activity by allowing the discussion of the bill among some unions.[62]

The corporatist-populist line of Díaz and Leigh was supported neither by Pinochet, who saw a danger in the revival of union activity, nor by the already emerging "economic team," whose stabilization program assumed a passive and mutilated labor force. The ousting of Díaz from the government marked the end to this short-lived corporatist attempt, and very likely signaled Leigh's decline, as he was removed from office some time later. Díaz was replaced by Minister Fernández, a neo-liberal who, faced with sporadic labor reactions to the harsh stabilization policies, enacted a number of measures aimed at reestablishing total discipline in the work force and at obtaining the "purification" of the labor movement.[63]

Both Ministers Fernández and Costa, his successor, began to legislate on issues affecting labor contracts, job stability, and working hours. One of the most important modifications introduced was to allow employers to dismiss up to 10 percent of the work force each month without severance pay. The law also allowed the employer to hire minors (fourteen to twenty-one years old) who were paid only 60 percent of the minimum wage in order to decrease the labor costs of both the industrial and the agricultural entrepreneurs.

The weakest point of the new legislation was the absence of a union structure, which deprived Chile of formal representation in international labor organizations and conferences. Costa's ineptitude in dealing with the AFL-CIO and the negative impact of the conflict prompted Pinochet to dismiss Costa from the Ministry and to replace him with one of the stars of the "economic team," José Piñera. Among the major tasks handed to Piñera was to restructure the union organization according to neo-liberal lines and to reform the social security system. He achieved both.

The Plan Laboral, a set of labor laws enacted during the first seven months of 1979, elaborated the main concepts behind the new union structure. This structure, based on the notion of "freedom of association," permitted the formation of one or several unions in each industrial plant, gave the worker the freedom to join any or none of these unions, allowed the worker to change from one union to another, and granted the unions the right of joining national confederations. Regarding collective negotiations, as in the 1924 law, they were the exclusive prerogative of the plant union (or unions, in this case) and were prohibited in the civil service and in all those enterprises in which the state contributed more than 50 percent of the budget. The apprentices in urban areas and the temporary workers in the rural sector were also forbidden to participate in collective negotiations.[64]

Although strikes were allowed in all those enterprises in which collective negotiations were allowed, the law discouraged the workers from resorting to strikes, since at any time during the strike the workers could be dismissed. Furthermore, after sixty days on strike, the law assumed that the workers had resigned their jobs. In other words, the new law did not attempt to control the forces participating in the labor market, but only to permit the undisturbed functioning of that market, transforming human labor into another commodity bringing whatever the market would bear. As Piñera argued:

> Collective negotiations should adjust themselves, but never substitute the economic reality that the labor market producers . . . . [T]he process of collective bargaining is not a mechanism through which the unionized workers are going to obtain salaries above those established by the market securing income generated by another factor of production.[65]

Nevertheless, the set of laws proved incapable of creating the perfect market conditions that the neo-liberals thought necessary for the proper functioning of the Chilean economy. Just as in England in the 1830s and 1840s, Chile between 1979 and 1981 saw an outburst of legislation repealing the previous system and trying to adapt labor to the needs of the economic model. In 1981, Miguel Kast, another prominent Chicago Boy, former Director of the National Planning Office, became Minister of Labor,[66] and new legislation was enacted that "liberalized" even more the labor market. The new laws geared to "flexibilize" the labor market eliminated the still-existing limitations on carrying out massive dismissal of workers and decreased the lump-sum compensation received by the dismissed workers. Kast also increased the daily working day up to twelve hours in some cases, decreasing the number of holidays and eliminating the obligation of the employer to pay gratuities.[67]

In order to assess the real impact of this legislation, one has to place it in the context of the labor situation in 1981. These reforms came at a time when the price of labor was very low as a result of years of repression, destruction of the labor organization, and stabilization policies that placed the burden of the economic adjustment on the backs of the workers. By 1980 real wages were just beginning to reach the levels they had in 1970. At the same time, the incipient economic recession that was beginning to cloud the bright skies forecast by the Chilean economists was already pushing unemployment rates up. High unemployment, which had been a constant problem for the regime, was going to be resolved according to the neo-liberal economists simply by lowering the cost of labor, while ignoring the structural conditions that were producing the high unemployment rates. Thus the new set of "liberalizing" laws were presented as an attempt to decrease the unemployment rate through an increase in the mobility of labor and the deregulation of the labor contract.[68]

The modernization of the labor law system was completed by Kast with the elimination of the last remnant of the old system, the Labor Courts. This decision was taken in spite of the opposition of the Supreme Court, the legal community, and the workers who argued for the need to maintain the Labor Court system, long recognized by international organizations and labor law specialists all over the world as a crucial element in the modern administration of justice.[69]

The Economic Results, 1975–1982

The impact of the stabilization policies and the implementation of the economic model were felt throughout the economy. In the analysis of the results it is important to distinguish between the anti-inflationary policies and the development model.

Regarding fiscal and monetary policies, the monetarist approach successfully eliminated the fiscal deficit and created a healthy situation in the balance of payments. Inflation was eventually brought under control by 1981 when the rate was reduced to 9.1 percent. The revaluation of the peso, in turn, reduced the price of imported goods which began to displace national products from the market. This approach to inflation culminated in 1979 with the freezing of the exchange rate at $39 per dollar, which equalized the external and the internal inflation rates; it was believed also that in the future Chilean inflation rates would not be higher than international rates.

Regarding economic growth, one clear effect of the program was to produce the largest contraction of economic activity ever experienced by the country since the Great Depression. In 1975 GDP decreased by 12.9 percent. After 1978, the economy recuperated growing at an average 8.7 percent per year for the next three years. A decline began again in 1980, which culminated in the economic depression of 1982 when the GDP decreased 14.5 percent.[70] On the average, then, the performance of the economy during this period was mixed. The average rate of growth for the period 1974–1984 was 1.0 percent, slightly lower than the average growth rate for the Allende period which was 1.3 percent, and well below the 4.5 percent average growth rate reached during the Frei administration.[71]

An analysis by sector of the economic growth data reveals that only the service sector was growing, an overgrown sector to begin with, and that both manufacturing and the agricultural sectors experienced a large decline as a result of the policy of *apertura*. In fact, the reduction of the protectionist barriers from an average of 94 percent in 1973 to 10 percent in 1979 changed the composition of the economy, reducing the relative weight of the manufacturing sector, which shrank in its relative share of the total product, in the employment it provided, and in absolute terms. The Central Bank reports that in 1982 the manufacturing sector was producing only 84.8 percent of what it produced in 1969.[72]

The behavior of the service sector was determined by two phenomena, the changes in the role of the state and the development of the financial service sector. The changes in the role of the state resulted in a decrease in the socioeconomic functions of the state, while the military and police functions increased. In the final analysis, overall state employment did not decrease, as many have argued, but increased by 13 percent.[73] The growth of the financial sector, on the other hand, resulted from the concern of the government economists with the liberalization of financial mechanisms and the development of large financial markets.

Since its inception, the proponents of the model had argued that, given the failure of the import substitution process, economic growth would be centered around those areas of the economy in which the country had natural advantages, such as certain agricultural products, e.g., timber, fruits, and wines. This would provide Chile with a new form of insertion into the international economic system and would put an end to Chile's mono-export economy through the development of non-traditional exports such as fruit. These non-traditional exports grew both in size, 4 percent between 1970 and 1980, and diversification during this period.[74]

The process of financial opening did not produce the inflow of foreign direct investment expected by the government, but a large inflow of credit from private lending institutions to the Chilean private sector. This capital neither spurred a process of domestic savings nor served as a source of productive investment. Instead it was used to finance the import of consumer goods. It sustained the growth of the financial service sector and created the largest indebtedness in Chilean history which, by 1982, amounted to 13.6 billion dollars.

Also, as a result of the changes in the relations between the private and the public sectors, the state restructured the entire economy around a few large economic conglomerates, the *grupos económicos*. By 1973, the state controlled, through different mechanisms, 533 enterprises. In the process of privatization that followed the coup, those enterprises were returned to the private sector, but not to their previous owners. The state-owned enterprises, as well as part of the expropriated farm land, were auctioned by the state. The auctions were all conducted in a very brief time period allowing the strongest economic conglomerates to obtain control of a very large number of enterprises at a cost that has been estimated to be between 50–70 percent of their book value.[75] Thus the sizable possessions that the economic groups accumulated were the result of the subsidized transference of state enterprises. The end result of this process was an unprecedented concentration of property in the hands of the five largest economic groups, which, by 1978, controlled the 250 largest private enterprises in the country.[76]

Particularly important was the concentration of financial capital in the hands of the *grupos* which resulted from a preferential access to both external and internal credit sources. The preferential access to external credit was, in turn, used to lend in the domestic market at rates which ranged from 64.2 percent per year in 1976 to 36 percent in 1981.[77] The large differences between the external and the domestic lending rates strengthened the position of the groups even further and fostered their expansion. At the same time they also controlled the access to domestic credit. By 1978 the six largest groups captured 25.3 percent of the domestic credit.[78] In view of the above, it is clear that, as Dahse argues, the economic recovery experienced by the country between 1977 and 1979 seems to have benefited mostly the five largest economic groups since they controlled 85 percent of the growing enterprises.[79]

Economic and Political Crises, 1982–1985

The political and economic scaffolding so carefully built by the Pinochet administration between 1978 and 1981 began to crumble in

1982. The economic debacle that followed was the result of the monetarist policies pursued by the administration, which produced the
largest recession that the country had yet experienced.

By 1979 the only economic problem that preoccupied the government economists was the inflation rate. The 30 percent-per-year inflation was unacceptable for the dogmatic Chilean policymakers. The
government decided to attack it directly by pegging the peso to the
dollar in order to bring inflation down to its international level. In
theory, the decision of pegging the peso to the dollar should have
brought the inflation rate down to the level of Chile's trading partners.
However, in practice, the overvalued currency allowed the financial
enterprises to borrow massively abroad, which undermined the process of automatic adjustment. The borrowed money, in turn, locked
the economy into a pseudo-growth spiral that accounted for an increase in consumption and imports and fueled financial speculation.
By the end of 1982 the foreign debt amounted to 80 percent of GNP
and the peso was overvalued by about 52 percent.[80]

Since inflation was still high, in early 1981 the monetary authorities decided to reduce the money supply in order to cool down the
economy. However, the economy had already entered a downward
cycle due to the combined effects of high interest rates and the overvalued currency. The reduction in the money supply acted as a catalyst to produce another recession. The full impact was felt in 1982
when the industrial sector decreased 21.6 percent.[81]

In the meantime, the combined effects of foreign borrowing and
the high interest rates had deepened the process of economic concentration. By mid-1981 the banks owned by the two largest groups had
issued 40 percent of total bank credit. In turn, more than 40 percent
of their loan portfolio was concentrated in their top thirty clients,
which often were enterprises owned by the same group.[82] By September overdue payments to these banks were growing rapidly. Particularly troublesome was the situation of the largest private bank, the
Banco de Chile (owned by the Vial group), which held a debt of
U.S.$2 billion.

The bankruptcy of the largest sugar refinery, CRAV, was the first
sign of the crisis, and it was followed by the decision of the government to take over the administration of the second largest bank,

Banco Español, and later on of three smaller banks, which accounted for 22 percent of the private sector lending, and three financial enterprises, which accounted for 49.9 percent of all the lending of these enterprises. By the end of 1982 the economy was in shambles. GNP had fallen 14.5 percent, the industrial sector had decreased 21.6 percent, and construction had fallen 29 percent. The unemployment rate reached 30 percent at the end of 1982 and despite the recession the inflation rate was 20.9 percent.[83] The price of labor fell again; and by the end of 1983 real wages were 14 percent below their 1970 level.

As in the past, the government decided to assist only the financial sector. The two largest banks, owned by the two largest economic groups, came under governmental management in January 1983. The government, at the same time, assumed full responsibility of the external debt that had been contracted by the private sector, and partially guaranteed the deposits in the "intervened" banks, while rejecting any responsibility for money deposited in the Savings and Loans that were now under the control of the state.

Given the pivotal role that the economic model had played in the construction and maintenance of the political system, the economic crisis was followed by the worst political crisis that the administration had experienced since coming to power. The end result of this dual process was not the overthrow of the Pinochet regime, as many expected, but the consolidation of its leadership around a new set of repressive policies. Nevertheless, in the process, political parties and unions reappeared and, although repressed and without power, they managed to put the regime on the defensive. In the short run there was a strengthening of the state both in its economic and political/repressive functions, but in the long run the crisis set the basis for the rebirth of political activity. To the extent that the economic model impinged directly on the political system, the economic crisis affected the regime's legitimacy, its relationship with society, and its attempt to generate an apolitical society in which consumption would replace political participation. The failure of the model destroyed, at least temporarily, the internal cohesion of the regime and affected its legitimacy. In order to restore both cohesion and legitimacy General Pinochet proceeded in August 1983 to form a new Cabinet led by

Sergio Onofre Jarpa. Jarpa, an old right-wing politician, was authorized to establish a dialogue with the political parties.

By early 1983 three simultaneous processes began to unfold: the formation of new political blocs, the revitalization of the trade union movement, and the movement of popular protest. The process of political organization was manifested in the formation of three political blocs, the Democratic Alliance, the socialist bloc, and the Popular Democratic Movement dominated by the communists. The leadership of the political process was taken by the Democratic Alliance, a coalition formed by a sector of the political right, the Christian Democrats, and the radical mechanisms. Thus, while the reestablishment of the state of siege, reduction of the political arena, and the ensuing repression did not solve any of the fundamental problems, they made perfect political sense for General Pinochet and allowed him to survive politically.

The Transition to Democracy

The nature of Chile's new democracy was determined by the 1980 Constitution and the modifications introduced during 1989. Central to the analysis is the notion that until 1998 Pinochet had a great deal of impact on Chilean politics and society. His impact was felt by all Chileans in terms of both the existing political and economic structures and the prevailing attitudes toward social, economic, and political issues. Pinochet might not have succeeded in eliminating politics from the face of Chile, but he certainly succeeded in transforming Chilean society. Pinochet's policies led to the creation of a society based on individualism and competition, undermining the importance of politics vis-à-vis the market.

With the collapse of the economy in 1982, the power of those who had applied the orthodox, or radical, monetarist policies in Chile collapsed as well. Between 1983 and 1984 the government produced a set of policies geared to simply manage the crisis, abandoning the orthodox monetary policies. In its early stage, those policies included the devaluation of the peso, the establishment of a preferential dollar, and wage reduction. The regime also attempted to disband the powerful economic groups since their economic activities had been at the center of the crisis. The purchase of unrecoverable loans from the banks led to the so-called statization of the debt, but not to the break-up of the conglomerates.

However, those measures were not enough. In January 1983, Rolf Lüders, the new Finance Minister, placed the conglomerates' major financial institutions in receivership. Government-appointed "intervenors" became the effective managers of the companies. With that, the state, paradoxically, took effective possession of approximately 80 percent of the private financial system and gained indirect control of firms that were deeply indebted.[84] As Edwards and Edwards note, by 1983, "the financial sector was in some way at the same juncture it had been ten years before. It had been nationalized and it was tightly controlled by the state."[85]

The combination of temporary measures, increased repression, and negotiations with the political parties did not solve the political problems of the regime. By 1984 the sharp decline in international lending and the internal contraction of the economy produced the total collapse of the financial system. In turn, these processes opened up the space for the introduction of new policies which responded to the needs not of the economic groups but of a broad spectrum of peak associations represented by the Confederation of Production and Commerce. In fact, the crisis had damaged the ability of the Chicago Boys to sustain the exclusive attention of Pinochet and destroyed the coalition that had all along supported the orthodox neo-liberal policies. The mystique that the market-oriented policies were faultless was partially destroyed as well.

Pragmatic Neo-liberalism

In 1985 the orthodox economic policies were replaced by a set of policies that some analysts have called pragmatic neo-liberalism. The implementation of these policies entailed the refurbishing of the political coalition which in the past was centered around the powerful economic groups. The new policies allowed the regime to regain control of the economic process and solve both the political and the economic crisis. The policies entailed a reactivation of the economy through reflationary policies. They included high real exchange rates, credits, and protective policies tailored to the requirements of specific economic sectors, as well as lower taxes. Key to the policies was the attempt to reduce unemployment, which had reached 30 percent by the end of 1983.[86]

In charge of the economy's readjustment was the new Minister of Finance, Hernán Buchi. Buchi maintained the neo-liberal model, but increased government intervention in the economy in order to either promote certain areas or control important economic actors. Central to Buchi's policies was the promotion of exports based on the notion of comparative advantages. The policy entailed increasing government support and promoting foreign investment in the non-traditional export sector of the economy. On the other hand, Buchi continued to pursue a stringent management of the fiscal deficit, inflation, and exchange rates. Thus, the minister designed an export-oriented development strategy based on the government support of non-traditional exports and a reactivation of the domestic market. Basic to the reactivation was a set of subsidies to the construction sector geared to build low-income housing and new mechanisms to support the agricultural sector. Fiscal austerity was combined with regulation of the financial sector and the privatization of government-owned assets.

Buchi's privatization strategy was quite different from the one pursued in the early stages of the regime. Buchi had to deal with two different sets of enterprises: those that had yet to be privatized and those that had come into government control as a result of the economic crisis. Under the label of popular capitalism the government proceeded to sell to the public the stock of selected companies creating a new private economy which was based neither on the powerful economic groups of the past nor on a broad spectrum of the population as claimed by the regime. The powerful economic groups had been disbanded or were bankrupt, and most Chileans were simply trying to recuperate some of what they had lost in the recession and could not afford to become stock owners. Thus this process of privatization led to the insertion or reinsertion of two actors in the economic process, foreign enterprises and the military.

The reinsertion of foreign enterprises in the Chilean economy involved the total or partial acquisition of a variety of enterprises, particularly in those areas that the government identified as key to the development strategy, such as the agro-export sector and forestry. The foreign companies also invested heavily in the financial, communication, and insurance sectors as well as pharmaceuticals, steel, and coal mines. Enterprises were either totally or partially acquired mostly through a novel mechanism known as debt/equity swaps. Debt/equity swaps were discounted debt notes—equity in Chilean companies—sold in world markets with the purpose of reducing the debt burden, bolstering the balance of payments, and privatizing state-owned assets.[87] In the final analysis the policy led to the creation of a new financial elite formed by a mix of Chilean and foreign entrepreneurs. About 8 percent of the stocks sold to the public were acquired by the military.[88]

Buchi's policies were very successful. During the 1985–1988 period the economy grew at about 5 percent per year while the debt was reduced by about $4 billion. Inflation remained stable at about 20 percent, and the process of privatization received a boost thanks to a new set of government policies geared to encourage investments in those sectors of the economy that offered the best export potential. Buchi's success can be measured also in terms of his ability to maintain a balance of forces within the new coalition.

The Long Road to the Plebiscite

Although the protest movement of 1982–83 did not achieve the goal of speeding up the process of democratization, it managed to destroy some of the administration's attitudes regarding the opposition. In the short run, the regime's answer to the protests was a new wave of repression combined with limited negotiations. In the long run, Pinochet reasserted control and reaffirmed his determination of conducting the process of democratization according to the deadlines established in the constitution.[89]

The popular protests were followed by the formation of the Democratic Alliance (AD), born in August 1983. The alliance, formed basically by the Christian Democrats and the moderate sectors of the Socialist Party, proposed the establishment of a constitutional assembly, the resignation of Pinochet, and the establishment of a transitional regime. The following month the Communist Party, the more radical sector of the Socialist Party, and the MIR formed the Democratic Popular Movement (MDP). The political right formed two different organizations: the Unión Democrática Independiente (UDI), which supported the policies and actions of the regime and proposed the establishment of an appointed Congress; and the Unión Nacional, which although supportive of the regime proposed a transition to democracy.

The responses of the regime were characterized by a mix of policies that allowed Pinochet to weather the storm and regain control. The appointment of Sergio Onofre Jarpa as Minister of Interior signaled the willingness of the government to pursue, temporarily, a policy of political opening characterized by talks with the AD coalition. Simultaneously, the regime launched an intensely repressive campaign geared to demobilize the society and end the protests. This new wave of repression was characterized by search and destroy missions, massive deployment of troops in Santiago, and the selective elimination of political leaders and human rights activists. The state of siege was renewed, freedom of the press was limited even further, and Santiago was "protected" by a military force of 40,000 soldiers.[90]

Jarpa's mission not only failed to produce a serious agreement with the opposition, but damaged the prestige of the regime even further. The talks had weakened the government cohesion since the initiatives taken by Jarpa questioned both the performance of the regime and the timetable set by the Constitution. General Pinochet could not accept either one, and in February 1985 he accepted Jarpa's resignation. Ricardo García, the new Minister of Interior, suspended the talks and continued with the repression. The Constitutional Court declared the MDP illegal.[91]

The AD had to come to terms with the fact that it was not going to speed up the process of democratic transition and that its best option was to force Pinochet to abide by the timetable that he had established and that he repeatedly said he would follow. Under the auspices of Monsignor Juan Francisco Fresno, the new head of the Chilean Church, a new set of talks among the democratic political parties took place. The talks ended with the signing of a document known as "The National Accord for the Transition to a Full Democracy." This document set an alternative timetable for the return to democracy, and it was signed by all the political parties except the UDI and the communists. For the UDI the timetable set by the Constitution of 1980 was sufficient, while for the Communist Party the timetable represented a compromise with an illegitimate ruler. The document called for the direct election of the president, a popularly elected congress, respect for political rights, and freedom of expression. It also called for the end of the political recess and the enactment of electoral laws. However, this attempt did not achieve its goals, due to the strength of the government and the weakness of the opposition.[92]

Here again the timely actions of the church leadership served the opposition very well. The actions of the church in defense of human rights during the dictatorship had taught the opposition lessons regarding interest representation and aggregation. The Vicaría had effectively included a broad range of people united not by political ideas, but by their opposition to human rights abuses. The same approach could now be applied to political issues. The unifying force now had to be opposition to the regime and desire for a transition to democracy. In order to achieve these goals both the Christian Democrats and the left had to abandon some of their sacred principles.

According to the former Minister of Interior Sergio Fernández, the National Accord "in essence, meant a return to the [political] system of 1925 with just minor corrections. To accept it meant to negate the significance of the military regime and its accomplishments."[93] Fernández, in the meantime, had been appointed head of a commission charged with studying constitutional laws geared to allow for the full application of the 1980 Constitution. The purpose of the laws was to regulate the reappearance of the political parties, to establish an electoral system, and to delineate the nature and functions of the future Congress. The first law produced by the Fernández Commission dealt with political parties. According to the commission's proposal 20,000 signatures were required to establish a party. The Consejo de Estado increased the number of signatures to 150,000, marking the beginning of a long process of discussions, both within the government and later with the opposition, regarding the nature of the parties.[94] In November 1985 a less controversial law regulating the Electoral Tribunal was approved.

The year 1986 was characterized by the end of the protest movement and the beginning of the process of economic recovery. At the same time, the government accused the opposition of resorting to violence and terrorism. The attempt to kill General Pinochet and the wave of repression launched by the regime became the trademarks of the year. The Fernández Commission continued drafting the electoral and political legislation required to conduct the now impending plebiscite. The recently drafted laws regulated the electoral process, including the establishment of norms dealing with radio and television advertising. Although the laws included important limitations to political freedoms, pluralism, and union rights, they provided the legal framework required to hold the referendum and to launch the transition process.

The impending plebiscite raised a series of political issues both within the regime and in the opposition. The strategy of the yes, or *si*, campaign launched by the government was to create fear among the population by associating democracy with disorder and chaos. The purpose was to convince the middle class that voting for the opposition or *no* campaign would mean a return to the chaos, scarcities, and conflict of the Popular Unity years. The Marxist threat and the war against Marxism continued providing the political foundations of the regime and its justification for survival. While the message was widely accepted by the upper-class groups, it failed to convince the majority of Chileans that their best option was another eight years of Pinochet.

The opposition, on the other hand, managed to resolve a number of internal differences and formed the Concertación de los Partidos por el No. The critical issue for the Christian Democrats was to get rid of the failed *camino propio*.[95] In mid-1987 the Christian Democrats elected Patricio Aylwin as the head of the coalition and presidential candidate. The official strategy called for a massive mobilization of all those sectors that opposed the dictatorship, mass electoral registration campaigns, and the legalization of the party. Although the party officially rejected the government timetable and continued calling for free elections, in practice it had no option but to accept the constitutional terms. As a result, a strategy geared toward confronting Pinochet in the plebiscite had to be developed.

The divisions in the Socialist Party between the "renovated" faction and the more radical faction set the tone for the role of these groups in the electoral process. For the renovated sector the central issues were the party's fragmentation, the need to form a broad political alliance, and the need to reexamine the Marxist foundations of the party. Under the leadership of Ricardo Nuñez, the renovated sector decided to abandon Leninism and to join forces with the Christian

Democrats to facilitate the transition.[96] However, the policies and actions of even the more moderate elements of the party were indecisive and contradictory. After joining the Alianza the Nuñez faction decided to leave in December 1986 to form a broad left-wing alliance. The meeting of the left-wing forces held in December 1986 failed to produce a joint program, and the Nuñez faction decided to maintain an independent position vis-à-vis the rest of the political system, insisting on the need for free, immediate elections.

At the same time, the more radical faction, or Almeyda faction, was also moving away from its close relationship with the Communist Party due to the communist insistence that the parties use all forms of struggle to end the regime, including arms. The socialists perceived this position as obstructing the unification of the opposition and the political process of transition. The increased power of the Frente Patriótico Manuel Rodríguez (FPMR), the armed wing of the Communist Party, and the failed attempt to kill Pinochet only deepened the differences between socialists and communists. The Almeyda faction began to look for other alliances and formed a new left-wing coalition without the communists, Izquierda Unida. The new coalition decided to opt for the political process and negotiations with the Christian Democrats.

Intense negotiations between the Christian Democratic leadership and the Almeyda faction led to the formation of the Agreement for the No, or *Acuerdo por el No*, which was to confront the regime's campaign.[97] In the final analysis, by the end of 1987 all the opposition parties, except the communists and the MIR, had joined forces to call for a massive electoral registration campaign and free elections.[98] The Concertación de Partidos por el No was officially established in February 1988 and included seventeen political parties.

The political position of the Communist Party vis-à-vis the Pinochet regime was defined in 1980. The new strategy called for the use of all forms of struggle, including popular rebellion, and the use of all available means to defeat the dictatorship. This major departure from the party's non-violent position resulted from the internal conditions as well as the impact of the revolutionary process in Central America. In the words of Luis Corbalán, the General Secretary of the party, "[W]e are not going to wait until the conditions are developed. We believe that the struggle is going to allow us to create those conditions."[99] The creation of the Manuel Rodríguez Patriotic Front (FPMR) in 1983 made clear the party's commitment to armed struggle and the implementation of the policy of popular rebellion.

The violent strategy failed. The FPMR did not become the engine of a revolution against General Pinochet and only managed to carry out isolated terrorist actions. The party became isolated from the other political parties and marginal to the political negotiations conducted prior to the plebiscite. An intense political debate that divided the party followed the implementation of the new strategy.[100] By 1989 the already existing divisions were reinforced by the changes taking place in the Soviet Union. The persistent rejection of the Perestroika approach produced the exit of an important group of members, the expulsion of others, and the creation of the PDI, Participación Democrática de Izquierda (Leftist Democratic Participation).

The No campaign emphasized the need for social peace and social justice and a new political regime. Appealing to Chile's long democratic traditions, the campaign asked the voters to choose between two distinct political regimes, democracy or dictatorship. The campaign emphasized the harsh traits of General Pinochet's personality as well as the damage to Chile's international prestige caused by his actions. Contrasting with the fear-based campaign of the Pinochet regime, the No propaganda was based on a happy and optimistic view of the future. The slogan of the *alegría ya viene* (happiness will soon arrive) contrasted with the Si campaign's emphasis on the tutelary role of Pinochet that argued that he was the only one capable of guaranteeing safety and progress. The No campaign stressed the notions of freedom and change after seventeen years of military rule and oppression and called for progress for all, as opposed to the very selective progress that had taken place during the dictatorship. Finally, the international economic and technical assistance provided to the No campaign made a great difference. Monies provided by the National Endowment for Democracy and the European Social and Christian Democratic parties allowed the opposition to finance a number of political activities and an excellent media campaign. Sergio Fernández writes that the music of the *alegria ya viene* was so good that even those who supported the regime liked to sing it.[101]

The overall performance of the economy during the dictatorship certainly did not help the regime. Although economic performance had improved since 1985, the overall economic picture was characterized by high unemployment and massive poverty. Average wages in 1989 were 8 percent below the 1970 level, while the minimum income had decreased by 9 percent. Income distribution data confirms that the impact of the neo-liberal policies was highly regressive. During the 1970s and 1980s the income of the highest 20 percent of the population increased from 44.5 percent to 54.5 percent, while the lowest 60 percent experienced a decline from 34 percent to 25 percent.[102]

The electoral results confirmed the notion that the neo-liberal polices had an adverse effect on the regime's electoral performance. The opposition won the referendum by a margin of 7.7 percent, and did very well in the large cities and among the low-income groups. For instance, the opposition received 65.4 percent of the low-income vote and 60 percent of the vote in the communes with more than 100,000 inhabitants.[103] Poverty and the economic performance of the regime certainly affected the referendum results providing a base of support to the opposition.

Pinochet's defeat in the October referendum led to a further recognition of the role and importance of the opposition. The administration agreed to begin preparations for the presidential elections and to initiate talks with the "Concertación" regarding the need to reform some aspects of the 1980 Constitution. The task of the opposition was to deal with the formation of electoral coalitions, the selection of candidates and programs, and the negotiations with the government regarding the enactment of political laws. These laws were essential to conduct fair and free elections. The presidential election was set for 14 December 1989.

In the new political spectrum the right-wing coalition was formed by two political forces: the Union Democrática Independiente (UDI) led by Jaime Guzmán, representing the hardliners; and Renovación Nacional (RN) representing the more democratic sectors of the right. RN was looking forward to participating in the new regime and, consequently, was willing to support partial reforms to the Constitution. UDI, on the other hand, opposed any democratization of the Constitution. While Pinochet and the UDI prevailed in the selection of Hernán Buchi as the presidential candidate, Renovación Nacional managed to get advantages in the selection of parliamentary candidates.[104]

The opposition, unified under the banner of the "Concertación," was able to solve its differences and accomplish two central tasks, to negotiate with the regime as a bloc and to select the Christian Democratic leader Patricio Aylwin as the presidential candidate. The parties that formed the coalition managed to reach electoral agreements regarding congressional elections as well.

The next step involved negotiations between the regime and the opposition regarding the content of the laws that would facilitate the transition to an elected regime. In fact, two parallel processes evolved after the plebiscite. One was the imposition on the part of Pinochet and the hardliners of a set of policies geared to maintain and strengthen the autonomy and political influence of the military and to maintain authoritarian structures in key areas of the economy and the society. The other was the negotiations between the regime and the opposition geared to reform the constitution. The regime had the upper hand in these negotiations.

The regime assured the continuation of the authoritarian structures through a set of laws, called the organic-constitutional laws, which established authoritarian enclaves in the future political regime. For example, one law determined the structure and autonomy of the Central Bank, forbidding government intervention in the decision-making process of the institution; another law made television independent from the executive branch; and a third prohibited Congress from investigating human rights abuses committed by the military regime. The most crucial of these organic laws was the Armed Forces Law that gave the military a tutelary role and made them financially and structurally autonomous from civilian control.[105] As Garretón argues, these laws consolidated the existence "of a state within the state." Finally, the regime projected itself into the future through a set of key appointments that guaranteed control of the universities, local government, and sectors of the bureaucracy.

On the other hand, there was a set of constitutional reforms suggested by the opposition and partially accepted by the regime. These reforms included the reduction of the first presidential period from eight to four years; reduction in the power of the National Security Council; measures geared to facilitate the process of constitutional reform, eliminating the requirement that the reform be approved by two successive Congresses; the incorporation of human rights treaties into Chile's legal system; reforms geared to augment the rights of the individuals under a state of siege; and the elimination of Article 8 of the Constitution that forbade the existence of Marxist parties. These reforms were approved by a referendum held in July 1989.[106]

For both the regime and the opposition these reforms were the product of internal struggles and compromises. The hardliners within the regime, led by former Minister of Interior Sergio Fernández, found these reforms unacceptable. According to him, "the reforms undermined the protective structure created by the 1980 Constitution, regressing to and becoming dangerously close to the norms of 1925 [constitution]."[107] The reforms were supported by the current Minister of Interior Carlos Cáceres and by the more democratic sector of the right led by Renovación Nacional.[108] The opposition, for their part, had to abandon the so-called 'maximalist' position that demanded an almost complete overhaul of the 1980 Constitution. Instead, they opted for the acceptance of a limited packet of reforms that would simply facilitate the process and provide a set of minimum guarantees. What is important to highlight is that throughout the process the regime maintained the upper hand and was able to determine the nature and extent of these reforms. Consequently, the role of the Armed Forces as independent "protectors" of the political system and the presence of non-elected members of Congress could not be changed. From the standpoint of the opposition, although the reforms were partial at best, they were perceived as a more compromising attitude on the part of the government. These reforms were also seen as a first step in what seems to be a long struggle between democratic and authoritarian forces in Chile.

As the Pinochet regime began to look into its political future it began to search for mechanisms and organizations that would allow the projection of its power beyond the elections. The major problem the regime encountered was the lack of a political structure that could operate during the transition period and beyond. General Pinochet's determination to create an apolitical system based on a combination of patrimonial concepts precluded the development of a strong political movement capable of capitalizing on the regime's support among the upper class and sectors of the middle class. In other words, the patrimonialist approach to politics held by Pinochet lacked a long-term political project and simply rested on the ability of the patrimonial ruler to stay alive and in power. The concentration of power in the hands of Pinochet was such that even the Armed Forces had been excluded from the conduction of the government and, true to its Prussian inheritance, simply obeyed the orders of the Commander-in-Chief.

Summary

The policy axis of the Pinochet regime had two poles: the replacement of the populist-inclusionary state by an authoritarian-exclusionary one, and the replacement of the import substitution model of economic development by the neo-liberal model, changing the role and the functions of the state.

General Pinochet forced the disappearance of other political actors through the very effective use of massive repression, propaganda, and a new constitutional structure. The policies produced at least the temporary elimination of societal organizations that could serve as foci of political activity and managed to atomize the society. Those goals were achieved through a set of legal norms, most importantly the 1980 Constitution, which institutionalized the authoritarian regime, and by way of a number of public policies, the modernizations, which while explicitly designed to facilitate the operation of the market also served the political needs of the system. Simultaneously, the personalistic rule of Pinochet was consolidated and legitimized through the plebiscite and other political processes and by his ability to exclude all other political players.

From a political standpoint, the 1980 Constitution established a form of authoritarianism that was made to the measure of Pinochet's needs. The concentration of power in the hands of the Executive, in practice, involved simply the concentration of power in the hands of Pinochet and a few trusted advisors. The military as an institution played a supporting role, following the basic Prussian principles of hierarchy and obedience that are central to the education of the Chilean military. What emerged in Chile during the first ten years of the Pinochet administration was a new set of political structures and a total redefinition of the relations between state and society, as well as a drastic reduction in the social functions of the state.

The transformation of the political, economic, and social functions of the state was profound. From an economic perspective, while the state reduced its socioeconomic functions, it did not disappear either as a direct or as an indirect economic actor. Throughout the period the state not only maintained control of Chile's most important economic resource, the copper mines, it reserved for itself a more permanent and fundamental set of prerogatives in transforming the economic structure of the nation, setting the rules according to which the new economic game was played, and deciding who were the central players. Thus the invisible hand of the free market genie required the very visible hand of the state to transform the existing economy and society.

The transition process in Chile was determined by the nature and ideology of the Pinochet regime. The personalistic type of authoritarian rule served General Pinochet well for about fifteen years.[109] However, at the same time this patrimonial-personalistic style of rule, based on the concentration of power in the hands of the authoritarian ruler, deprived Pinochet of a political organization that he could use if the economic model did not produce the expected political results.

Second, the entire political edifice was built on the success of the economic model and the ability of the regime to keep the society atomized and passive for about one generation. That the sixteen years of military rule resulted in a very mixed record of economic successes and failures seems relevant here.[110] Most of the success can be attributed to the "revised" application of the model made by Buchi, who managed to increase exports, reduce the debt, increase foreign investment, reprivatize the banks, and obtain high rates of economic growth. The model also generated a process of concentration of capital in the upper income sectors, while increasing poverty. By 1985, 45 percent of the population were living below the poverty level and 20 percent were in conditions of extreme poverty.[111] As I have argued elsewhere, the economic model, both in its initial form and under Buchi's leadership, had both economic and political goals. The model was designed to give economic power to a small elite. The elite, in turn, provided support to a repressive political regime.

The efforts to keep the society passive and atomized were only partially successful. The enormous human rights violations instilled fear in the society and destroyed political organizations while a whole generation of political leaders of the left disappeared from the political arena. However, the protest movement represented a forceful response to a regime that had failed to achieve its own economic goals and was single-handedly responsible for the economic crisis. In the wake of the protests a political coalition emerged that pressured the regime to comply with its own timetable for the transition to democracy. Moreover, the actions of the Catholic Church and of the human rights organizations that emerged during the repression provided a new model of political action that was used during the transition process. These organizations taught the politicians a lesson about the possibilities of "cohabitation" and the need to abandon rigid ideological pronouncements in favor of a unified opposition to the regime.

The combined effect of relentless repression, a very well-orchestrated propaganda campaign, and the "modernizations" was intimately connected to the transformation of the social narrative. The old narrative with its emphasis on democracy and equality was defined as old fashioned, outmoded, inefficient, and impregnated with Marxist ideas that would effectively destroy the society. Instead, the new narrative stressed individualism and the market. Both concepts served the regime well since they were used to justify the destruction of previous organizations, augmenting the power of the ruler.

The importance of the Pinochet regime rests not only in having ruled the country for seventeen years. His regime transformed Chile's political and economic institutions and changed the society as well. The analysis of the social security reform will illustrate the new policy-making style, the new principles, and the new narrative.

CHAPTER 8

Winners and Losers
The Privatization of Social Security

T he vital and intimate connection between politics and policies is again seen in the analysis of the Pinochet regime and
the 1980 social security reform. The exclusionary, repressive
regime established by General Pinochet was complemented by a neo-
liberal economic model and the destruction of the labor law system.
The "modernizations," in turn, changed the relations between the state
and the private economic actors and enhanced the power of a new economic elite. It is at the level of policies such as the modernization/
privatization of social security that the complementarity between the
needs of the political regime and the neo-liberal economic model are
best seen. The policies were an essential component of both the new
economic policies and the political need to atomize and disintegrate
the society. The establishment of a market economy was the product of
the actions and decisions of a very powerful regime. Pinochet's social
security reform reflects the power arrangements that existed in Chile
in 1980. The policies have concentrated capital and power in the
hands of the Administadoras de Fondos de Pensiones (AFPs), coverage
has been reduced, and the state bears a large financial burden, although
it performs limited functions.

The Chilean social security system was the subject of a variety of
modifying schemes between 1973 and 1980 and a sweeping reform in
1981. A prevalent concern of the administration was not only to restructure the social security system in order to eliminate some of its
vicious practices, but to create a system attuned to the new economic

model. Neither goal was achieved until the "economic team" consolidated its position within the administration.

In this analysis of the social security reform the new roles assumed by the state and by the private sector will be stressed in addition to the principles that guided the reform itself. Those principles involved a reduction of the role of the state, the transformation of social security into a compulsory private insurance system, and the privatization of the administration of the social security funds. The policy analysis gives an indication of the depth of the societal transformation carried out by the Pinochet regime and the impact of the market principles and their proponents. The policy is also indicative of the many policies used by the regime in its attempt to disarticulate the society.

The social security reform was not only a reflection of the new societal arrangements, it was a method of transforming the existing social, political, and economic organization. This reform in conjunction with the other modernizations was designed to atomize the society and to enhance the role of the market as a regulator of socioeconomic relations. It has changed the nature of the role of the state in this area and it has transformed basic principles of social welfare.

The rhetoric that accompanied the reform reflected the new social narrative. The reform was presented as a symbol of modernity and progress, a step forward. Those who did not join the new system were, according to the propaganda, *los quedados*, those who are left behind or are not smart enough to keep up with the rest. Those who join would become active participants in the new economy and the new system; they would be at the forefront of a process that would revolutionize social security.

The central thesis of this chapter is that, although the reform entailed a revolution in the way of making social security, its benefits have been limited. The extent of those limitations is analyzed below.

The First Attempt to Reform the Social Security System

Just as previous governments had done, the Pinochet regime decided to initiate a reform of the social security system very early in its administration and, following previous patterns, asked the Superintendencia of Social Security to report on the main problems of the system. The report came in November 1973 and focused on the well-known problems of high costs, inequality of benefits and contributions, and chaotic administration.[1] Upon receiving the report, the Junta de Gobierno asked ODEPLAN, the National Planning Office and the central agency of the economic sector, for an evaluation of the social security system. ODEPLAN was asked to formulate a blueprint for reform. The Superintendencia was also asked to elaborate a reform proposal.

Following its traditional line which, under the military regime, has contemptuously become known as *estatista*, the Superintendencia's report to the Junta in April 1974 called for the creation of a new social security system administered by the state through four major institutions that would cover workers on a functional basis, the establishment of a universal and sufficient system of benefits, the maintenance of the financial system based on tripartite contributions, and the continuation of the common fund system, but eliminating the existing inequalities.[2]

ODEPLAN's proposal, on the other hand, called for the replacement of the existing financial structure by an individual capitalization fund, the creation of private institutions charged with the administration of the individual capital accounts, and the investment of those funds in private capital markets. It was the view of ODEPLAN that the new system would generate enough resources to maintain, and even improve, the quality and the quantity of the benefits.[3]

It is not difficult to perceive the contrasting nature and the enormous conceptual and practical differences of the schemes. Despite these differences both projects were combined in a bill known as Anteproyecto del Estatuto Fundamental de Principios y Bases del Sistema de Seguridad Social, henceforth referred to as the Anteproyecto, which was announced to the public in November 1975.

The Anteproyecto was the result of a compromise between two government bureaucracies with totally different institutional interests and ideologies. ODEPLAN was already in the hands of the neo-liberal economists, and the Superintendencia of Social Security was still dominated by its "statist cadres." While the first was concerned with the implementation of a given economic scheme and with the role of the social security system in this scheme, the second was concerned with the reform of an inefficient, unjust, and costly social security system.

As discussed elsewhere, this conflict was not limited to the area of social security. It was part of a much larger political battle, the conflict between the neo-liberals and the corporatists to capture the ear of General Pinochet. In this context, the Anteproyecto was an attempt to compromise two irreconcilable positions, involving different political and economic alternatives and different groups of political actors within the administration. It reproduced in microcosm the larger political conflict.

The Anteproyecto, following the principles of the subsidiary state, reduced the functions of the state to a general supervisory role and, based on the notion of freedom of choice and competitiveness, proposed the creation of new administrative units, the Corporations of Social Security. The project also attempted to maintain the basic social security principles of universality, uniformity, unity, and sufficiency of pensions, while eliminating the discriminatory pensions based on years of service. Thus, while the Superintendencia influenced the administrative organization and the inclusion of minimum pensions, ODEPLAN prevailed in all the financial aspects, which included the creation of a system based on individual accounts and a reduction in the payroll tax.

As part of his program of controlled reactivation of the labor movement, General Díaz, the Minister of Labor, submitted the Anteproyecto to the analysis and criticism of various labor organizations. At the same time it was submitted to the analysis of the Junta and other authorities. Publicly, the project generated mixed reactions. Suggestions and criticisms dealt with the nature and management of the corporations, the nature of the individual capital accounts, and the elimination of pensions based on years of service.

The period of public discussion ended abruptly in April 1976 with the replacement of Minister Díaz by the neo-liberal Sergio Fernández, who announced that the social security reform would be made into law in the future. From this moment on, an aura of mystery surrounded the social security reform. The reform was neither publicly discussed nor approved during the remainder of 1976 nor during 1977, and the few official declarations on the topic never amounted to more than evasive answers.

What was not revealed to the public was that throughout 1976 and 1977, the Anteproyecto was being revised and discussed by the different members of the Junta and their advisors, and by the Superintendencia; neither was it revealed that the reform as it has been delineated in the Anteproyecto was very far from having the support of the Junta.[4] In fact, an analysis of the reports exchanged by the members of Junta shows that there were disagreements regarding both the need for a total reform and the nature of the reform. Members of the Junta argued that the total transformation of the system was unnecessary. General Leigh, for instance, questioned the need to reform all the programs and proposed simply a unification of the system around three funds, each of them with similar benefits and financial provisions. General Leigh also opposed the establishment of individual accounts and the replacement of the common fund system. General Leigh and Mendoza (the Commander-in-Chief of the Police) argued that the new system would benefit more the new financial enterprises created to administer the system than the workers.

The discussions of the bill ended in August 1977. Neither during the remainder of 1977 nor during the next year did the government take any action concerning social security reform. It was not until José Piñera was named Minister of Labor in December 1979 that the government again mentioned the problem, but this time the existence of the Anteproyecto was totally ignored.

Undoubtedly, the government paralysis in the area of social security can only be understood in the context of the major political disputes that took place between the neo-liberals and the corporatists during this period. The Anteproyecto, even though a compromise between the neo-liberal and the corporatists, reflected to a larger extent the power of Leigh and Díaz. As their power began to decline in mid-1977, the neo-liberals knew it was only a matter of time until they could obtain a bill that fully expressed their ideas in the area of social security. The reappearance of the issue in early 1980 coincides with the consolidation of the power of the neo-liberals. But now they did not need to consider the Anteproyecto as the basis for a reform, nor had they to contend with a powerful Superintendencia, which had been reduced to little more than an appendage of the Ministry of Labor.

The analysis of the written responses of the Commander-in-Chiefs of the Air Force, Navy, and Police to the Anteproyecto sheds light on the conflicts among the Junta members. These documents are indicative of the relations among Pinochet, Leigh, Merino, and Mendoza.[5] One sees that Leigh opposed the neo-liberal project and was not interested in the total transformation of the society the project proposed, while Merino and Mendoza stood somewhere in the middle. General Pinochet soon realized that a coalition with the neo-liberals would nicely complement his long-term political goals. As seen in the previous chapter, the removal of General Leigh the following year was the result of this conflict.

Partial Reform in the Interim

Although decisions regarding the total reform of the system were postponed until the power of the neo-liberals was totally consolidated, the administration did not stay completely inactive in the area of social security. The Pinochet regime showed concern with two important issues, the insufficiency of pensions and the problem of family allowances.

The government as well as the public knew that pensions were highly insufficient. The reason for the insufficiency resulted from the form in which pensions were calculated and the constant inflationary process experienced by the Chilean economy. In periods of skyrocketing inflation such as those experienced by Chile between 1973 and 1976, it is easy to imagine the inadequacy of an income based on a part of the wages of years past. The government's attempts to partially solve this problem through dozens of pension readjustment laws always fell short of their purpose. By 1978 the average monthly pension was only U.S.$54. In the words of the Superintendent of Social Security, Ricardo Schmidt, "[T]here is no hope of an improvement in the situation of the retirees." He added that "in the long run the only solution was the total reform of the system."[6]

From the beginning, the Pinochet administration demonstrated special interest in the area of family allowances. In fact, only nineteen days after the coup on 1 October 1973, the government unified by decree all the family allowances funds, replacing the numerous systems of benefits with the Sistema Unico de Prestaciones Familiares.

Further modifications took place in 1978, when the administration of the family allowances program was taken away from the pension funds and given to newly created entities, the Cajas de Compensación de la Asignación Familiar. The new Cajas could be formed by up to 6,000 workers and followed the principle of self-management that had already been proposed by the Superintendencia and the Novoa Commission during the Frei administration.

D.L. 2448 and the Elimination of Privileged Pensions

In February 1979, the Pinochet government, without previous announcement or discussion, enacted D.L. 2448, which introduced the most important reforms of the social security system to date. D.L. 2448 dealt basically with equalizing benefits, eliminating pensions based on years of service, and establishing uniformity in pension readjustments.

Regarding retirement age, D.L. 2448 established a general minimum retirement age of sixty-five years for males and sixty years for females and a general requirement of at least ten years of contributions. Furthermore, the decree eliminated all the pensions based on years of service, repealed all the existing legislation regarding readjustment of pensions, and established a general, uniform system of readjustability that tied pensions to the consumer price index. With the same stroke of the pen, the administration eliminated the *perseguidoras*.[7] The financial and political importance of D.L. 2448 cannot be overlooked. There is no doubt that this decree addressed the two most critical problems of the social security system, inequities and insufficiency of pensions, while it eliminated its most costly vices, pensions based on years of service and the *perseguidoras*.

The administrative reforms contained in D.L. 2448 and the reforms to the Family Allowance system enacted between 1973 and 1978 were very similar to the reforms proposed by the Frei administration. But what President Frei could not achieve in a democratic context, the authoritarian regime had no trouble accomplishing. The group most affected by the reform, the civil servants, who in the past had proven to be powerful enough to obstruct any substantial reform of their system, was unable to do anything on this occasion. The civil servants learned, just as others had already learned and still others will undoubtedly learn in the future, that an authoritarian government operates with a large degree of autonomy even from the most organized and powerful social groups.

The 1980 Reform

If 1978 was the year of the consolidation of power for the neo-liberals, 1980 was the year of the great reforms or "modernizations" which materialized the power that this faction had over the process of economic policymaking. Among those modernizations, the reform of the social security system, or Modernización de la Previsión, occupied a central place and Minister José Piñera was charged with the role of leading the process.

Piñera's personal career is very similar to that of many of the other Chicago Boys who filled the top ranks of the Chilean administration during the Pinochet regime. Harvard educated, but a Chicago Boy in his economic beliefs, Piñera was associated with the Cruzat family economic group, one of the two largest. Piñera was also a close associate of Minister Sergio de Castro, the dean of the Chicago Boys and certainly the most influential person in the policy-making arena during the years 1978–1982. The thirty-year-old minister was assigned three specific tasks: (a) to coordinate the labor and economic sectors of the government; (b) to institutionalize a new system of labor relations, creating a depoliticized labor organization; and (c) to reform of the social security system.[8]

Soon after his designation Piñera named a commission to be headed by Martín Cóstabal, Director of the National Budget Office. The commission was instructed to draft a reform that included the application of the principle of subsidiarity of the state in the administration of the funds, the reduction of the principle of social solidarity, and the elimination of the portion of the social security tax paid by the employers.[9] Most of these ideas were already part of the reform proposal presented by ODEPLAN in 1975. The only new element was the elimination of the social security tax paid by the employer, which was an idea that also originated at ODEPLAN, principally by its director Miguel Kast. This proposal had been developed in an important policy paper drafted by Kast known as the "Plan to Foster Employment and Efficiency in Social Action" (Plan de Fomento del Empleo y Eficiencia de la Acción Social). In that paper Kast suggested that the most important distortions in the labor market, those which had limited the growth of employment, were the social security tax, the existence of a minimum wage, and a law which limited the freedom of the employers to dismiss labor. Regarding the social security tax, the Plan proposed the progressive elimination of the payroll tax within a four-year period. According to the Plan that measure would produce 320,000 new jobs in two years in Santiago alone.[10]

While Kast provided the intellectual justification for the elimination of the social security tax, Piñera had already elaborated an administrative reform. Piñera argued that the provision of social security services is a function that can be performed by either private or public agents, and that the only acceptable criteria to assign this function to one or the other was efficiency. Piñera also argued that these functions can be best performed by the private sector since the production of such services requires sophisticated financial techniques and complex administrative systems, and it does not entail a redistributive function.[11] Accordingly, Piñera proposed: (a) to authorize the creation of private corporations charged exclusively with the administration of social security funds; (b) to establish a compulsory individual social security system; (c) to subsidize the lowest income pensions through a system of minimum pensions; and (d) to ensure competition among the private corporations by fostering the establishment of multiple administrative entities.[12] A reform of this nature would disperse economic power diminishing the gigantism of the state, reduce the financial burden of the state, and strengthen the private sector. A final element of concern for Piñera was the potential criticism that the proposal would generate and the fear that the reform would give excessive power to the private enterprises. However, according to him, this fear was just a remnant of the past that had to be ignored and fought.

Given the contributions of Kast and Piñera, the commission's role was limited to applying and integrating their ideas into a coherent law. The commission worked in an environment of total secrecy. Until the day of its public announcement nothing was known about the content of the reform. Following the public announcement, Piñera introduced the reform to the most important unions with a purely educational purpose since it became law on 4 November 1980 through D.L. 3500. In the words of Minister Kast, "Chile was again at the forefront of social security reform in Latin America."[13]

Before analyzing the different aspects of the reform it is important to note that the reform covers only the pension system for all blue- and white-collar workers, dependent or independent, and both in the private or the public sector, except the military. The existing family allowances and occupational accident insurance programs were not included since they had been reformed early in the administration.

The Financial Structure

The 1980 legislation introduced a number of substantial reforms which changed the very basis of the financial system, altered the principle of solidarity, and reinforced individualism. It involved the elimination of employers' contributions to the social security system and the transformation of the common fund into individual funds.

The reduction of the employers' contribution to the pension system had began in 1975 when contributions were reduced from 43.3 percent of the taxable wages to 20.3 percent in 1980.[14] The 1980 legislation maintained only a 1 percent contribution to the workmen's compensation fund and a temporary 2.85 percent tax to finance the family allowance and the unemployment insurance programs. By 1988 all the employers' contributions had been eliminated. The purpose of these reductions was to lower the cost of labor and in turn reduce unemployment rates. Employees' and workers' contributions to the system were also reduced, but only for those workers who transferred their social security funds to the new system, providing a very strong incentive to do so. The insured pays a 10 percent contribution to the old age pension system. Additional contributions of 2.5 percent to 3.7 percent are required to finance the disability and survivors pensions. The insured can also make additional contributions of up to 10 percent to augment the old age pension fund and they have to deposit another 7 percent of their wages to obtain health and maternity benefits. Consequently, the total compulsory contribution in the private sector amounts to 19.5 percent to 20.7 percent, while the contribution in the public sector is about 27 percent.[15]

The large reduction in the contributions to the pension plan resulted from the reduction in social security expenditures that was mandated by D.L. 2448, specifically, the elimination of the pensions based on years of service, the increase in the retirement age, and the elimination of the *desahucio* or cash benefit paid in relation to the years of service. Better fiscal policy and compliance with the laws also produced an increase in revenues.[16]

Officials in the administration argued that the elimination of the social security tax would reduce the cost of labor, which in turn would reduce the very large unemployment rates. Martín Cóstabal, chairman of the commission and director of the National Budget Office, argued that the reform would produce in the medium and long range between 100,000 and 200,000 jobs.[17]

The common fund system, *sistema de reparto*, which had been under the attack of the neo-liberals since 1974, was replaced by the individual capitalization fund. For Piñera the common fund had not only failed to achieve its fundamental purpose of social solidarity, it had generated and encouraged the inequalities, inefficiencies, and insufficiencies that characterized the whole social security system.[18] Logically, then, the problem had to be attacked at its roots, replacing a system based on the collectivist ideology with one based on an ideology which "establishes a clear relationship between the personal effort and the reward," and "that gives the individual the freedom of choosing and deciding."[19] The elimination of the common fund system, in fact, complemented the elimination of the social security tax and established a system that might be defined as a compulsory private insurance system.

There is little doubt that the prime reason behind the replacement of the common fund by the individual fund was the individualistic ideology sustained by the regime. What Piñera calls the collectivist philosophy of the past is what had served as the foundation for the prevailing social narrative: the notion that the state could be used to bring about a better society for all. Piñera's argument was that the old system, instead of creating a better society for all, created a better system for those with enough power to get the benefits from the politicians. For the others it created simply a hope and also a deception.

Elsewhere in this book I have analyzed the connection that existed between politics and policies and between politicians and interest groups. There is little doubt that the old system was unequal and dependent upon a set of clientelistic relationships. However, what Piñera failed to recognize was that while in the new system there were no politicians, there was still a clear relationship between policies and politics. In the context of an authoritarian, personalistic regime the power is not found in the interest groups operating in the society at large, but in the interest groups operating from within the regime. Under a scientific, semi-religious disguise the Chicago Boys represented political ideas and economic interests. They represented and often acted on behalf of specific economic groups. The connection between the large economic groups and the technocrats has been widely demonstrated.

Why was the military excluded from the system? Here the issues of modernity and self-reliance were conveniently abandoned. It appears that in this case the old system was not as bad as depicted by Piñera. It is quite obvious that the military would rather have the safety and security provided by the state instead of the uncertainty of a system based on one's personal effort. That the military acted as an interest group within the regime is also quite obvious.

It is also important to mention that the connection between effort and reward is mediated by one's socioeconomic situation, or to paraphrase Anatole France, "the law in its majestic equality prohibits the rich and the poor alike to steal bread, sleep under the bridges and to beg." In the new Chile, everyone has the right to get a substantial pension, the question is simply to have a well-paid job that allows the person to save enough for the future. As we will see below, there are groups that due to gender, income, or age do not have the same right to choose.

The Administrative Reform

The principle of subsidiarity of the state, the need to enhance the role of the private sector, and the need to improve the administration led Piñera to argue that the social security funds should be put in the hands of the private sector. The administrative reform was expected to reduce the administrative costs and integrate the social security system into the national economy.

It is important to note that, for the government economists, one of the major obstacles to Chile's economic development—and one that the market approach had proven unable to resolve—was the low savings rate. The low savings rate resulted from the underdevelopment of the local capital markets. The social security reform was crucial both for the development of the capital markets and to achieve economic growth. According to Martín Cóstabal,

> The growth of the capital markets produced by the new pension system will be oriented, by and large, to produce long-term effects. The long-term characteristics of the social security savings will be geared to develop long-term credit instruments, which would contribute to structure a more integral capital market, something we have not had until now.

> The development of these long-term capital markets would bring stability and longer terms to the credit system, improving credit conditions for activities such as housing, and for medium and small entrepreneurs, who are intensive credit users.[20]

The transfer of the administration of social security funds to the private sector involved the creation of a new type of enterprise, the Administadoras de Fondos de Pensiones, or AFPs (Pension Funds Managing Corporations). They are exclusively charged with the administration of the individual funds and the provision of the social security benefits established in the law.

In order to understand the nature and functions of these new private entities, one has to keep in mind that D.L. 3500 contains both free market and regulatory principles. The free market principles encouraged the formation of a plurality of AFPs that would compete among themselves, offering the highest interests in the capital accounts and charging the lowest commissions. The AFP is a lucrative corporation, whose profit results from the commissions it charges for the administration of the funds. Originally, those commissions could be structured as a flat rate, as a percentage of the insured deposit, or as a combination of both. In order to ensure efficiency and the lowest commissions, the insured was free to move from one AFP to another.

Given the under-development of the Chilean economy, and especially the under-development of the capital markets, the state chose to regulate the investments of the newly created corporations. The law establishes that each AFP has to maintain two separate funds: a minimum capital fund required to establish an AFP, and a second one formed by the individual deposits. The law also prescribes investment policies and the profitability of the latter fund.[21]

In regard to benefits, the 1980 legislation and the modifications to the law approved in August 1987 established that once the basic requirements to obtain a pension have been fulfilled the pensioner has three options: (a) to buy an immediate life annuity from an insurance company with the funds accumulated in the account; (b) to obtain the pension directly from the AFP—however, in this case, the capital fund has to be large enough to provide for a pension that is at least equal to 120 percent of the value of the minimum state pension—and (c) to combine a temporary annuity paid by the AFP with a deferred life annuity bought from an insurance company. In the case of disability and survivors pensions, the pension received by the beneficiary is a proportion of the taxable income of the last twelve months, fluctuating between 50–100 percent of the taxable income. The benefit is paid by the AFP directly.[22]

Finally, D.L. 3500 created a system of minimum pensions for those affiliated with the new system to be applied in case of depletion of the individual capital account, or if the rent produced by the fund were smaller than the minimum pension. In order to qualify for this pension the insured must have at least twenty years of contributions. The original value of the pension was about U.S.$45 monthly.

The New System in Operation

Launching the new system involved the actions of both the private and the public sector: the former had to create the AFPs and the latter had to make the affiliation to the new system compulsory for all those who became employed for the first time after December 1982 and to ensure that all transfers to the new system were permanent. The state also created two new agencies, the Superintendencia of AFP and the Instituto de Normalización Previsional, or Institute for the Normalization of the Social Security System, charged with coordinating the transition from the old to the new system.

The AFPs and Enrollment in the New System

The launching of the reform on 1 May 1981 was followed by the massive adoption of the new system. In the first month, half a million people changed to the new system and by December 1981, 1,604,908 persons, out of an economically active population of 2,890,000, had moved to the new social security system. Neither the government nor the leadership of the AFPs had predicted such a large move.[23] Four elements seem to have prompted people to abandon the old social security system: (a) a very expensive and well-orchestrated propaganda campaign; (b) the net increase in income of those that moved to the new system; (c) the desperate situation of the pensioners; and (d) the pressure applied by some employers.

Both the AFPs and the government launched what was the most expensive publicity campaign in Chile's history.[24] This campaign stressed the issues of modernity and self-reliance involved in the new system, as opposed to the politicization, chaos, and crisis involved in the old one. Just during the months of May and June 1981 all of the AFPs spent over U.S.$8 million in advertising.[25] The acceptance of the new system can be explained in terms of the skillful propaganda campaign, the changes in societal values stressed in the publicity, and the importance of propaganda in the context of a tyrannical regime in which the society is deprived of alternative views or ideas.

The net salary increase obtained by those workers who chose to move to the new system also contributed to their decision. The salary increase ranged from 7.6 percent for those who had belonged to the Blue-Collar Workers Fund to 17.1 percent for the Bank Employees. The salary increase was well publicized by both the government and the AFPs. It is reasonable to believe that the desperate situation of the retirees might have also acted as an incentive for people to move to the new system since the combined effect of several years of high inflation, declining real wages, and the system used to compute the pensions had withered away their pensions.

The beginning of the new system was preceded by the creation of several AFPs. However, the large degree of concentration in the Chilean economy thwarted the free market principles that inspired the reform. Of the twelve corporations that were originally created, nine of them were owned by Chile's largest economic groups and covered

91.99 percent of the affiliates that changed to the new system.[26] Furthermore, the two largest AFPs, Provida and Santa María, owned by the two largest economic groups, captured 63 percent of the insured. By the end of 1987, Provida had 30 percent of the affiliates while Santa María had 20 percent. By the end of 1998 one third of the insured were using Provida while Santa Maria ranked third with about a sixth of the affiliates.[27]

The Role of the State

The social security reform did not eliminate the role of the state as one might be led to believe by the neo-liberal rhetoric, but simply transformed it. The new role of the state exhibits three important characteristics. Because of the compulsory nature of the Nueva Previsión, the state had to enforce the system. The law established that all new workers were obligated to join while old workers were forced to remain in it once they decided to change. In order to enforce the new rules and facilitate the transition from one system to the other, two new bureaucracies were created. From a financial perspective the role of the state changed and the reform entailed a massive budget deficit.

The establishment of a state-enforced private insurance system is certainly unique. Its creation reflects some of the contradictions that the application of neo-liberal principles with extensive state involvement can exhibit, especially in the context of authoritarian politics. In order to understand the extent of this contradiction it must be remembered that the government consistently claimed that the new system was designed to enhance the freedom of the Chilean workers. The compulsory aspects of the system reflect both the authoritarian nature of the regime as well as a paternalistic approach to policymaking. Both created a perception among policymakers that the state must make critical decisions for the society because the individual is unable to do it.

The two new social security bureaucracies that were created for the new system were the Superintendencia de Administradoras de Fondos de Pensiones and the Instituto de Normalización Previsiónal. The Superintendencia de Suguridad Social was maintained to control the old system.

The Superintendencia of AFP was created to supervise and control the newly established AFPs, authorize their constitution, supervise the structure of commissions, control the pension funds, regulate the agreements with the insurance companies, and dissolve an AFP in case of violation of the law. Why did the government create this new supervisory agency? The question is particularly relevant since the regime had done the utmost to reduce the size of the civil bureaucracy and reduce government involvement in the economy. Behind the stated technical reasons seem to be political motives: to create an institution responsive to the needs and ideas of the neo-liberal economists and to put an end to the life of the old Superintendencia.[28]

The Instituto de Normalización Previsional has financial functions. It was created to facilitate the transition from one system to another. Its fundamental function is to administer a social security fund formed with all the funds received by the different Cajas. The old Cajas had ceased to be autonomous and were under the financial control of this institute. The creation of the institute was the culmination of the process of fiscal centralization that had began in 1978 and that drastically reduced the power and functions of the Cajas. The Instituto also administers the Bono de Reconocimiento, or recognition bond. The bond represents the number of years that the insured contributed to the old system and is given to the AFP at the time of retirement, disability, or death.[29]

The Impact of the Reform

As Piñera correctly argued,

> The social security reform has been one of the most important steps taken by the present regime. It constitutes a new and original scheme which will contribute decisively to change the economic, social and political culture of all Chileans.[30]

Of the seven modernizations carried out by the government, this one stands out as having a profound impact on both society and the individual, as being significant to Chile's economy and to its politics, and as touching not only the present, but the future of the entire population. The impact of this reform has to be analyzed in at least two ways: from an economic perspective regarding both the public and the private sector of the economy, and from a socio-political perspective. In order to assess the economic impact we will look at data from the late 1980s and the late 1990s.

The Economic Impact

confuses two regimes

It is useful to distinguish two levels of the reform's economic impact, the impact on the pensions and on the general economy. Regarding the first we will look at the reform's effects on coverage and the value of pensions as well as the impact on women. Regarding the second, the analysis will focus on those areas identified as critical by the proponents of the reform such as the impact on the state and on the capital and labor markets.

The question of coverage under the new system appears to be quite complex. While in the old system Chile had about 80 percent of the labor force covered, in the new one the measurement of the coverage has been problematic. In 1996 the Superintendencia reported that 107 percent of the labor force was covered by the new system, but that figure did not take into account that 89 percent of the self-employed were not covered, that a small percentage remained in the old system, and that the military had its own separate system. After a preliminary revision of the data the Superintendencia admitted that the figures were marred by statistical deficiencies produced by the constant changes from one AFP to another one. The agency now estimates that about 80 percent of the labor force is covered and 90 percent of that is in the private system. However, this data is still being revised.[31] The data for 1998 indicates that the total number of people registered in the AFP system amounted to 5,966,143 while the active contributors to the system were 3,149,755. This means that only 62 percent of the insured were actually paying the monthly contribution, which entails a substantial reduction of the number of people actually covered by the private pension system. Revised government data for the year 2000 indicates that only 60 percent of the work force is covered. The self-employed which amount to about 28 percent of the work force still do not have any coverage (only 4 percent are contributing to the pension system).[32]

The value of the pension received by the insured depends on the deposits made by the insured plus the interest accrued, less the commissions charged by the AFP. The pensions awarded under the new system are therefore the direct result of the level of wages and the real rate of capital return. Between 1981 and 1987 one observes at least two contradictory phenomena: the decrease in the real value of wages, which by 1985 were estimated to be 13 percent below their 1970 level, and the high real yield of the pension fund investments which on average amounted to 13.8 percent per year. The situation changed dramatically in the 1990s. Between 1990 and 1998 the real value of wages increased by 35 percent.[33] On the other hand, the real yield of the investments decreased. The performance of the pension funds has been quite unstable, oscillating from a real yield of 28.6 percent in 1991 to –2.5 in 1995. There were moderate gains in 1996 and 1997 and the real yield was again negative in 1998 (–1.6 percent). The average yield since the inception of the system until December 1998 has been 10.9 percent.[34]

In 1987, the Superintendencia de Administradoras de Fondos de Pensiones estimated that the average value of a pension paid by the new system was 1.24 times higher than those paid by the old system, while the disability pensions were 2.23 times higher. However, it is important to note that by the time this estimate was done the AFPs had granted only 10,099 old age pensions and 12,383 disability pensions out of an insured population of almost 3 million people. By the end of 1998 the system was paying 290,000 pensions and the average value of a retirement pension was about U.S.\$200, while the average value of a disability pension was about U.S.\$280.[35]

A very interesting issue raised by the reform is the question of gender inequities. The central issue here is that the reform reinforces the existing gender inequalities. To the extent that the value of the pension depends on the value of the wages, the years of contribution, and the life expectancy after retirement, the situation of women is certainly worse than that of the male retirees. As Arenas de Mesa and Montecinos argue,

> women should clearly understand that . . . every year in the labor market is considered in the calculation of their pensions. This means that women who take time off the labor market . . . will

receive lower pensions than those who have worked without interruptions.

Women should also know that the actuarial factors used to calculate their pensions are different from the ones used for men's pensions. The pensions that women receive in the new system are lower than the pensions of men, because the average life expectancy of women is longer than men's life expectancy. Women should consider that although the system allows them to retire five years earlier than men, early retirement reduces even further the amount of their pensions.[36]

The government, women, and those interested in women's rights have entirely ignored this critical issue. The value of the pensions has a direct effect on the life of women and also on state finances. One can expect that a very large number of women will not qualify for a retirement pension due to the fact that they earned less (a recent study indicates that, on the average, the salary of a woman is 31.1 percent lower than that of a man performing the same job[37]), took time off, or simply live longer than men and that they will have to obtain a minimum pension from the state. Women are being penalized and discriminated against by the system, yet nothing has been done to remedy the problem. Pensions for women are estimated to be between 52 and 76 percent of men's pensions.[38]

The structure and size of the commissions charged by the AFPs for the administration of the fund also impinges directly on the pensions. Originally the law established that the AFP could charge a flat rate, plus a percentage of the deposit to administer the fund, plus an additional commission geared to finance disability pensions which amounted to a percentage of the wages. Changes in the law introduced in 1987 have separated the premium and the percentage commission. Although this change makes it easier for the insured to know how much he or she is paying for the administration of the fund, it does not deal with the main problem, the regressive nature of the flat rate. For instance, at the beginning of 1988 Provida charged $954 to administer the fund when the taxable wage was $20,000 and $3,728 when the taxable wage was $100,000.[39] This regressive element affects not only the poorest sectors of the population, it has an impact on the fiscal deficit, given the fact that the government has to subsidize those pensions that are smaller than the minimum pension. Because of its regressive impact the fixed commission has been widely criticized, but the AFPs have opposed any reform geared to eliminate them. Differences in the commissions charged by the AFPs have been reduced.

The data for 1998 indicates that the regressive effects and the high administrative costs continue. For instance, for an insured with an income of about U.S.$160, the administrative costs fluctuate between 25.6 percent and 37.9 percent of the mandatory contribution, while for an insured with an income of U.S.$1,300, the costs fluctuate between 24.1 percent and 30.2 percent of the contribution.[40] The data also indicates that in spite of the reforms and the freedom of the insured to move from one AFP to another, the administrative costs did not decline between 1988 and 1998. The net cost of the pension system was 2.09 percent of the average income in 1988 and 2.10 percent in 1998.

What has decreased is the premium for disability and survivor insurance which is managed by commercial insurance companies . . . the premium decreased from 1.22 percent to 0.62 percent from 1990 to 1998, but the commission rose from 1.73 percent to 2.34 percent from 1990 to 1995 and then declined to 2 percent (still higher than in 1990). Conversely, the commission for old-age insurance has oscillated but tended to increase in the long run. The net result has been rising or at best stagnant administrative costs, a strong indication that competition does not work properly.[41]

Strongly related to the question of commissions is the overall nature of the administrative system designed by the framers of the program. Essential to the reform was the notion that the private sector would create the pension fund–managing companies and that the public would be free to choose among them and to change from one to another. Ideally this would create a system characterized by low administrative costs and high coverage and efficiency. In practice, the number of AFPs has not changed much. There are today thirteen AFPs (initially there were twelve) and the three largest concentrate 69 percent of the insured. Initially the insured was permitted to change AFPs as often as he or she wished and the data indicates that large numbers of people have changed from one AFP to another.

According to Mesa-Lago, between 1984 and 1996 the proportion of insured changing AFPs increased from 10 percent to 52 percent, which amounts to a total of 1.3 million transfers. Most of these changes were the result of the promotional activities of the AFPs. The number of salespeople reached almost 19,000 by 1996 or one per 160 insured. The cost of this amounted to 37 percent of the total operating costs of the AFPs and 60 percent of the commission charged by the AFP to the insured.[42] New legislation in effect since 1998 has made the changes more difficult and drastically reduced the transfers from one AFP to another. This reform has lowered the administrative costs from 4.9 percent of the average income in 1983 to 2.75 percent in 2000.[43]

Perceptions about the efficiency of the AFPs have changed since the inception of the system. A survey conducted in 1987 indicates that these institutions have a serious image problem. For instance, over 50 percent of the interviewees believed the state was more likely to pay a higher pension and an indexed pension than the AFP, while only 9 percent preferred to leave the administration of the pension programs to national private enterprises.[44]

It is interesting to note that during the 1980s the three largest AFPs charged the highest commissions; however, that has changed and currently they exhibit the lowest costs. During that same period the largest institutions had the lowest rate of return. Consequently, it appears that the selection was not made on the bases of performance or cost, but as a result of the actions of the sellers and the publicity. It could also be the result of a generalized dissatisfaction with the performance of the AFPs.

The economic effects of the reform have not been limited to the pensioners; the reform has had also a large impact on the private sector at large, representing a huge transference of funds from the public to the private economy. By the end of 1985, the capital accumulated by the AFPs amounted to 9.73 percent of GDP and by the end of 1998 the capital accumulated in the hands of the AFPs was about U.S.$30 billion which amounts to about 40 percent of the GDP. By 2000 the capital accumulated amounted to over U.S.$35 billion or 52 percent of the GDP.[45]

In order to protect the fund the law closely regulates the investment of the pension funds and establishes that the AFPs have to distribute their investment among government instruments, fixed term deposits, mortgage bonds, and stocks. By the end of 1985, 42.6 percent of the funds were invested in government instruments, 35.3 percent in mortgage bonds, and 20.5 in fixed term deposits.[46] In 1987, 1990, and 1993 some of these regulations were modified in order to liberalize the investment opportunities, reducing the investment in government paper while increasing the investment in stocks and allowing investment in foreign stocks and bonds. By December 1998, 40.9 percent of the funds were invested in government bonds, 16.6 percent in mortgage bonds, 14.5 percent in stocks, and 13.6 percent in fixed term deposits.[47]

The Chicago-trained economists argued that the private pension system would be a critical element in the establishment of a local capital market. Although there is no question about the growth of the capital markets in Chile, there is a strong debate about the role of the AFPs in that process. Some analysts argue that the pension funds have had a critical role, promoting foreign investment in the local market and reducing the foreign debt by transforming debt into a capital investment. Others argue that the growth of the Chilean capital market is not different from that of other Latin American markets during the same period and that the pension system did not make a strong contribution to that growth.[48] The most complete study to date has been made by Robert Holzmann. He suggests that the pension funds made the financial markets deeper and more liquid and that the pension fund activities enhanced efficiency and risk allocation. Holzmann's econometric studies also indicate that the overall impact of the pension fund on growth rates fluctuates between 1 and 2.9 percent.[49]

Finally, the expected positive impact on national savings is also a matter of intense debate and there is no conclusive evidence that the new system has had a positive impact on the rate of savings. In fact a recent study shows that the net effect on national savings has been negative (−2.4 percent of GDP) since the fiscal cost was higher than the capital accumulation.[50]

Ministers Piñera and Kast argued that the elimination of the employers' contribution would reduce the price of labor and that, in turn, would produce a drastic reduction of unemployment. The behavior of the unemployment rates between 1981 and 1985 show that the social security reform did not produce this effect. Again the neo-liberals seemed to have ignored the fact that the high unemployment rates were linked to the very nature of the economic model and its consequences. Unemployment was the result of the reduction in the size of the industrial sector due to the combined effect of the policy of trade liberalization, the reduction or elimination of subsidies to the industrial sector, and the reduction in the internal demand produced by the shock therapy. In fact, between 1975 and 1983 unemployment rates were at least three times higher than in the previous decade while the price of labor had dramatically decreased. Since unemployment was not the result of the price of labor, as Kast and others repeatedly argued, there was very little the reduction or elimination of the social security tax could accomplish. By the same token the growth of employment between 1986 and 1997 cannot be attributed to the social security reform, but to the modifications introduced in the model and the success of the export sector.

Unemployment has again increased since 1997 and in May 1998 reached 10 percent, the highest level in a decade. The main reason is the collapse of Asia's demand for copper, which accounts for about two fifths of Chile's exports. Chile's exports of manufactured goods have also suffered due to the recession in Argentina and Brazil in the late 1990s.[51]

The effects of the social security reform on the public sector are just as important as those it produced on the private sector. The preeminent theme of the social security reform, the same refrain that echoed throughout the Pinochet regime, is the subsidiary role that the state should play in this area. However, the financial impact of the reform was never estimated.[52] In fact, the social security reform is having and will continue to have a large budgetary impact that will seriously affect the finances of the Chilean state.

The reform carried a budget deficit which was the result of the transference of the administration and payment of contributions to the private sector while the state maintained a high level of expenditures. The transference of about 90 percent of the economically active population to the new system involved a net decrease of the government social security receipts. But this reduction was not accompanied by a decrease in social security expenditures for a number of reasons. First, in order to allow the AFPs to capitalize, the law established that they would not pay retirement pensions during the first five years. As a result, during those five years, the state was faced basically with the same social security expenditure, since workers close to retirement chose not to move to the new system.

After the first five years the state continued paying pensions to those who chose to remain in the old system as well as the *bono de re-conocimiento* (or recognition bond) of those who retire in the new system. This bond, which represents the number of years that the insured contributed in the old system, becomes effective at the time of retirement, disability, or death.[53]

The pattern of transfer to the new system added a new financial burden. Those affiliated with the Civil Servants Fund, which required the largest state contribution, were reluctant to move to the new system, while those affiliated with the self-financed funds such as white-collar workers and bank employees moved in a very large proportion because of the increase in take-home pay. In brief, "the state contributes to the private pension fund through two mechanisms: the recognition bond, that amounts to half to two thirds of the capital of those who are going to retire before the year 2000; and the difference needed to pay the minimum pension of those individuals who at time of retirement do not have enough funds in the AFPs. Furthermore, the state covers the deficit of the civil servant and armed forces funds, pays all the welfare pensions and the unemployment compensation, and the family allowances and the health benefits for the indigents."[54]

The question of the fiscal cost of the transition has been at the forefront of the discussion for some time. The study made by Alberto Arenas de Mesa, Director of Research of the National Budget Office, and published in September 1999 is the most comprehensive since it includes not only the cost of the recognition bond, but the cost of minimum pensions, welfare pensions, and the social security system of the police and the military. Arenas de Mesa estimates that since its inception the social security system has produced a budget deficit that grew from 3.8 percent of GDP in 1981 to 6.1 percent in 2000. After 2001 the deficit is expected to begin a slow decline. By 2040 the deficit is estimated to be of 3.3 percent of GDP.[55] Currently the deficit amounts to approximately $4 billion per year.[56] According to Arenas de Mesa, "The fiscal involvement in the AFPs was substantially under-estimated and the budget deficit resulting from the state's obligation to pay the minimum pensions could reach unexpected dimensions in the future."[57] In fact, Arenas argues that the state involvement in this area is expected to grow and that the deficit will be directly linked to the increased number of persons receiving minimum pensions. Thus, while today only 6.5 percent of the workers receive minimum pensions, the same study estimates that in the future between 50 and 70 percent of the affiliates will be receiving them. The study also argues that there are 637,5000 affiliates who have not contributed to the system for seven years and that those people will be receiving either a minimum or a welfare pension in the future.

It is not clear how the state is financing the deficit. According to Carmelo Mesa-Lago, the state has three options—taxes, public debt, and a combination of the two—and up to 1994 the government has opted for the use of public debt, which in turn would increase the public debt to as much as 67 percent of GDP.[58]

The real rate of return of the pension funds will also affect the size and impact of the budget deficit. Here a new study done by C. B. Capitales estimates that the Superintendency of AFPs has consistently overestimated the rate of growth of the pension funds since it has not considered the negative impact that the commissions have on the funds. Since the average commission for 1998 was estimated to be 18 percent of the contribution, only 82 percent enters the fund. Consequently, the actual real rate of growth of the fund between 1982 and 1998 was 5.1 percent and not 11 percent which was the estimate of the Superintendency for the same period. According to the same study, the affiliate would have done better if the money had been invested in 90 day certificates of deposit.[59]

In August 1999, presidential candidate Ricardo Lagos declared that "during the next administration we are going to have to deal with the problem of the AFP . . . since the majority of the pensioners will not be able to [save enough to] obtain a pension that is equivalent to the minimum pension. Who is going to pay the difference? The state."[60]

In conclusion, the reform has not involved a reduction of government expenditures, but a very peculiar application of the principle of subsidiarity of the state, as the state maintains a secondary role only regarding the administration of the funds, but not regarding financial responsibility.

Social and Political Impact of the Reform

The unavoidable question from a social point of view is to what extent this reform altered the traditional social security principles. There is little doubt that, at the very least, the reform substantially transformed the principle of social solidarity since the new system is based on the notion of individual insurance combined with a social system of minimum pensions. In other words, providing for old age is an individual responsibility, except in the case of military personnel and the extremely poor. As the under-secretary of labor pointed out, the reform transforms the notion of solidarity both in its role and in its content. Solidarity is not a fundamental notion, but a complementary notion and as such is not expressed in the entire system, but it is reserved for those cases in which the principle of individual responsibility cannot be applied as in the system of minimum pensions and the system of welfare pensions.[61] To a large extent, then, the reform has transformed the social security system into a private insurance system in which the state intervenes at two different stages, at the onset by enforcing enrollment into the new system and at the final stage by providing pensions to the military and to the lowest income groups.

From a political perspective, the reform has to be analyzed in the context of the other reforms enacted by the government between 1981 and 1982. It is clear that the neo-liberal economic model and the authoritarian regime converged in their need to disarticulate the entire society. It was especially important to disarticulate those groups perceived as having political power and the power to interfere with the free functioning of the market, such as organized labor, professional associations, and the organizations representing white-collar workers and civil servants.

Throughout the last fifty years there has been a close relationship between the organization of the labor movement, its pattern of interaction with the state, and the evolution of the social security system. After having reformed the role and functions of the state and the nature of the labor movement, the Pinochet regime found it necessary to create a social security attuned to those reforms. Of course, in an authoritarian context, the reforms came from the regime itself, without the participation of the society.

The social security reform has been crucial to destroy large bureaucratic entities, such as the pension funds, as well as the groups of
workers organized around them, who in the past had proven to have a
major role both in the formulation and in the obstruction of public
policies. The social security reform during this period, as well as in the
past, reflected the existing political organization and the principles
that guided the relations between the regime and the society. At the
same time, those policies have been a key political mechanism used to
shape future political arrangements. In this case the policy has served
to atomize the society and depoliticize critical groups, reinforcing the
power of the authoritarian regime.[62]

Moreover, the social security reform was an integral part of the
new economic and social logic of the Pinochet regime and it was used
to destroy the old narrative and create a new one. In the words of José
Piñera:

> For many democracy meant a complex game of pressure and force
> geared to gain privileges and power. According to this perverted
> notion of politics the priority was to gain a position in Congress, a
> job in the civil service, to gain control of the country's economic
> management, gain power in the universities, control the streets. . . .
> To call this system a democracy was hypocritical. But it was a
> tragic, institutionalized and shared hypocrisy.
>
> This degraded concept of democracy was responsible for creating
> the social security system of the past. Strictly speaking it was its
> mirror image. . . . The national profile of privileges coincided in a
> rather scandalous form with the political power of the different
> groups of Chileans.[63]

Speaking about the new system and the new ideology Piñera argues,

> This was not the first time that the government increased para-
> doxically and substantially the political space of all Chileans. . . . I
> recognized that the reform would have never been approved by
> democratic political institutions. . . . The reform was not the
> daughter of the representative democracy, but it was the daughter
> of the direct democracy. . . . The true liberalism is here. One must

trust the individual, one must have confidence in his freedom and sense of responsibility, otherwise one must trust other institutions that will make decisions for him. . . . The subterfuges used to give to others the power to make the decisions that need to be made by each person are many, and the socialist ideology took advantage of all of them.[64]

Here and elsewhere the words of Piñera are a true expression not only of the form in which the regime depicted the old narrative, but the use of the social security policies to both destroy the old narrative and foster the new one. What Piñera does not recognize is that this reform, just as in the past, is a product of the existing sociopolitical arrangements and the power of certain groups—that while the old system was a product of a clientelistic political system, this one is the product of a system in which economic decision making was concentrated in the hands of a small group of advisors who felt entitled to transform the entire economic structure because of their privileged relationship with an authoritarian ruler. In fact, these economists were part of an authoritarian/patrimonial system of rule and not a democratic system as he claims. It is also clear that like in the past there were groups favored by the system and others ignored by the system. However, due to the nature of the regime these interest groups acted from within the government. Very much favored by the reform are those who own or control the pension industry as well as the major banking and publicity concerns involved in the reform. The real measure of their economic power is that they control more than 50 percent of the country's GDP. On the other hand, there are those with temporary, low-paying jobs, those who have to abandon the labor market because of either a downturn in the economy or personal reasons, and those who are not even in the system. What is their freedom? I suppose they are free to choose between a state pension of about U.S.$50 or no pension at all.

The Reforms in the Health Area

Due to the historical and financial connections between social security and health policies the remainder of this chapter contains an overview of the health policies carried out by the Pinochet regime. The analysis will be centered on the partial privatization of health, its cost and impact. What has to be emphasized is that the health policies, just like the social security policies, evolved from the simple reduction in public health expenditures of the initial years to a total administrative restructuring of the system in 1979, and to a partial privatization of health in 1981. As in the social security area, the most important problem of the system was a huge fiscal deficit which in this case resulted from the combined effect of high cost, evasion, extensive coverage, and administrative inefficiencies. And as in the social security area, the most important reforms were inspired by the neo-liberal ideology and implemented by the Chicago Boys in 1981.

Between 1974 and 1977 the Pinochet regime consistently reduced the health budget. By 1979 the health budget had just recuperated its 1970 level, but the budget was reduced again in 1980 and 1981, falling behind its 1974 level.[65] Since the reduction in the health budget was followed by a reapportionment of expenditures within the health area, it did not produce an immediate reduction of health services. However, the budgetary reductions certainly produced a reduction of investments and a decrease in the real value of wages and salaries of those employed in the health delivery system. Thus, while elsewhere health care costs were rising all throughout the 1980s, in Chile they were reduced. In 1989 only 3.2 percent of total fiscal expenditures were devoted to the public health care sector as opposed to 7.2 percent in 1974. As a result, there was a sharp decrease in medical personnel and equipment. The number of doctors in the public health area declined from 0.49 to 0.42 per one thousand inhabitants while the number of low-level personnel increased three times. The reduction of funds also had an impact on the physical plant. As President Aylwin argued in his inaugural speech, despite the aging infrastructure public expenditures devoted to maintenance and repairs decreased by 0.4 percent throughout the 1980s.[66]

Present both in the reduction of health expenditures and in the other health policies pursued by the administration was the question of the role of the subsidiary state in the provision of health. Although the Pinochet government rejected a total privatization of health, it also rejected the notion of a total commitment to public health as in the past. The situation was resolved with a partial privatization. In September 1981 the Minister of Health, M. E. de la Jara, declared that the state would continue to play a central role in the provision of curative and preventive care for low-income groups, but that the private sector would be increasingly responsible for the provision of curative attention for middle- and upper-income groups.[67] In practice, the government reforms included changes in the system of contributions and in the administrative system as well as the establishment of private health insurance organizations.

In July 1979 the government proceeded to reorganize the entire health system, creating the National System of Health Services, Sistema Nacional de Servicios de Salud, which merged the functions of the National Health Service and SERMENA. The newly created system is divided not along occupational lines, but into regional services which are charged with the provision of preventive and curative attention to all the insured population and indigents in an area. Each unit is led by a general director who is responsible directly to the president.[68]

The administrative reform involved also a centralization of the financial aspects of health. To this end, the government created a common fund, the United Health Fund, Fondo Unico de Salud (Fonasa), which has consolidated the finances of the entire health system. The past association between the Blue-Collar Workers Fund and the National Health Service, and between the White-Collar Workers Fund and SERMENA was eliminated. Instead all the contributions from the Cajas as well as the state go into this unified fund, which in turn distributes the money among the twenty-seven regional services. Each of these services is expected to be profitable. The financial reform also included the elimination of the employer's contributions. The new system was initially financed with a 3 percent contribution made by the employee and in 1986 this contribution was increased to 7 percent. A government subsidy of up to 2 percent was offered to low-income groups as an incentive to subscribe to one of the private plans. Indigents receive free medical attention in the public health clinics.

The public sector serves the curative medicine needs of about 80 percent of the population and is also responsible for preventive medical services such as vaccination programs, milk and food distribution programs, the prevention of contagious diseases, and the maintenance of water and sewage services for the entire population.

Although the reform has solved the old problem of excessive centralization, it has entailed a dramatic reduction of funds. Between 1974 and 1989 public expenditures as a percentage of total health care expenditures declined from 61.7 percent to 47.3 percent. The combined effect of decentralization, privatization, and limited state subsidies have resulted in the transference of a large part of health care costs to the municipalities which are not equipped to deal with this financial responsibility. Moreover, the policy has left secondary and tertiary levels of health care ill equipped to detect and treat the growing number of diseases associated with development.[69]

The most important innovation in the health area has been the creation of the Institutos de Salud Previsional, ISAPREs, which are an optional form of health insurance modeled around American private health insurance organization. Their purpose was to increase the role of the private sector and to give, at least theoretically, an opportunity to the blue-collar workers to have access to private medicine.[70]

According to the legislation passed in 1981 the insured can choose between directing its health contribution either to the public sector or to one of the ISAPREs. The ISAPREs "are private entities that offer a series of medical insurance and workman's compensation packages in return for the basic 7 percent payroll contribution plus an additional premium of 2–3 percent, depending on the size of the package."[71] Given the cost of medical care and the low level of wages, the ISAPREs are authorized to set a minimum income for their subscribers. Both in practice and conception the ISAPREs are institutions geared to provide health to middle- and upper-income groups.

The creation of the ISAPREs had a profound effect not only on the provision of health for middle- and upper-income groups, but on the entire system. From a financial standpoint, the issue here is that those who moved to the ISAPREs were in the highest income groups and consequently they made a significant contribution to the entire health system. This money has been transferred to the ISAPREs. Thus the combined effect of the reduction of the contributions and the migration of the higher income groups to the ISAPREs has produced a major deficit in the health system. This deficit, in turn, forced the government to increase the contributions from 3 to 7 percent, to reduce services for those in the public health area, and to transfer to the municipalities part of the financial responsibilities.

Furthermore, those remaining in the public health sector are the poor and the elderly who are more prone to serious and more costly health problems.

The 2 percent subsidy offered to low-income groups to join the ISAPREs also had a negative effect on the public system and on the health of the low-income groups. The subsidy allowed low-income people to buy the most basic package offered by the ISAPRE which is no better than what the public system offers. In fact, that level of care is often substandard and that group has to continue relying on the public system. Although, legally, the ISAPREs should repay the public system, those payments often do not materialize. After lengthy discussions the Congress decided to eliminate that subsidy altogether in 1998.[72]

By 1997 there were thirty-nine ISAPREs which provided coverage to 27 percent of the population. However, just as in the case of the AFPs a large percentage of the insured is concentrated in the top three insurers which account for 54 percent of the insured. The affiliates are mostly males, not only because males are a larger proportion of the work force, but because up to 1990 the system discriminated against women by charging higher premiums. The reforms introduced in 1990 eliminated this problem, but established that the ISAPREs are exempt from paying for maternity leave, which is now paid by the state. Regarding age, the population insured in the ISAPRES is very young. By 1997, 63 percent of the affiliates were less than sixty-four years old, while 1.7 percent were sixty-five years or older. This phenomenon results from discriminatory policies implemented by the ISAPREs until 1990.[73] The situation has improved somewhat as a result of the 1990 legal reforms and currently the proportion of people older than sixty-five years is 6.6 percent.

While AFPs were heavily regulated from the very beginning, the ISAPREs were fairly unregulated until 1990. Before the creation of the Superintendency of ISAPREs, the beneficiaries had no means to protect themselves against discrimination and fraud. The ISAPREs have been accused of discriminating against women, the elderly, and the terminally ill. The new agency is responsible for regulating and controlling the ISAPREs and of serving as a channel for the resolution of conflicts between an ISAPRE and the insured.[74] The Superintendency has had a positive impact: the proportion of women and the elderly in the ISAPREs has increased and the structural discriminations against these two groups have been reduced. Between 1990 and 1996 the percentage of affiliates sixty to sixty-nine years old increased from 2.15 percent to 2.5 percent while the proportion of female affiliates decreased from 31.8 percent in 1990 to 30.7 percent in 1993 and then increased to 31.8 percent in 1997.[75]

From a political perspective the reforms in the health area point to processes that are now familiar. As in other areas the government not only acted without consulting those involved in the provision of health nor those who received medical attention, it acted against their explicit wishes. For instance, in the area of administrative reorganization, the government ignored the views of white-collar workers and physicians, who opposed the fusion of SERMENA and the SNS. In the economic area, the physicians, who in a very large majority are government employees, have seen their real salaries constantly reduced as a result of the reduced power of the Colegio Médico de Chile and increased regulation of the physicians' activities. As the former Government Delegate to the Unified Fund argued, "the principal reason behind the problem has been the fact that this government is not concerned with the opinions of interest groups, and as such it has constantly ignored the policy recommendations of the physicians."[76]

Throughout the Pinochet regime, the reform of the health delivery system was an ongoing process based on a redefinition of the state's role in health care. The reforms have produced a number of contradictory effects on the health status of the population. On the positive side the government statistics indicate that the infant mortality rate had been reduced to 19.5 per thousand live births, that the general mortality rate had declined to 6.1 per thousand inhabitants, while life expectancy had increased to seventy-five years by 1995. On the other hand, there has been a constant reduction of public health expenditures which by 1985 were 36 percent less than in 1970. This process has continued during the Aylwin and Frei administrations.[77] Moreover, there is an increasing disparity between the medical services that can be obtained in the rural and the urban areas and great disparities concerning the rights and services provided to females and the elderly.[78]

It has become quite common that individuals who are subscribing to one of the twenty-six ISAPREs seek medical attention in the public system either because their plan does not cover a particular ailment or because of the poor distribution of the services provided by the ISAPREs throughout the country.[79] In fact, the Minister of Health Doctor Alex Figueroa declared that by the winter of 1998, about 20 percent of those served by the public health system were actually enrolled in the private system.[80] Thus, the state is deprived of resources, is burdened with the cost, and in practice is subsidizing the medicine of those who remain in the ISAPREs. Typically in case of an emergency, such as a heart attack, the patient is often taken to an emergency room in a hospital and not to the clinic of the ISAPRE. In this case, the ISAPRE will pay just a small portion of the cost and the rest has to be absorbed by the state. After intense political discussion, the 2 percent subsidy to the private system was eliminated which increased the funds of FONASA, but these new funds will not be enough to solve the existing problems. According to the former minister Figueroa, "what is needed is an integral reform of the Chilean health care system, including the ISAPREs, FONASA and the other public agencies."[81]

The Colegio Médico de Chile is also demanding a structural reform of the system, attacking the private health care providers. The most serious conflict between the ISAPREs and the Colegio revolves around the issue of the "medical licenses" which are the authorizations for referral that the primary care physician gives to the patient. The intensity of the conflict led Doctor Enrique Accorsi, the president of the Colegio, to declare that "the ISAPREs tarnish our reputation."[82] According to the Colegio the reform should include the establishment of a mechanism that would integrate the ISAPREs into the public health care system, regulations to improve their performance, and an increase in the state funding for health. The remarks of the representative of the Colegio defined the entire situation as bleak, particularly in the area of emergency room attention.[83]

The year 1999 was the worst in the history of the ISAPREs since 461,950 people, or 12.2 percent of the affiliates, abandoned the system (the total number of people served by the ISAPREs declined to 3,232,506 by mid-2000).[84] The industry also registered heavy losses. The high level of unemployment and the elimination of the 2 percent subsidy were the major reasons for the debacle. As a result, FONASA has become the only real alternative for most Chileans.

Accusations of discrimination against the elderly, women, and new-born children have also been at the forefront of the discussion. According to the Superintendent of ISAPREs Alejandro Ferreiro, the ISAPREs follow entirely arbitrary policies to determine the cost of a plan for women or the elderly. In some cases the difference is up to three times higher for women than for men.[85] In the case of the newborn, one plan may be up to thirteen times higher than another.[86]

Under the leadership of Minister Figueroa the government not only withdrew the 2 percent subsidy, it initiated legislation to increase the funds of FONASA which serves nine million people. According to the Frei administration, this 2 percent was regressive, inefficient, and unnecessary since it had been established to support the initial development of the private system.[87] The governmental actions against the ISAPREs were combined with a deterioration in the prestige of these institutions. A study done by Adimark established that the public perception of the ISAPREs has deteriorated quickly due to accusations of fraud, discrimination against those who are older and sicker, and lack of coverage for catastrophic diseases.

As a result, in May 2000 the Health Committee of the Chamber of Deputies established a special commission geared to study the viability of the system. The legislators are expected to find a formula through which the private and the public system are better coordinated and complement each other. Directly or indirectly, the private system has invested about $5 billion dollars in the health care system, and through the modifications approved in 1997 the actions of the ISAPREs have become more transparent and the control more effective.[88] On the other hand, the ISAPREs discriminate on the bases of pre-existing illness, lack a preventive approach, and essentially serve those who are young, healthy, and have a high income. The Lagos administration, on the other hand, has promised to increase the health budget by 7.1 percent for 2001.

Summary

The analysis of the Pinochet regime's social security reforms illustrates the nature of politics under an authoritarian regime, the multiple impacts of the policies, and the importance of the regime's narrative.

The first years of the process of reform, 1974–1977, were unproductive, indicating the extent to which the administration was unable to adopt an overarching political and economic model, or to decide on the basic features of the regime. During this period two ideological and political factions, the corporatists and the neo-liberals, struggled for control. After 1978, and especially during 1980 and 1981, the adoption of the neo-liberal model resulted in a set of public policies geared to adapt the society to the requirements of the new political and economic ideology.

The reform reflects the ideology of the neo-liberal cadres. They were committed to use their control of the policy-making process to transform the nature of the state involvement in socioeconomic policies and to enhance the power and role of the private sector. In the area of social security this meant the elimination of the social security tax, the transference of the administration of the funds to private corporations, and the creation of private medical insurance institutions. The state's role, on the other hand, has been transformed. The state pulled out from the direct management of the new funds, centralized the administration of the old ones, and it has continuously regulated the operations of both the old and the new systems. Most importantly this is state-enforced private insurance and the state has important supervisory and budgetary functions.

Advocates of the reform have argued that only a total overhaul would bring equity and rationality into the system and it would improve the pensions themselves. D.L. 2448 achieved a great deal in this regard by eliminating some of its most discriminatory aspects and by creating a universal indexing system. In the final analysis, the question of how adequate pensions are, or will be, under the private system depends on macroeconomic conditions, such as the level of wages, the performance of the capital markets, and on individual conditions such as the level of income and the stability of employment.

Several sociopolitical aspects of the reform need to be highlighted. First is the use of authoritarian mechanisms to impose a policy that in fact was developed and supported only by a cadre of administrators in control of the policy process. Moreover, the policy served not only the philosophical and practical needs of the subsidiary state, but the purposes of the authoritarian, patrimonial regime. Although the rhetoric emphasized that the individual will "be free to choose how to save for old age," that freedom operates only after the state has compulsorily decided about the main features of the system. Again, to quote the former under-secretary of labor, the patrimonial nature of the state forces its intervention to protect the immature elements of the society.[89]

The social security reform, just like the other modernizations, was premised on the assumption that the market was the most efficient and neutral mechanism to allocate resources, but the effects of the social security reform were anything but neutral. Politically speaking the reform was instrumental in destroying important interest groups and contributed to a process of social atomization that clearly enhanced the power of the authoritarian ruler. The economic impact of the reform has not been neutral either. As discussed in the body of this chapter the extent of effective coverage has declined and the old, women, and the poor have gained little from the new system. The owners of the AFPs, on the other hand, have acquired an enormous amount of economic power since they control over 50 percent of the country's national product.

The new narrative reinforced the effects of the policies and cannot be separated from them. The well-publicized notion of modernity served to create an environment in which the past institutions and policies were looked at with disdain. To be modern meant to move to an AFP and to an ISAPRE, to abandon the old and inefficient state system. The regime stressed the importance of self-reliance and of having a competitive, modern attitude. However, in order to get a decent pension or a decent health package one needs more than just a positive attitude toward modernity, one needs to be a young male, to have a stable job, and a high income. Only under those conditions is modernity a blessing. If one does not fulfill those conditions modernity does not look any better than the old system. In fact, modernity appears to be worse since the effective coverage of the social security system has declined dramatically. All that is left for those at the bottom of the income scale is the hope that maybe one day they will also get the benefits of modernity. In the meantime, they have only hope.

Epilogue
The Limits of Chilean Democracy

The nature of Chile's new democracy was determined by the 1980 Constitution and the modifications introduced during 1989. From an economic standpoint the elected regimes continued applying the neo-liberal model. The manner in which the country dealt with the human rights issues was also determined by General Pinochet's policies, particularly the 1978 Amnesty Law, and his continued control of the military until 1988. Finally, the dominant social narrative still emphasizes individualism, competition, and the importance of the market.

Central to this analysis is the notion that, until 1998, Pinochet had a great deal of impact on Chilean politics and society. His impact was felt by all Chileans in terms of both the existing political and economic structures and the prevailing attitudes toward social, economic, and political issues. Pinochet might not have succeeded in eliminating politics from the face of Chile, but he certainly succeeded in transforming Chilean society. His policies led to the creation of a society based on individualism and competition, undermining the importance of politics vis-à-vis the market. Until 1998 these policies created an environment that precluded a serious discussion of socioeconomic and human rights issues.

The Political System

The nature of Chile's democratization process was determined by the constitutional and legal framework inherited from the military regime and the impact of seventeen years of military rule. The legacy left by the Pinochet regime includes not only a new institutional framework

241

and a new economic organization, but a society that had suffered the impact of years of human rights abuses.

As one tries to understand the nature of this transition to democracy and its outcome, it is important to analyze some of the most salient characteristics of the new democracy. Among those are the nature of the electoral system and its impact, the presence of appointed senators, the continuation of the economic policies designed by Minister Buchi, the transformation of the left, the tutelary role of the military, and the form in which the new regime has dealt with human rights issues.

This section deals with the macropolitical and the macroeconomic characteristics of this new democracy. The focus here is on the analysis of the central characteristics of the new democracy, including not only the structural characteristics of the system, but the form in which the new regimes have dealt with the human rights issues and the nature of civil-military relations until 1998. Central to the argument presented below is the notion that we have seen a limited transition to democracy and a limited attempt to deal with the legacy of socioeconomic inequities and human rights abuses.

From a purely political standpoint, the nature of Chile's current political system was determined not by a cadre of democratically minded politicians or legal experts, but by a group of individuals handpicked by General Pinochet; they held authoritarian political ideas and did their best to legitimize the power of Pinochet even after he had left office. They created a semi-democratic political system. The most salient characteristics of the post-Pinochet democracy were defined by the nature of the electoral system, the impact of the end of the Cold War and of the authoritarian system on the left, and the approach toward past human rights abuses.

The Electoral System

The electoral system established by the Pinochet regime is known as *sistema binominal mayoritario*. According to the law each party can present up to two candidates and each district elects two representatives. Voters choose one candidate and the winners are determined by the total vote received per list. The list with the largest number of votes gets one seat and the second seat is elected from the second list that has at least half of the number of votes. Its purpose was to transform the nature of the political party system from the traditional three thirds to a two-party system and to give the right a permanent veto power. Valenzuela points out that "if there are two lists presented, the top list, presumably the opposition, could earn as high as 65 percent of the vote and still win only one seat, while the second list (presumably pro-Pinochet) needs only 33 percent to earn another seat."[1] The laws also designed the congressional districts in such a way that rural areas supportive of the regime elected more deputies than urban areas where the opposition was stronger. Thus the "20 smallest districts, with a population of 1.5 million, elect 40 deputies, while the seven larger with a comparable population, can choose only 14."[2]

In the short term, the electoral laws gave the right a sizable parliamentary representation fostering the formation of a coalition between UDI and RN (the right obtained 34 percent of the Senate seats and 40 percent in the Chamber of Deputies in the first elections). In the long run, the system gives the right a veto power over constitutional reforms that secures the continuation of a political farce, prolonging the life of the Pinochet regime and its policies. As a result, attempts on the part of both the Aylwin and the Frei administrations to reform the constitution have largely failed.[3]

In 1992, the Aylwin administration put together a set of constitutional reforms that included the elimination of the appointed senators, changes in the nature and functions of the Security Council, and restrictions to the autonomy of the military as well as reforms to the electoral system geared to establish a proportional system. The bill also called for changes in the composition and nomination of the members of the Constitutional Court to eliminate the participation of the military in the court. The proposed reforms were rejected because of the opposition of UDI and RN. These parties argued that the reforms undermined the principles established in the 1980 Constitution. The only major constitutional reform approved during the Aylwin administration increased the length of the presidential period from four to six years. In 1995 President Frei tried again to reform the Constitution and although this time the President had the support of at least a sector of Renovación Nacional he could not obtain the elimination of the appointed senators.

In fact what we see today is that although the right does not control either the executive or the legislative branch, it has the power to maintain the system as it was designed by Pinochet. Consequently, the right has been able to obstruct reforms dealing with the electoral laws, the structure and power of the Supreme Court, the autonomy of the military, and the presence of the appointed senators, who have no popular mandate. As a result, the political system remains highly undemocratic.

The Left

A central characteristic of the current political landscape is the absence of the traditional Marxist left. Here one has to analyze the combined effect of years of repression and the process of reform launched by Michael Gorbachev in the former Soviet Union. The impact of both processes has been radically different on the Socialist and Communist parties.

As discussed above, the Socialist Party responded to both the domestic and the international situation by launching a process of ideological renovation, stressing the importance of political democracy and reducing or eliminating their commitment to Marxism. Although the process produced important ideological divisions within the party, i.e., the Nuñez and Almeyda factions, in practical terms the renovation facilitated the alliance with the Christian Democratic Party and the formation of the Concertación. Since 1990 the socialists have been an integral part of the ruling coalition.

The communist response to both the domestic and international changes has been characterized by isolation and denial. Throughout the 1980s the party proposed the armed struggle against the regime, a policy that was not supported by the U.S.S.R. and that the Chilean communists had great trouble applying. As a result, the communists were excluded from the transition process both by their own attitude and by the policies of the Pinochet regime. As the electoral process advanced they failed to abandon the policy of popular rebellion and refused to accept the new electoral system which only increased their isolation. At the same time the leadership had to confront the impact of Gorbachev's reforms. Throughout 1989 and 1990 Perestroika and Glasnost were dismissed as simply a reinterpretation of the traditional dogma and the result of the failure of one specific form of socialism, bureaucratic socialism. Pressure to follow a Perestroika approach was contained by the leadership and prompted the formation of a dissident movement based on a process of ideological renovation. Former communists have divided into three groups: the orthodox group, those who abandoned the party because they supported Perestroika, and those who were expelled because of disagreements with the leadership.

Human Rights Issues

A central dimension of the democratization process in both Chile and elsewhere is the question of human rights and the power of the military in the current political structure. In Chile, in spite of the transition to an elected regime, the Armed Forces remain financially and organizationally autonomous. The military obtains its resources directly from CODELCO (Chilean Copper Corporation), receiving a percentage of the sale of copper. Organizationally, the military not only enjoys total autonomy, but it has a tutelary role over the government and the society. And, from a judicial standpoint, the military has been protected by the 1978 Amnesty Law. Any analysis of the human rights policies then needs to deal with the fact that in practice the military has veto power over the civilian authorities. The alliance between the military and the political right makes it all but impossible to reform the Constitution and curtail the power of the military. The fact that until March 1998 General Pinochet was the Commander-in-Chief of the Armed Forces only reinforced the legal and juridical autonomy of the military and the inability of the civilians to control it.

The Aylwin administration promptly recognized the importance of human rights issues and took a number of important initiatives during the first year, including failed attempts to reform the Penal Code, pass a new Anti-Terrorist Law, and reform the Internal Security and Arms Control Laws, the Military Code of Justice, and the Press Law. Again, given the veto power that the right had over the political system, these reforms were not approved. As a result, the criminal procedure is highly inadequate, the rights of prisoners are not protected, the military tribunals have a broad jurisdiction, and the criminal legal system needs to be reformed. The government managed to obtain the transfer of only a handful of cases from the military to the civilian courts, but until 1998 those cases moved very slowly or were dismissed by the civilian courts. Only the case of the assassination of Orlando Letelier was successfully concluded by the courts.

In order to uncover the truth and repair some of the damage produced by the human rights abuses of the Pinochet regime, the administration appointed the Commission on Truth and Reconciliation, also known as the Rettig Commission, after the name of the commission's head, the prominent lawyer Raúl Rettig. In order to fully appreciate the work of the commission one has to look at the nature of the mandate, the resources, and the time in which the commission was operating. Although the commission had the mandate to investigate all forms of human rights abuses, in practice its activities were limited to executions and disappearances. The commission argued that the use of torture was so widespread that given the limited resources at its disposal torture could not be investigated. Furthermore, the commission was empowered to identify only the victims, not the authors of the crimes, and it had no judicial powers. In spite of the personal commitment of its members, the commission could only produce a partial report of the human rights abuses carried out by the military and police between 1973 and 1987, yet it was able to identify 2,279 deaths. The commission's report presented to the President in December 1991 criticized the courts, the military, and the society at large for their behavior: "as people became aware of what was happening, major sectors of the public opinion allowed, tolerated, supported and even concealed the violation of human rights. . . . The deep conviction that every person's human rights must be respected . . . did not win the day in our country."[4] The report also argued that by 1990 this attitude of indifference and disbelief had yet to change.[5]

President Aylwin, in turn, endorsed those accusations and responded by suggesting that moral and economic reparations were necessary. He concluded by accusing the military of human rights violations. As soon as President Aylwin announced the results of the investigation the political right and General Pinochet initiated a campaign to again use the Marxist threat as a justification for the abuses. It is clear that the goal of the campaign was to undermine the effects of the commission's report. The Armed Forces, on the other hand, were protected by the very presence of General Pinochet as Commander-in-Chief, the 1978 Amnesty Law, and their political and economic autonomy. The tutelary functions of the military and the veto power of the political right reinforced the situation and limited the powers of the new political leaders. In this context, neither the

Aylwin nor the Frei administration could do very much against those who had violated human rights. The Aylwin administration took some measures such as granting freedom to all the remaining political prisoners, allowing the return of the remaining political exiles, and creating a program that grants reparations and medical attention to the victims of repression (PRAIS). However, the law authorizing the reparations was not passed by Congress until February 1992. By 1994 it had granted benefits to about 4,000 persons.[6] The work of the Rettig Commission was continued by the National Corporation of Reparation and Reconciliation established in February 1992, which has added about 400 new names to the list of people killed by the Pinochet regime.

In regard to the responsibility of the Armed Forces the central issue is the existence of the Amnesty Law of 1978. Solá Sierra, the former Chilean human rights leader, effectively described the feelings of many Chileans, saying that "the families [of those who disappeared or were detained and tortured] feel that there is 'a veil of impunity' over the human rights abusers and that the amnesty law should be either annulled or reformed."[7] The General Secretary of the Presidency, Enrique Correa, responded that "the government will not promote any initiatives geared to modify the Amnesty Law because the political conditions are not favorable."[8] The words of Correa are quite useful in understanding the dilemma of the regime in this area. Regardless of the actual commitment of the administration to the human rights issue, the existing political structure and the continuous presence of General Pinochet simply limited the ability of the government to prosecute those members of the military and police involved in human rights violations.

Until 1998 General Pinochet managed to maintain control of the Armed Forces, exercise a veto power over the elected officials, and threaten civilian authorities. For instance in May 1993 heavily armed soldiers appeared in the streets to protest the evolution of the trials against a handful of military officers not protected by the Amnesty Law. Under pressure, President Aylwin attempted to seek a political solution to the problem of the trials of military officers through the so-called Aylwin Law. The proposed legislation sought to reconcile the demands of the relatives of the army officers and the relatives of those who suffered the abuses, but failed in the midst of disagreement within the ruling coalition.

On 11 December 1993 Eduardo Frei won the presidential elections with 58 percent of the vote. The Concertación also kept control of the Chamber of Deputies with seventy seats, with only fifty won by the right. In the new senate the balance of power was again held by the appointed senators. In January 1994 the newly appointed Minister of Defense, Peréz Yoma, indicated that the human rights policy is not part of a permanent policy of the Ministry of Defense and that the question of the autonomy of the Commander-in-Chief was not a priority. Given his career as Auditor General of the Armed Forces, one could not expect anything else.[9] President Frei confirmed this position declaring that he was not going to promote new legislation nor a political dialogue in regard to human rights because he believed that "the actions of the courts were promoting national reconciliation."[10] As usual, Pinochet made sure to remain at the center of the political discussion. In September 1995 he declared that "his rule was too soft to be called a dictatorship" and that those who fought to keep the country's peace and protect the country against terrorist aggression should not be tried.[11]

dicta blanda

Before the detention of Pinochet in London in October 1998, Chile's institutional and political realities were such that only outside forces could make a difference in this case. The only two military officers convicted for human rights abuses have been General Contreras, the former director of DINA, and his assistant, Colonel Espinoza, for the assassination of Letelier and Moffitt in Washington. Those actions were clearly linked to pressures from the United States government.

The detention in London of Pinochet and the subsequent decision of the House of Lords to authorize the process of extradition to Spain in response to the actions of the Spanish judge, Baltazar Garzón, who accuses General Pinochet of the assassination of about 300 Spanish citizens, highlights the international nature of human rights abuses. These are crimes that because of their nature should not be subject to the limitations imposed by those who committed the crimes.

The lack of power of the elected regimes to deal with the human rights issues results not only from the institutional limitations established in the 1980 Constitution. It is quite clear that the repression had an impact not only on the victims but on the entire society. There is by now a body of work developed by psychoanalysts, psychologists, and other health professionals that speaks about the social impact of repression in terms of fear and paralysis. Fear has a paralyzing effect and leads to what Elizabeth Lira calls chronic fear, which is the impact that the widespread use of repression had on the society.[12] Consequently, the impunity of the military results not only from the institutional arrangements, but from the fear of the people to challenge the power of the oppressor. Until 1998, the presence of General Pinochet as Commander-in-Chief of the Armed Forces served as a clear reminder of his power and his ability to instill fear in the society.

Here again one sees another example of the success of Pinochet's policies. The massive repression was a result of a well-planned and organized set of state policies and not the actions of demented leaders. "These leaders and their followers alike shared a psychology characterized by a set of primitive defenses: the splitting of the world into good and evil—Western civilization versus subversion; the projection of everything bad onto a hated object—the subversive—with the consequent need to control it for fear of being controlled by it; an infantile sense of omnipotence that promotes attacks on free inquiry and political difference with a corresponding incapacity for empathy."[13] Thus the transition to a more democratic regime has not entailed a transformation of the society's mind. Those who suffered the repression will continue feeling the effects of their trauma for a long period of time; those who exercised the repression and those who approved of it still maintain the kind of mentality that led them to torture and kill or to support those who tortured and killed. On 14 September 1995 General Pinochet advised Chileans to forget and not to reopen court cases against the military. Forgetting was certainly the best policy for the military, but not for the society. Pinochet's advice was followed by many in Chile while he was in control of the Armed Forces. His detention in London seems to be lessening the power of the message.[14]

The Socioeconomic Policies

From a socioeconomic standpoint, the Aylwin and the Frei administrations inherited a situation which was also institutionally and practically defined during the pre-transition period. To the extent that the economic model was an integral part of the 1980 Constitution, the basic features of the economic policies could only be changed through major institutional transformations requiring the support of the parties in the rightist coalition. More specific institutions and policies were determined through the "modernizations," while others were determined through the "organic laws" that determined the functions of key institutions such as the Central Bank. To reform them the administration needs congressional approval which means having the support of the right. Consequently, it is clear that given the institutional arrangements left in place by Pinochet the new regime could only attempt marginal modifications to the system.[15]

When President Aylwin took office the macroeconomic landscape was characterized by high rates of economic growth, profound distributive inequities, a high social debt, and the reduction in the social functions of the state. Between 1986 and 1989 the economy grew at an average of 7.4 percent, inflation reached 18.3 percent, unemployment was still high at 8.8 percent (average), and real wages were growing at an average of 2.5 percent.[16] During this period one sees the consolidation of Minister Buchi's approach based on an export-oriented model of development, strict monetary policies, moderate inflation, and the promotion of savings, investments, and exports. The social dimension was characterized by a severe contraction of social spending, which affected not only social policies, but investments and salaries in the social sector. For instance, social spending in the health area was 40 percent below the 1974 level and 35 percent below the 1981 level; educational spending was 6 percent below the 1974 level and 25 percent below the 1981 level. Most importantly, according to a CEPAL study, by 1987, 5.5 million people or 45.1 percent of the population were defined as poor, while the indigent (extremely poor) amounted to 27.7 percent of the population. According to the same study 17 percent of the population was defined as poor in 1970. Poverty was clearly the result of the high rates of unemployment and the low level of wages experienced by the economy throughout the 1980s. For the 1986–1989 period unemployment declined to an average of 10 percent, while real wages, despite some growth in 1987 and 1989, were still 29 percent below the 1981 level.[17] The Pinochet regime tried to reduce the impact of the combined effect of poverty and the reduction in social spending through the creation of programs geared to provide a minimum amount of cash support to the extremely poor.

There is no doubt that both the Aylwin and the Frei regime have been committed to the existing economic model and that their economic policies have reinforced the role of the market as the central economic agent. The bases for the policies remain the same: an open economy based on an export model and a fiscal policy characterized by austerity, low inflation rates, increased savings, and reduction of the external debt. The macroeconomic results for the period 1990–1998 were excellent: the economy grew at an average 7 percent, inflation decreased to 5 percent in 1998, unemployment was reduced to an average of 6.7 percent, and the real wages grew by 4.3 percent

Between 1990 and 1998, the Aylwin and the Frei regimes managed not only to consolidate the gains of the old one, but to improve performance in economic growth, fairly low inflation rates, and debt reduction. Simultaneously, the regimes recognized the depth of the socioeconomic problems, particularly the need to deal with the question of poverty. Social spending for the 1990–1996 period grew at about 7.4 percent, and the rate of poverty was reduced from 45 percent in 1987 to 23 percent in 1996, while extreme poverty was reduced from 17.4 percent to 5.8 percent in the same period.[18] The key to improvements in the reduction of poverty and social inequity have been the high rates of economic growth and the strong performance of the economy. Thus the reduction in poverty has been intimately linked to the growth in some sectors of the economy and in some sectors of the society. It is interesting to note that people living in the rural areas, women, and the youth are still affected by high rates of poverty. The International Labor Office (ILO) reports that by 1994, 40.3 percent of the population under fifteen years of age was below the poverty level, and that 28.9 percent of the women and 31.8 percent of the rural inhabitants lived in poverty.[19] Undoubtedly, there is a clear connection between unemployment and poverty and to the extent that the rates of unemployment declined until 1998 poverty was reduced. However, having a job is not enough. The same ILO document reports that 70 percent of the indigents and 90 percent of the poor had a job in 1994.[20] To combat poverty what is needed is not only a good job, but a set of social policies that will deal with the reasons behind the high levels of poverty in the rural sector and among children, youth, and the elderly. As presented in chapter eight at least 40 percent of the elderly will be receiving a minimum pension that only guarantees poverty since they do not have enough savings to obtain a private pension.

Finally, Chile exhibits one of the worst income distributions in Latin America.[21] By 1996 the highest 20 percent of the population captured 56.7 percent of the income, while the lowest 20 percent received only 4.1 percent of the income. The income of the highest quintile is 13.8 times higher than that of the lowest quintile, even when government subsidies are added to the basic income. There are also huge income disparities between the urban and the rural areas, urban income is 87 percent higher than the rural income. What is also remarkable is that the disparities and income differences grew throughout the 1990s, a period of high economic growth.[22]

The government of President Aylwin defined its social policy along four fundamental lines: equity, solidarity, efficiency, and an integral approach to the social problems. The most important elements of the policy were a tax reform and a set of labor laws that reformed some aspects of the Plan Laboral, the regressive labor legislation designed by José Piñera during the Pinochet regime. The agreements reached by representatives of the government, entrepreneurs, and unions involved substantial wage improvements for the workers who participated in the process, changed the legislation regarding collective negotiations and the right to strike, protected the rights of the union leaders, and established a policy of limited compensation for workers who are dismissed after seven years of work.[23]

The tax reform passed in 1990 involved an increase of the tax burden of about 3 percent between 1990 to 1993. The reform allowed the regime to increase social expenditures by about 3 percent of GDP. In 1993 a new set of negotiations led to new tax legislation, which reduced the tax burden and destroyed any possibility of having a more redistributive tax system.[24] Given the magnitude of the social problems there is no question that the 3 percent increase in social spending was highly insufficient; however, it allowed the government to at least indicate its intention to reverse the policies of the previous administration. The Aylwin and the Frei administrations have also continued the policy of providing small, and certainly insufficient, subsidies to the lowest income groups. The continuation of the market approach to pensions and health means that the inequities in those areas continue as well. For instance, in the health area, 1990 data shows that while the private sector spent U.S.$228 per capita, the public sector spent only $75 per capita. The importance of this difference is compounded by the fact that the private sector provides services for about 20 percent of the population, while the public sector is responsible for the reminding 80 percent.[25]

In brief, in the area of social policy we also see the continuation of the policies designed during the authoritarian regime, with marginal changes geared toward dealing with extremely pressing issues. The most important accomplishment here is the reduction of the number of people living in poverty.

Summary

Aylwin declared at the end of his presidency,

> In Chile we have public freedoms; the political parties function; and the state power is generated by the people except for the appointed senators, the existence of a non-representative electoral system, and the Constitutional Court. The power of the president is limited by the fact that he cannot remove the Commanders-in-Chief of the Armed Forces and by the Organic Law of the Armed Forces. . . . This is a restricted democracy . . . a military officer can insult the President and the President does not have the power to ask for his removal.

In regard to human rights, he said that

> that there is nothing more disturbing for a society than lies, injustices and hatred . . . the law cannot mandate to forget. Nobody can believe that the state can mandate the wives, parents and children [of the victims] to forget what happened to them. Just attempting to do it involves a new offense. Besides it is not good for countries to forget their tragedies. On the contrary, in order to avoid the repetition [of these acts] they should be conserved in the memory of the nation.[26]

This honest assessment summarizes the nature of Chile's political system very clearly. Although Aylwin argued that in Chile there are public freedoms a recent Human Rights Watch report effectively demonstrates that "freedom of expression in Chile is subject to restrictions perhaps unparalleled among Western democracies."[27]

In his remarks Aylwin also mentioned that there were still four million poor people in the country. In the body of this chapter we have analyzed the three main dimensions of the limited transition to democracy in Chile: the economic system remains unchanged, the political system has important undemocratic features, and the human rights abuses of the military remain by and large unpunished.

Finally, the dominant social narrative did not change; it was only adapted to the new necessities of those with power and as in the past it has been used to reinforce the existing constitutional and socioeconomic arrangements. The narrative continues to emphasize the importance of the market ideology, the policies, and the institutions created by the the Pinochet regime. The limited transition to democracy, the great socioeconomic inequities, the impunity of the military, have been largely ignored or justified by the notion that the military established order and a rational and efficient economic system. Until 1998, before the latest economic recession and the arrest of General Pinochet, the new myth stressed the importance of Chile as a model and Pinochet as the patriarch that made that model possible.[28] What mattered was that Chile was a strong economic power: Chile was the jaguar of that jungle called South America, or even the world. And Chile had become the jaguar because of the actions and policies of General Pinochet. He had had the foresight to lead the country into this new path. He had demonstrated that politics and politicians were irrelevant and the best thing he had done was to kill and torture to eliminate those who stood in the way of greatness. Human rights issues were to be forgotten and the role of the military in those abuses was to be seen as heroic.

According to the new myth, unity and equality were going to be achieved through access to the market. The shopping mall emerged as the most powerful symbol of this new narrative. The economic data presented in the body of this chapter clearly indicates that this was just another myth and that at best the only right that most Chileans had was *to go* to the mall—only a few could afford to buy what was sold there.

Throughout the book I have argued that social security policies played a substantial role in sustaining an "official history" and an "official story" that emphasized the uniqueness of Chileans and of Chilean politics. At the core of that "uniqueness" there is a myth of unity that can be traced back to the 1830s. However, what is clear is that both in the 1830s and in 1973 unity was imposed on the society through force and violence.

While the history and the story stressed the establishment of a unified society through the shared effort of the people and the government, the policies and politics reflected a discriminatory attitude.[29] Before 1973, the stratified nature of the social security policies reflected that discriminatory attitude. However, the policies were very useful not so much to the poor retirees, but to those receiving the privileged pensions and to the politicians that appeared as the providers of some magnificent gift. The policies also served to provide legitimacy to a political system built on profound inequities. The old narrative, the old policies, and the old politics died with the 1973 coup.

The new regime developed a new political system, new policies, as well as a new history and a story that, just as in 1830, stressed the importance of redefining the economic system for both internal and external purposes. The narrative and the policies were sustained through a repressive system. The new official story called for modernity, competitiveness, the importance of the market, and the dangers of state intervention in the economy. The rhetoric has certainly succeeded in prolonging the undemocratic values and principles that inspired the Pinochet regime and that are still present in the Chilean political system and Chilean society. It has also succeeded in justifying the reduction of the role of the state on behalf of the lower income groups. However, this has been only a partial withdrawal of the state. As shown in chapters seven and eight, all throughout the Pinochet years the state pursued a large number of policies that strengthened the power of those privileged groups that had access to the regime. The privatization of social security is not only one of the clearest expressions of those policies, but it also reflects the vital and intimate connection between la política and las políticas, between politics and policies.

Notes

Notes to the Introduction

1. Hugh Heclo, *Modern Social Politics in Britain and Sweden* (New Haven, Conn.: Yale University Press, 1997), 3.

2. Kenneth Dyson, *The State Tradition in Western Europe* (New York: Oxford University Press, 1980), 7.

3. Brian Loveman and Elizabeth Lira, *Las suaves cenizas del olvido: Vía chilena de la reconciliación política 1814–1932* (Santiago: LOM Ediciones, 1999). See also Gabriel Salazar and Julio Pinto, *Historia contemporánea de Chile*, vols. I and II (Santiago: LOM Ediciones, 1999).

4. Margaret R. Somers uses the concept of narrative identity and she argues that social identities are constituted through narrativity, that social action is guided by narrativity, and social processes and interactions—both institutional and interpersonal—are narratively mediated. See her "The Narrative Constitution of Identity: A Relational and Network Approach," *Theory and Society* 23 (October 1994); see also Jeffery M. Paige, *Coffee and Power: Revolution and the Rise of Democracy in Central America* (Cambridge, Mass.: Harvard University Press, 1997), 341.

5. I stress the notion of the "official story" or dominant narrative. I am certain that there were, and still are, other narratives.

Notes to Chapter 1

1. Alberto Edwards, *La fronda aristocrática* (Santiago: Editorial Ercilla, 1936); Francisco Encina, *Historia de Chile* (Santiago: Zig Zag, 1954); Julio

Cesar Jobet, *Ensayo crítico al desarrollo económico y social de Chile* (Santiago: Editorial Universitaria, 1955).

2. Mario Góngora, *Ensayo sobre la noción del Estado en Chile en los siglos XIX y XX* (Santiago: Editorial Universitaria, 1986).

3. Henry Kirsh, *Industrial Development in a Traditional Society: The Conflict of Entrepreneurship and Modernization in Chile* (Gainesville, Fla.: University Press of Florida, 1977), 67. For a similar analysis, see Frederick Pike, *Chile and the United States* (Notre Dame, Ind.: University of Notre Dame Press, 1963), and Tulio Halperin, *Historia contemporánea de América Latina* (Madrid: Editorial Madrid Alianza, 1969).

4. Maurice Zeitlin, *The Civil Wars in Chile (or the Bourgeois Revolutions that Never Were)* (Princeton, N.J.: Princeton University Press, 1984), 23.

5. For an analysis of this period, see Francisco Antonio Encina, *La presidencia de Balmaceda* (Santiago: Editorial Nacimiento, 1952); Hernan Rámírez Necochea, *Balmaceda y la contrarevolución de 1891* (Santiago: Editorial Universitaria, 1969); Luis Vitale, *Interpretación marxista de la historia de Chile,* 2 vols. (Santiago: Prensa Latinoamericana, 1969 and 1971).

6. The Civil Code was enacted in 1855, the Banking Law in 1860, the Commercial Code in 1864, and the Mining Code in 1874. For an analysis of the role of the state during this period, see Oscar Muñoz, "Estado e industrialización en el ciclo de expansión del salitre," *Estudios Cieplan,* no. 6 (January 1977).

7. On the Radical Party, see Peter Snow, *Radicalismo chileno* (Buenos Aires: Editorial Francisco de Encina, 1972).

8. A. Edwards, *La fronda aristocrática,* 119.

9. James O. Morris, *Elites, Intellectuals and Consensus: A Study of the Social Question and the Industrial Relations System in Chile* (Ithaca, N.Y.: Cornell University Press, 1966), 83.

10. Ibid., 87.

11. Cited in Julio C. Jobet, *Recabarren y los orígenes del movimiento obrero y del socialismo chilenos* (Santiago: Editorial Prensa Latinoamericana, 1973), 45.

12. In 1913 the death rate was 31 per 1,000, and the infant mortality rate was 304 per 1,000 (Morris, *Elites, Intellectuals and Consensus,* 85).

13. According to Albert Hirschman, prices increased almost nine times between 1880 and 1920 (*Journeys toward Progress: Studies of Economic Policymaking in Latin America* [New York: Twentieth Century Fund, 1963], 160). On the other hand, by 1900 over 90 percent of public revenues were generated by export taxes, and the only remaining local taxes were on seals, documents, and newspapers, all of them indirect taxes (Jobet, *Ensayo crítico*).

14. Alejandro Venegas, *Cartas al Excelentísimo Señor don Pedro Montt* (Valparaíso, 1909); Eduardo Ross, *South of Panama* (New York: Twentieth

Century Fund, 1915); Frank Fetter, *Monetary Inflation in Chile* (Princeton, N.J.: Princeton University Press, 1931); Tom Davis, "Eight Decades of Inflation in Chile, 1879–1959: A Political Interpretation," *Journal of Political Economy* 181, no. 4 (1963); John Stevenson, *The Chilean Popular Front* (Philadelphia: University of Pennsylvania Press, 1938).

15. Jobet, *Ensayo crítico*, 37.

16. By 1910 there were 433 mutual aid societies with an affiliation of about 35,000 members (Jorge Barría, *Breve historia del sindicalismo chileno* [Santiago: INSORA, 1967], 12–15).

17. Sergio Grez, *De la "regeneración del pueblo" a la huelga general: Génesis y evolución histórica del movimiento popular en Chile (1810–1890)* (Santiago: Ediciones Ril, 1997), chs. 19 and 20. This is the most detailed analysis of the history of the labor movement and other popular organizations written to date.

18. For an analysis of anarchism in Chile, see Julio Heise, *Historia de Chile: El período parlamentario, 1861–1925* (Santiago: Editorial Andrés Bello, 1974), 382–89.

19. Grez, *De la "regeneración del pueblo,"* 756.

20. For an analysis of Recabarren's position, see Jobet, *Recabarren y los orígenes del movimiento obrero*.

21. The Democratic Party appeared as a branch of the Radical Party in 1887, calling for political, social, and economic emancipation of the masses and emphasizing education and the provision of social services as fundamental roles of the state.

22. Recabarren's role has been studied by Jobet in *Recabarren y los orígenes del movimiento obrero* and by Alan Angell, *Politics and the Labour Movement in Chile* (London: Oxford University Press, 1973).

23. Grez lists about forty strikes between 1860 and 1880 (*De la "regeneración del pueblo,"* 446–50).

24. Ibid., 569–75.

25. Jobet, *Ensayo crítico*, 101. See also Hernan Rámírez Necochea, *Historia del movimento obrero de Chile* (Santiago: Siglo XXI, 1956).

26. Jobet, *Ensayo crítico*, 135.

27. For a detailed history and interpretation of the events, see Eduardo Devés, *Los que van a morir te saludan: Historia de una masacre, Escuela Santa María, Iquique, 1907* (Santiago: Ediciones Documentas, 1989). See also Jobet, *Ensayo crítico*, 138.

28. Moisés Poblete, *La organización sindical en Chile* (Santiago, 1926), Annex 5. The reliability of this figure is under discussion. Poblete was the first director of the Office of Labor, and he seemed to have included in this number the membership of the mutual aid societies.

29. Crisóstomo Pizarro, "El rol de los sindicatos en Chile," *Colección Estudios CIEPLAN*, no. 22 (1978).

30. Francisco Valdés Vergara, Conferencia en el Centro Conservador, Santiago, 1919, quoted in Jobet, *Recabarren y los orígenes del movimiento obrero*, 40. Valdés was a leader of the Conservative Party and a well-known politician.

31. In 1906 the first blue-collar housing law was adopted and the following year Sunday was declared a day of rest.

32. Carmelo Mesa-Lago, *Social Security in Latin America: Pressure Groups, Stratification and Inequality* (Pittsburgh: University of Pittsburgh Press, 1978), 24.

33. James M. Malloy, *The Politics of Social Security in Brazil* (Pittsburgh: University of Pittsburgh Press, 1980), 49.

34. For a similar conclusion regarding the Brazilian case, see ibid.

35. Arturo Alessandri, "Programa Presidencial," Convención de la Alianza Liberal, Santiago, April 1920.

36. Arturo Alessandri, speech in la Escuela de Caballería, Santiago, 1924.

37. Stevenson, *Chilean Popular Front*, 24.

38. Loveman and Lira, *Las suaves cenizas del olvido,* 256.

39. The best analysis of these bills has been done by Morris in *Elites, Intellectuals and Consensus.*

40. Ibid., 128.

41. Ibid., 163–65.

42. Charles C. Praeger Roman, "The Origin and Development of the Bourgeoisie in the Nineteenth-Century Chile," *Latin American Perspectives* 10, nos. 37 and 38 (Summer 1983).

43. Arturo Alessandri, *Recuerdos de Gobierno, Administración 1920–1925,* vol. 1 (Santiago: Editorial Universitaria, 1952); Carlos Vicuña, *La Tiranía en Chile* (Santiago: Editorial Aconcagua, 1987).

44. Morris, *Elites, Intellectuals and Consensus,* 221–40.

45. Bergquist, *Exports and the Left,* 43.

46. Stephen Skowroneck, *Building a New American State: The Expansion of National Administrative Capacities* (London: Cambridge University Press, 1982), 10.

47. Loveman and Lira, *Las suaves cenizas del olvido,* 255–56.

Notes to Chapter 2

1. Frederick Nunn, *Chilean Politics 1920–1931, The Honorable Mission of the Armed Forces* (Albuquerque: University of New Mexico Press, 1970), 110.

2. For an analysis of Chile's unique form of populism, see Silvia Borzutzky, "Chilean Politics and Social Security Policies," doctoral dissertation, University of Pittsburgh, 1983. See also Salazar and Pinto, *Historia Contemporánea de Chile*, vol. I, *Estado, legitimidad, ciudadanía*, ch. 1.

3. Few authors have analyzed this problem. One exception is Brian Loveman, *Struggle in the Countryside: Politics and Rural Labor in Chile, 1919–1973* (Bloomington, Ind.: Indiana University Press, 1977), 293–94, and *Chile, the Legacy of Hispanic Capitalism* (New York: Oxford University Press, 1979), 257.

4. The rightist and central parties argued throughout the years that acceptance of the new census would mean a constant increase in the number of deputies, which would necessitate building a new Congressional Palace. See José M. Navasal, "La distribución de los disputados," *El Mercurio*, 21 June 1984.

5. The D'Hont system involves a complicated process. First, total votes are tabulated for all candidates as well as all the parties running under the same coalition. Second, a quotient is obtained for each district, and this quotient is divided by the total number of votes obtained by the party if it runs alone, or by the list in case of a coalition. The resulting figure determines the number of candidates elected in each list. Those with the higher number of individual votes in each list are elected.

6. On the Socialist Party, see Julio Cesar Jobet, *El partido socialista de Chile* (Santiago: Editorial Prensa Latinoamericana, 1971), and Paul Drake, *Socialism and Populism in Chile* (Chicago: University of Illinois Press, 1977).

7. Drake, *Socialism and Populism,* 37.

8. Traditional sources for the study of the Christian Democratic Party are: George Grayson, *El partido demócrata cristiano chileno* (Buenos Aires: Editorial Francisco de Aguirre, 1968); Jaime Castillo Velasco, *Los caminos de la revolución* (Santiago: Editorial del Pacifíco, 1972) and *Las fuentes de la democracia cristiana* (Santiago: Editorial del Pacífico, 1963); Eduardo Frei, *El social cristianismo* (Santiago: Editorial del Pacífico, 1951), *La verdad tiene su hora* (Santiago: Editorial del Pacífico, 1955), and *Pensamiento y acción* (Santiago: Editorial del Pacífico, 1958); Ricardo Boizard, *La democracia cristiana en Chile* (Santiago: Editorial Orbe, 1963); Sergio Molina, *El proceso de cambio en Chile* (Santiago: Editorial Universitaria, 1972); Patricio Dooner, *El conflicto político nacional durante el Gobierno de Eduardo Frei (1964–1970)* (Santiago: CPU-ICHEH, 1984); Tomás Moulián and Isabel Torres, *Discusiones entre honorables: Las candidaturas presidenciales de la derecha 1938–1946* (Santiago: FLACSO, 1988); Alan Angell, *Chile de Alessandri a Pinochet: En busca de la utopía* (Santiago: Editorial Andrés Bello, 1993); and Michael Fleet, *The Rise and Fall of Chilean Christian Democracy* (Princeton, N.J.:

Princeton University Press, 1985). Alberto Cardemil, *El camino de la utopía: Alessandri, Frei, Allende Pensamiento y obra* (Santiago: Editorial Andrés Bello, 1997) has an excellent comparison of the policies of the three presidents. Frei's life and work are analyzed by Cristian Gazmuri, Patricia Arancibia, and Alvaro Góngora in *Eduardo Frei Montalva (1911–1982)* (Mexico: Fondo de Cultura Económica, 1996).

9. Quoted by Eduardo Frei in *Política y espíritu* 13 (July 1957): 31.

10. Ibid., 32.

11. Charles Anderson, *Politics and Economic Change in Latin America* (Princeton, N.J.: D. Van Nostrand, 1967).

12. J. Samuel Valenzuela. "The Chilean Labor Movement: The Institutionalization of Conflict," in *Chile: Politics and Society*, ed. Arturo Valenzuela and Julio Valenzuela (New Jersey: Transaction Books, 1974), 161.

13. Robert Kaufman, in his excellent analysis of the politics of land reform in Chile, makes a similar point when he argues that the distinctive features of the Chilean political order were the containment of the struggles between the established social groups within the parliamentary framework, the capacity of the party politicians to establish informal patronage ties with small clusters of voters "within a particular plant or enterprise, within a city or neighborhood or within relatively small occupational or locational communities," and finally the maintenance of political stability by the political elites at the top of each sector (right, center, left) with all having a strong interest in the status quo (*The Politics of Land Reform in Chile, 1950–1970: Public Policy, Political Institutions, and Social Change* [Cambridge, Mass.: Harvard University Press, 1972], 20). For an analysis of the political parties, see Federico Gil, *The Political System of Chile* (Boston: Houghton Mifflin, 1966); Manuel Antonio Garretón, *The Chilean Political Process* (Boston: Unwin Hyman, 1989); Arturo Valenzuela, *Chile: The Breakdown of Democratic Regimes* (Baltimore, Md.: Johns Hopkins University Press, 1978); Timothy R. Scully, *Rethinking the Center: Party Politics in Nineteenth- and Twentieth-Century Chile* (Stanford, Calif.: Stanford University Press, 1992).

14. See, for instance, Muñoz, "Estado e industrialización."

15. Michael Monteón, *Chile and the Great Depression: The Politics of Underdevelopment, 1927–1948* (Tempe, Ariz.: Arizona State University Press, 1998), 18–24.

16. Loveman, *Struggle in the Countryside*, 247–48.

17. Speech quoted in Monteón, *Chile and the Great Depression*, 23.

18. Salazar and Pinto, *Historia contemporánea de Chile*, vol. 1, 242–43.

19. Quoted in ibid., 242.

20. Barbara Stallings, *Class Conflict and Economic Development in Chile, 1958–1973* (Stanford, Calif.: Stanford University Press, 1978), 46.

21. On the bureaucracy, see German Urzúa, *Evolución de la administración pública chilena. 1818–1968* (Santiago: Editorial Jurídica de Chile, 1970); German Urzúa and Ana M. Barzelatto, *Diagnóstico de la burocracia chilena* (Santiago: Editorial Jurídica de Chile, 1971); and Loveman, *Chile*.

22. The decentralized sector is divided into four types of institutions: (a) autonomous institutions such as the universities; (b) semi-public institutions formed mainly by the different social security funds; (c) state enterprises such as railroads, transportation, etc., that serve the community as a whole, but must operate with a profit; and (d) semi-public enterprises which are corporations in which a percentage of the shares is owned by the state. These enterprises had a central role in the process of industrial development and by 1969 there were more than sixty of them.

23. For an analysis, see Loveman, *Chile*, 277–78.

24. Monteón, *Chile and the Great Depression*, 257.

25. See the speech by Recaredo Ossa, President of the Confederación de la Producción y del Comercio, *El Mercurio*, 27 May 1964; also *El Mercurio*, 8 April 1964, p. 3.

26. There are few studies that deal with the relations between the organized business and the public sector. The most important are Constantine Menges, "Public Policy and Organized Business in Chile: A Preliminary Analysis," *Journal of International Affairs* 20 (1966), and David Cusack, "The Politics of Chilean Private Enterprises under Christian Democracy," doctoral dissertation, University of Denver, 1970.

27. Quoted in Loveman, *Chile*, 283.

28. Overvaluation has been estimated between 45 percent and 68 percent for the early 1960s (World Bank, *Chile: An Economy in Transition* [Washington, D.C., 1980], 15).

29. Marcos Mamalakis, *The Growth and Structure of the Chilean Economy* (New Haven, Conn.: Yale University Press, 1976). See also Patricio Meller, *Un siglo de economía política chilena* (Santiago: Editorial Andrés Bello, 1996).

30. World Bank, *Chile: An Economy in Transition*, 40.

31. Hirschman, *Journeys toward Progress*, 183.

32. Aguirre Cerda, Mensaje Presidencial, 1941. The Mensaje Presidencial is the speech given at the beginning session of Congress.

33. Hirschman, *Journeys toward Progress*. See also Anibal Pinto, "Desarrollo económico y relaciones sociales en Chile," *Aportes*, no. 20 (April 1971): 40–66.

34. See Anibal Pinto, "Ni estabilidad ni desarrollo" (Santiago, 1960).

35. For a complete analysis of the political economy of the Alessandri government, see Ricardo Ffrench-Davis, *Políticas económicas en Chile; 1952–1970* (Santiago: Ediciones Nueva Universidad, 1973), and Stallings, *Class Conflict*.

36. This is the structuralist position best represented by Osvaldo Sunkel. See "Un esquema general para el analisís de la inflación," *Economía*, no. 62 (1962): 55–99.

37. Anibal Pinto, *Chile, un caso de desarrolo frustrado* (Santiago: Editorial Universitaria, 1962), 99.

38. Ibid., 135.

39. Labor Code, Article 367.

40. For an analysis of this period, see Cole Blasier, "The Cuban and Chilean Communist Parties: Instruments of Soviet Policy (1935–1948)," doctoral dissertation, Columbia University, 1954.

41. Loveman, *Chile*, 285.

42. Jorge Barría, *Historia de la CUT* (Santiago: Editorial Prensa Latinoamericana, 1971).

43. The Law of Permanent Defense of Democracy was not repealed until 1958.

44. Angell, *Chile de Alessandri a Pinochet*, 77. Landsberger corroborates this point. His survey of labor leaders shows that only 10 percent of them thought they had much influence on issues of national importance, while 57 percent thought that they did not have any influence (Henry Landsberger et al., *El pensamiento del dirigente industrial chileno* [Santiago: INSORA, Universidad de Chile, 1963]).

45. Angell, *Chile de Alessandri a Pinochet*, 77; C. Fuchs and L. Santibañez, *Pensamiento, política y acción del ejecutivo industrial* (Santiago: INSORA, Universidad de Chile, 1967), 46.

46. Pizarro, "Rol de los sindicatos," 40.

47. CUT, *Principios, métodos de lucha, estatutos y programa immediato* (Santiago, 1953).

48. Nicholas Kaldor, "Problemas económicos de Chile," *Trimestre Económico* (April-June 1959): 179.

49. Isabel Heskia, "La distribución del ingreso en Chile," in *Bienestar y probreza*, ed. CEPLAN (Santiago: Universidad Católica de Chile, 1974), 45.

50. For a detailed anlaysis of the behavior of wages and inflation, see Joseph Ramos, *Política de remuneraciones e inflaciones persistentes: El caso chileno* (Santiago: Instituto de Economía, Universidad de Chile, 1970).

51. Anderson, *Politics and Economic Change*.

52. Tomás Moulián, "Desarrollo político y estado de compromiso: Desajustes y crisis estatal en Chile," *Colección Estudios CIEPLAN*, no. 8. (July 1982): 105–160; Manuel Antonio Garretón, "Democratización y otro desarrollo: el caso chileno," *Revista Mexicana de Sociología* 42, no. 3 (September 1980): 1167–213.

Notes to Chapter 3

1. Mesa-Lago, *Social Security in Latin America,* 22.

2. This was explicitly stated by President Alessandri in a letter written to Moisés Poblete. See Moisés Poblete, *El derecho del trabajo y la seguridad social* (Santiago: Editorial Jurídica de Chile, 1949), 18–29.

3. Morris, *Elites, Intellectuals and Consensus,* 165.

4. For two excellent analyses of these events, see ibid., and Nunn, *Chilean Politics*; also Raul Aldunate, *Ruido de sables* (Santiago, 1969), and George Strawbridge, *Ibañez and Alessandri: The Authoritarian Right and the Democratic Left in Twentieth-Century Chile,* Buffalo Council on International Studies (New York: State University of New York at Buffalo, 1971).

5. See D.F.L 837 and D.L. 454 and 767 of 1925. D.F.L. (Decreto con Fuerza de Ley) and D.L. (Decreto-Ley) are two different forms of law used in cases of de facto governments and in cases in which the Executive has obtained special authorization from Congress to legislate on specific issues.

6. Mesa-Lago, *Social Security in Latin America,* 33. This estimate dates from the late 1960s. My own estimate is that by 1973 the number of social security laws was more than 2,000. They still remain uncompiled.

7. Ibid.

8. This legislation is known as Ley del Nuevo Trato.

9. Comisión de Estudios de la Seguridad Social Chilena, *Informe sobre la reforma de la seguridad social Chilena* (Santiago: Editorial Jurídica de Chile, 1965), 322–39.

10. Article 10, No. 14 of the Constitution assured to all inhabitants the benefits of a social security system and established the obligation of the state to care for the public health and the welfare of the nation.

11. Comisión de Estudios de la Seguridad Social Chilena, *Informe sobre la reforma,* vol. 1, p. 51.

12. Mesa-Lago, *Social Security in Latin America,* 41.

13. One of the few studies on the sectors of the population not covered by the social security systems in Latin America is found in Carmelo Mesa-Lago, "Seguridad social y pobreza," in *Se puede superar la pobreza?* (Santiago: United Nations, 1980).

14. Article 582, Chilean Civil Code.

15. For an excellent study of the situation of rural labor in Chile, see Loveman, *Struggle in the Countryside.*

16. Labor Code, Articles 77 and 78.

17. Loveman, *Struggle in the Countryside,* 63.

18. See ibid., 124–32.

19. *El campesino chileno le escribe a su Excelencia,* ed. Brian Loveman (Santiago: ICIRA, 1971).

20. Eduardo Miranda, "El Sector agrícola en la seguridad social chilena," *Boletín de Estadísticas de Seguridad Social* 27–28 (December 1965).

21. The approval of a minimum agricultural wages in 1953 somewhat improved the pensions received by the rural workers and the finances of the Blue-Collar Workers Fund. The agricultural workers did not reach wage parity with the urban workers until 1965, when the minimum industrial wage was extended to the rural areas.

22. Carlos Briones et al., "Antecedentes básicos y ánalisis del estado actual de la Seguridad Social en Chile," *Seguridad Social,* no. 98 (1968): 13; Luis Orlandini, *Características básicas de la Seguridad Social en Chile* (Santiago: Insora, 1966).

23. See Law 10383, Article 53; Briones et al., "Antecedentes," and Orlandini, *Características básicas.*

24. Briones et al., "Antecedentes," 14.

25. Ibid., 13.

26. The first report on the subject was made by the Klein-Saks mission in 1956. The most complete report was prepared by the Special Commission on Social Security Reform named by President Alessandri. This report, called "Informe sobre la reforma de la Seguridad Social Chilena," is known also as the Prat Report, after the name of its chairman, Jorge Prat. Henceforth it will be cited as the Prat Report. In 1968 the Superintendencia de Seguridad Social, the organism charged with the supervision of the entire social security system, also recorded a thorough analysis of the issue. Its authors were Carlos Briones, Luis Orlandini, and other top social security administrators, and it is entitled "Antecedentes básicos y análisis del estado actual de la Seguridad Social en Chile," published in *Seguridad Social,* no. 98 (Briones et al., "Antecedentes"). Finally, Carmelo Mesa-Lago has probably the best quantitative analysis of these inequalities, and the only comparative study on the subject in the Latin American context in his *Social Security in Latin America.*

27. Mesa-Lago, *Social Security in Latin America,* 49.

28. Prat Report, Informe No. 5, secciones 3 and 4.

29. Briones et al., "Antecedentes," 71–79.

30. ODEPLAN, *Informe Económico Anual* (Santiago, 1971), 104, cited in Mesa-Lago, *Social Security in Latin America,* 54.

31. Mesa-Lago, *Social Security in Latin America,* 55.

32. Prat Report, 1391.

33. Prat Report, 1424.

34. Luis Romero. "La seguridad social en Chile. Incidencias económicas en el período 1958–1978," Memoria de Prueba, Escuela de Economía (Santiago: Universidad de Chile, 1978).

35. See Prat Report, 1391–433, and Patricio Novoa, *Derecho de la seguridad social* (Santiago: Editorial Jurídica de Chile, 1977), 295–97. Social security experts revel in telling stories about people who receive three, four, or even five pensions at the same time, all legally obtained.

36. Briones et al., "Antecedentes," 19.

37. Historical health statistics are found in Julio Bustos, *La previsión y la medicina social en Chile,* Memoria anual presentada por el Director General de Previsión Social, Santiago, August 1946.

38. Eduardo Cruz-Coke, "Medicina preventiva y medicina dirigida" (Santiago, 1938), 16–17.

39. Bustos, *La previsión,* 20, 53. Bustos makes a general assessment of the system arguing that it had enabled the early detection and treatment of tuberculosis, syphilis, and cardiovascular diseases. Special attention was given to pregnant women and the newborn, and by 1947 the health system controlled 25 percent of all pregnancies and provided attention to 38 percent of the population under two years old.

40. Infant mortality rate declined from 117.8 per thousand live births in 1952 to 101.9 in 1986. See Servicio Nacional de Salud, "15 años de labor, 1952–1967," (Santiago, 1968), 12.

41. Prat Report, 1471. For a detailed description of the administrative chaos, see Prat Report, informe No. 1, Anexo 1–4.

42. Prat Report, 85.

43. Mesa-Lago, *Social Security in Latin America,* 55.

44. Prat Report, 1465–66.

45. Prat Report, p. xvi.

Notes to Chapter 4

1. Jorge Ahumada, *En vez de la miseria* (Santiago: Editorial del Pacífico, 1965), 54.

2. See A. Valenzuela, *Breakdown of Democratic Regimes,* 19.

3. Ahumada, *En vez de la miseria,* ch. 2.

4. A. Valenzuela, *Breakdown of Democratic Regimes,* 33–39; also Tomás Moulián, "Desarrollo político," 105–160.

5. Jacques Maritain, *The Rights of Man and Natural Law* (New York: Charles Scribner and Sons, 1943), 17–22.

6. Castillo Velasco, *Los caminos de la revolución*, 370.

7. Frei developed his political ideas in a number of books and articles. This quote was first published in the journal *Política y Espíritu*, June 1947, and later in *Pensamiento de Eduardo Frei: Selección y Notas de Oscar Pinochet* (Santiago: Editorial Aconcagua, 1982), 28.

8. Frei obtained 56 percent of the vote.

9. Analyses of the economic program of the Frei government are found in Stallings, *Class Conflict*; Ffrench-Davis, *Políticas económicas*; Edward Thomas, *Economic Development and Reform in Chile: Progress under Frei, 1964–1970*, Michigan Latin American Studies Center, Monograph No. 8, Michigan State University, March 1972.

10. Ffrench-Davis, *Políticas económicas*, 55.

11. It was a common claim among the Christian Democrats that they would govern Chile for thirty-six years.

12. Stallings, *Class Conflict*, 196.

13. Eduardo Frei, Cuarto Mensaje Presidencial, 21 May 1968.

14. L. Cereceda and F. Dahse, *Dos decadas de cambio en el agro chileno* (Santiago: Cuadernos del Instituto de Sociologia, Universidad Católica de Chile, 1980), 98.

15. T. Edwards, *Economic Development and Reform*, 18. The GNP growth is estimated in 1965 market prices.

16. Text of the Reformas Constitucionales, *El Mercurio*, 1 December 1964.

17. Eduardo Frei et al., *Reformas Constitucionales 1970* (Santiago: Editorial Jurídica de Chile, 1970).

18. For a detailed study of the passage of the Agrarian Reform Law and the tactics employed by the opposition to link it with the approval of the copper reform, see Kaufman, *Politics of Land Reform in Chile*.

19. Eduardo Frei, Sexto Mensaje Presidencial, 21 May 1970. For an analysis of the Chilenization process, see Theodore Moran, *Multinational Corporations and the Politics of Dependence* (Princeton, N.J.: Princeton University Press, 1977).

20. T. Edwards, *Economic Development and Reform*, 27.

21. Eduardo Frei, Primer Mensaje Presidencial, 21 May 1965.

22. The most important contributions on this topic have been made by Anibal Quijano, José Nunn, and Gino Germani. In the Chilean context, Father Roger Vekemans, S.J., and Armando Mattelart are the most important contributors. Among the many writings of Vekemans, see "La marginalidad en el subdesarrollo de América Latina," *Razón y Fe*, nos. 808 and 809 (October 1973): 140–56; *La pre-revolución latino-americana* (Buenos Aires: DESAL, 1969); Roger Vekemans and Ismael Silva, *Marginalidad, promoción*

popular y neo-marxismo (Bogota: Cedial, 1976); and *La Marginalidad en América Latina* (Buenos Aires: DESAL, 1970).

23. *Callampas,* the popular name for the Chilean slums, means mushroom. The name reflects their external appearance and the fact that they grow rapidly, especially in winter after it rains.

24. Armando Mattelart and Manuel Garretón, *Integración y marginalidad* (Santiago: Editorial del Pacífico, 1966), 77; this study is one of the most complete on marginality in Chile.

25. President Frei repeated this idea several times during his long political career. See, for instance, the interview in *Il Giorno de Milan,* 1 July 1965, published in *El pensamiento de Eduardo Frei,* 61.

26. Roger Vekemans, S. J., *Marginalidad incorporación e integración* (Santiago: Desal, 1966), Documento No. 2, pp. 9–15.

27. Ibid.

28. Frei et al., *Reformas Constitucionales 1970,* 42.

29. *El Mercurio,* 13 September 1965, p. 3. See also *El Mercurio* editorials on 9 October 1965, p. 3; 10 May 1966, p. 3; 17 May 1966, p. 3; 10 June 1966, p. 3.

30. See INDAP, "Qué es? Cómo esta organizado? Cómo actúa? Qué ha conseguido?" mimeo (Santiago, 1966.)

31. Amino Affonso et al., *Movimiento campesino chileno* (Santiago: ICIRA, 1970), 258.

32. Loveman, *Struggle in the Countryside,* 266.

33. See Kaufman, *Politics of Land Reform,* especially 154–58, and the letter of Aníbal Correa, editor of the SNA monthly journal, quoted by Kaufman on p. 153.

34. Loveman, *Struggle in the Countryside,* 262; S. Gomez and S. Arroyo, *Una etapa conflictiva en la reforma agraria* (Santiago: ICIRA, 1971), 11.

35. ABC de la Democracia Cristiana. Also see Jorge Ahumada, *El desarrollo integral de Chile* (Santiago: Fundación Jorge Ahumada, 1966).

36. Thayer, a labor law professor, developed each of these points in his book *Trabajo empresa y revolución* (Santiago: Editorial Zig-Zag, 1968), especially 45–46.

37. Carlos Walker, "Líneas de una moderna organización sindical en Chile," *El Mercurio,* 2 April 1965, p. 3.

38. For a full description of the program, see Sergio Molina, "Explosición sobre el estado de la Hacienda Pública," Dirección de Presupuesto No. 12, Santiago, November 1967. Sergio Molina, the Minister of Finance, had been the author of the financial provisions of the plan while Thayer had argued for the inclusion of the labor provisions.

39. Speech by Rafael A. Gumucio, *Punto Final,* 30 May 1969.

40. Quoted by Edward Glabb, "Christian Democracy, Marxism and Revolution in Chile: The Election and Overthrow of Salvador Allende," doctoral dissertation, Northern Illinois University, 1975, p. 189.

41. Since the Congress had only 200 members, each member introduced an average of 125 articles (*El Mercurio,* 10 April 1968, p. 1). The information on the social security articles was provided by Professor Novoa.

42. Eduardo Frei, interview with *The Economist,* 17 November 1967, published in *El pensamiento de Eduardo Frei,* 190.

43. Hernán del Canto, Secretario General de la CUT, interview to *Punto Final,* 2 January 1968.

Notes to Chapter 5

1. Prat Report, vol. 1, pp. xvii–xviii.

2. See declarations of Ramón Santander, Undersecretary for Social Security, *El Mercurio,* 31 December 1964, p. 17.

3. Text of the Reformas Constitucionales, published in *El Mercurio,* 1 December 1964, p. 1.

4. Eduardo Frei, Primer Mensaje Presidencial, 21 May 1965.

5. Ibid.

6. Superintendencia de Seguridad Social, "Costo de la Seguridad Social Chilena" (Santiago, 1981), 27, 35; *El Mercurio,* 7 February 1967, p. 3.

7. Foreword, Proyecto de ley de reforma del regimen de Asignaciones Familiares, *El Mercurio,* 6 January 1966, p. 1.

8. Interview with Alvaro Covarrubias, Santiago, July 1981.

9. See laws 16610 and 16612 of 1967.

10. Eduardo Frei, Tercer Mensaje Presidencial, 21 May 1967.

11. Eduardo Frei, Primer Mensaje Presidencial, 21 May 1965.

12. The emphasis on children and pregnant women was not an original idea of the Christian Democratic planners. As early as 1939 the public health experts were focusing on those two groups. As a result a law called the Mother and Child Law, *Ley de la madre y del niño,* was designed to improve the medical attention to the mother and the child. In 1953 another law defined the pre- and post-partum benefits available to working women.

13. See Partido Demócrata Cristiano, "Informe Preliminar para un Programa de Gobierno" (Santiago, 1962); R. Valdivieso and B. Juracic, "El Sistema Nacional de Salud en Chile," *Boletín de la Oficina Sanitaria Panaméricana* 68, no. 6 (1970); see also Eduardo Frei, Sexto Mensaje Presidencial, 21 May 1970.

14. Fernando Rodríguez, "Estructuras y características del sector salud," in *Salud pública y bienestar social,* ed. Mario Livingstone and Dagmar Raczynski (Santiago: CEPLAN, Universidad Católica de Chile, 1976), 81.

15. Prat Report, p. viii.

16. The total SNS budget increased from $592 million pesos in 1964 to $902 million pesos in 1967. These figures are estimated in real pesos. Eduardo Frei, Cuarto Mensaje Presidencial, 21 May 1968. For an analysis of the program, see Emanuel De Kadt, Mario Livingstone, and Dagmar Raczynski, "Políticas y programs de salud, 1964–1973," in *Salud pública y bienestar social,* ed. Mario Livingstone and Dagmar Raczynski (Santiago: CEPLAN, Universidad Católica de Chile, 1976), 111–48.

17. Adela Lagarreta, "Factores condicionantes de la mortalidad en la niñez," in *Salud pública y bienestar social,* ed. Mario Livingstone and Dagmar Raczynski (Santiago: CEPLAN, Universidad Católica de Chile, 1976), 219–30; Fernando Monckeberg et al., "Estudio del estado nutritivo y de las condiciones de vida en la provincia de Curicó," *Revista Chilena de Pediatría* 38 (1968) and "Malnutrition and Mental Development in Pre-School Children," *American Journal of Clinical Nutrition* 25 (1972); G. Solimano and F. Monckeberg, "Desigualdades alimentarias y estado de salud de la población," in *Salud pública y bienestar social,* ed. Mario Livingstone and Dagmar Raczynski (Santiago: CEPLAN, Universidad Católica de Chile, 1976), 239–49.

18. Curative services were limited to pulmonary, cardiovascular, and neurological diseases.

19. Raúl Gútierrez, "Acceso a los beneficios de la medicina socializada," in *Salud pública y bienestar social,* ed. CEPLAN (Santiago: Universidad Católica de Chile, 1976), 92.

20. Ramón Valdivieso, Minister of Public Health, *El Mercurio,* 4 July 1965, p. 39. Also *El Mercurio,* 5 October 1965, p. 3.

21. See, for instance, the articles written by Dr. Benjamin Vial, Professor of Public Health, University of Chile, and one of the most respected public health specialists, *El Mercurio,* 20 July 1965, p. 3, and 25 July 1965, p. 3.

22. *El Mercurio,* 5 November 1965, p. 1.

23. Law 16781; also G. Cáceres and R. Aguirra, *Analisis crítico del seguro social de medicina curativa, Ley 16781* (Santiago, Editorial Encina, 1971).

24. Minister Valdivieso argued that about 25 percent of the services provided by the SNS were received by this group and their families.

25. For a discussion on the salaries received by the physicians, see speech by Minister Valdivieso, *El Mercurio,* 5 May 1967, p. 24.

26. Colegio Médico de Chile, "Problemas y soluciones de la salud en Chile," informe del Colegio Médico de Chile Santiago, 1974.

27. Gútierrez, "Acceso a los beneficios," 102.

28. Loveman, *Struggle in the Countryside,* 247–51.

29. Letter from peasants in Pullally to the Director of the Labor Department, 12 November 1966, quoted in Loveman, *Struggle in the Countryside,* 251.

30. Miranda, "El sector agrícola," 15.

31. Oficio 4205, 26 August 1963, quoted in Loveman, *Struggle in the Countryside,* 231.

32. *El Mercurio,* 1 October 1966, p. 31.

33. Patricio Novoa, Anteproyecto de la reforma de la seguridad social (mimeo).

34. Alvaro Covarrubias, interview, Santiago, 1982.

35. For an account of Thayer's problem, see Alan Angell, *Politics and the Labour Movement in Chile.*

36. *El Mercurio,* 11 December 1967, p. 3.

37. Alvaro Covarrubias, interview, Santiago, 1982.

38. *El Mercurio,* 2 September 1968, p. 23.

39. Central Unica de Trabajadores, Posición de la Cut frente a la reforma previsional.

40. Ibid.

41. Ibid.

42. The bill was introduced by Senator Jaramillo from the Liberal Party.

43. Eduardo Frei, Primer Mensaje Presidencial, 21 May 1965.

Notes to Chapter 6

1. In order to keep a consistent analytical focus the impact of U.S. policies on this process will not receive as much attention as it deserves.

2. Allende himself was proud of these qualities. A rather fateful reference to his fame as a great compromiser was made by the President in a Cabinet meeting on 2 July 1973. in the midst of the political and economic crisis, when he said: *"veré si mi muñeca me acompaña una vez mas"* (I shall see if my ability to maneuver is still with me), quoted in Sergio Bitar, *Transición, Socialismo y Democracia: La experiencia chilena* (México: Siglo XXI Editores, 1979).

3. For an analysis of the Convention, see Jobet, *El Partido Socialista,* vol. 1.

4. Ibid., 130.

5. Electoral data obtained from James W. Protho and Patricio E. Chaparro, "Public Opinion and the Movement of Chilean Government to the

Left," in *Chile: Politics and Society*, ed. Arturo Valenzuela and J. Samuel Valenzuela (New Jersey: Transaction Books, 1976), 91.

6. Unidad Popular, *Programa básico del Gobierno de la Unidad Popular* (Santiago, 1970). For a summary and analysis of the policies, see Lois Hecht Oppenheimer, *Politics in Chile: Democracy, Authoritarianism, and the Search for Development*, 2d ed. (Boulder, Colo.: Westview Press, 1999); Verónica Montecinos, *Economists, Politics, and the State: Chile 1958–1994* (Amsterdam: CEDLA, 1998). Other sources are Alberto Cárdemil Herrera, *El camino de la utopía: Alessandri, Frei, Allende, pensamiento y obra* (Santiago: Editorial Andrés Bello, 1997), and Manuel Garretón and Tomás Moulián, *La Unidad Popular y el conflicto político en Chile* (Santiago: Ediciones Minga, 1983).

7. Salvador Allende, Mensaje Presidencial, 21 May 1971.

8. Bitar, *Transición, Socialismo y Democracia*, 67.

9. Ibid., 54.

10. Quoted in G. Palma and A. Zammit, *La Via Chilena al Socialismo* (México: Siglo XXI, 1973), 37. For a similar explanation of the Chilean Road, see Salvador Allende, Discurso Inaugural, 5 November 1970, in Salvador Allende, *Historia de una ilusión* (Santiago: La Señal, 1973), 11–23.

11. Allende's thoughts on the social property area are clearly stated in Regis Debray, *Conversaciones con Allende* (Mexico: Siglo XXI, 1971); for an analysis, see Pio García, "The Social Property Sector, Its Political Impact," in *Chile at the Turning Point: Lessons of the Socialist Years, 1970–1973*, ed. Federico Gil et al. (Philadelphia: Institute for the Study of Human Issues, 1979), 160–89.

12. The enterprises that were socialized during the Allende period were managed by a representative of the Executive and by Workers Councils. See Clarissa Hardy, "Participación obrera y gestion económica," in *El Gobierno de Allende y la lucha por el socialismo en Chile*, ed. Alonso Aguilar et al. (México: Universidad Nacional Autónoma de México, 1976), 225–37.

13. Several authors have analyzed this process; see, for instance, Stallings, *Class Conflict*; Bitar, *Transición, Socialismo y Democracia*; Gonzalo Martner, *El pensamiento económico del gobierno de Allende* (Santiago: Editorial Universitaria, 1971); Pedro Vuskovic, "La experiencia chilena: Problemas económicos," in *Transición al socialismo y la experiencia chilena*, ed. Lelio Basso et al. (Santiago: Rodolfo Alonso Editores, 1972); and Alejandro Foxley, *Política fiscal como instrumento redistributivo: La experiencia chilena* (Santiago: CEPLAN, Universidad Católica de Chile, 1977).

14. For an analysis, see Ian Roxborough et al., *Chile: The State and the Revolution* (New York: Holmes and Meier), 71–103.

15. Bitar, *Transición, Socialismo y Democracia*, 85.

16. Paul Sigmund, *The Overthrow of Allende and the Politics of Chile* (Pittsburgh: University of Pittsburgh Press, 1979), 234, 281.

17. For an analysis of these divergences, see Hugo Zemelman, "The Political Problems of Transition," and Jorge Tapia, "The Viability and Failure of the Chilean Road to Socialism," both in *Chile at the Turning Point: Lessons of the Socialist Years, 1970–1973*, ed. Federico Gil et al. (Philadelphia: Institute for the Study of Human Issues, 1979). For a study of the extent to which the actions and ideas of Allende and the communists differed from those of the official line of the Socialist Party, see Carlos Altamirano et al., *El proceso chileno* (Buenos Aires: Quatro Editores, 1974), especially the articles by Allende and by Altamirano. For a chronology of the conflict with the Christian Democratic Party, see Patricio Dooner, *Crónica de una democracia cansada: El partido Demócrata Cristiano durante el gobierno de Allende* (Santiago: Instituto de Estudios Humanisticos, 1985).

18. Loveman, *Chile,* 338.

19. Robert Moss, *Chile's Marxist Experiment* (Newton Abbot David and Charles, 1973), 61–65; Stefan de Vilder, *Allende's Chile* (London: Cambridge University Press, 1974), 146.

20. Moss, *Chile's Marxist Experiment,* 54 and 76.

21. Valenzuela, *Breakdown of Democratic Regimes,* 73.

22. Several authors have analyzed this issue; see Liliana de Riz, *Sociedad y política en Chile (De Portales a Pinochet)* (México: Universidad Nacional Autónoma de México, 1979), ch. 5; Armando Mattelart, *La burguesía en la escuela de Lenin: El gremialismo y la linea de masas de la burguesía chilena,* Boletín No. 4 (Lima: Documentación política económica y educatival, 1974); Sigmund, *Overthrow of Allende.*

23. Quoted in Mattelart, *La burguesía,* 3.

24. Several documents and reports deal with this issue. See, for instance, U.S. Congress, Senate, Select Committee on Intelligence Activities, *Covert Actions in Chile, 1963–1973,* Staff Report, 94th Congress, 1st session; U.S. Congress, *Multinational Corporations and United States Foreign Policy: Hearings 93rd Congress,* 1st session, 20 March–2 April 1973; U.S. Congress, Senate, Select Committee on Intelligence Activities, *Alleged Assassination Plots Involving Foreign Leader: Interim Report 1975.*

25. Sigmund, *Overthrow of Allende,* 156.

26. Nathaniel Davis, *The Last Two Years of Salvador Allende* (Ithaca, N.Y.: Cornell University Press, 1985), 308.

27. Oficina de Planificación Nacional, 1971–1976, Santiago, 1971.

28. Law 17418 dealt with an improvement of the welfare system, while Law 17595 produced an expansion of the population covered.

29. Francisco Zapata, *Las relaciones entre el movimiento obrero y el gobierno de Salvador Allende* (México: Colección de Estudios Sociológicos, El Colegio de México, 1974).

30. Romero, "La seguridad social en Chile."

31. Cited by Ivan Ljubetic Vargas, *Historia de la asociación de pensionados de Chile (1963–1973)*, vol. 2 (Santiago: Impresión y Diagramación Diamopij, 1999), 218.

32. Ibid., 228.

33. Ibid., 204.

34. *Los mil dias de Allende,* ed. Miguel González Pino and Arturo Fontaine Talavera (Santiago, Centro de Estudios Públicos, 1997), 42–43.

35. Jorge Barría, "Organización y políticas laborales en la Gran Minería del Cobre," in *El cobre en el desarrollo nacional,* ed. R. Ffrench Davis and E. Tironi (Santiago: CEPLAN 1974), 198.

36. Salvador Allende, "El niño, único privilegiado," in *Salvador Allende: Obras escogidas (1970–1973),* ed. Patricio Quiroga (Santiago: Editorial Crítica, 1989), 245.

37. Convenio SNS-SERMENA, Santiago, 1971.

38. *El Mercurio,* 11 September 1968, p. 36.

39. "Enunciados básicos del Gobierno de Chile para la IIIa Reunión de Ministros de Salud," Ministerio de Salud Pública, October 1972, p. 1, quoted in De Kadt, Livingstone, and Raczynski, "Políticas y programs," 121.

40. *El Mercurio,* 5 March 1968, p. 3.

41. Interview with Luis Orlandini, former chief lawyer of the Superintendencia of Social Security and professor of social security and labor law.

42. *Los mil dias de Allende,* 543.

43. De Kadt, Livingston, and Raczynski, "Políticas y programas," 129.

44. Prat Report, vol. 1, pp. xii–xiv.

45. Vargas, *Historia de la asociación de pensionados,* vol. 1, p. 59 and vol. 2, pp. 52–53. My own research also shows that the retirees from the Blue-Collar Workers Fund could barely buy food for part of the month. They had to either live with a family member or depend on the kindness of strangers to survive.

46. Briones et al., "Antecedentes," and Romero, "La seguridad social," 57.

47. Interview with Alvaro Cobarrubias.

48. Mesa-Lago, *Social Security in Latin America.*

49. Quoted in Tapia, "Viability and Failure," 297.

50. References to this flexibility can be found in several of Allende speeches. See for instance his inaugural speech on 5 November 1970.

51. Peter Winn, *Weavers of Revolution: The Yarur Workers and Chile's Road to Socialism* (New York: Oxford University Press, 1986), 7.

52. *El Mercurio Electrónico,* 9 September 2000, at the website elmercu rio.cl.

53. Nicola Miller, *Soviet Relations with Latin America 1959–1987* (Cambridge: Cambridge University Press, 1989), 144–47.

54. *New York Times,* 12 December 1998, pp. A1, A8. See also *New York Times,* 13 September 1998, "All the President Had to Do Was Ask; the C.I.A. Took Aim at Allende."

55. Interview, Mexico City, August 1982. Isla Dawson, an isolated naval base located near the Straight of Magellan, was used as a concentration camp for political prisoners. The most vivid description of life in the island is found in Sergio Bitar, *Isla 10* (Santiago: Editorial Pehuén,1987). Bitar also went voluntarily to the ministry thinking that it was a mistake and that if one had done nothing wrong, there was nothing to fear. See also Fernando Alegría, *Allende: Mi vecino el Presidente* (Santiago: Editorial Planeta, 1989), 280–83.

56. Ibid.

57. Ibid., 9. A malón is a type of violent party typical of the Araucanos.

Notes to Chapter 7

1. See *Algunos fundamentos de la intervención militar en Chile, Septiembre 1973* (Santiago: Editora Nacional Gabriela Mistral, 1974), 13–19.

2. For analysis of the role of the military during this period and the nature of the divisions within the Armed Forces, see Frederick Nunn, *The Military in Chilean History, Essays on Civil-Military Relations, 1810–1973* (Albuquerque: University of New Mexico Press, 1976); Albert Michaels, *Background to a Coup: Civil-Military Relations in Twentieth-Century Chile and the Overthrow of Salvador Allende,* Special Studies Series, Council on International Studies (Buffalo: State University of New York at Buffalo, 1975); Alain Joxe, *Las Fuerzas Armadas en el sistema político chileno* (Santiago: Editorial Universitaria, 1970). For a personal account, see Carlos Prats, *Una vida por la legalidad* (Mexico: Fondo de Cultura Económico, 1976), and Genaro Arriagada, *Pinochet: The Politics of Power* (Boston: Unwyn-Hyman, 1988).

3. Prats, *Una vida,* 79.

4. Jon Lee Anderson, "The Dictator," *The New Yorker,* 19 October 1999.

5. Raquel Correa and Elisabeth Subercaseaux, *Ego Sum* (Santiago: Editorial Planeta, Santiago, 1996), 11.

6. María Dolores Souza and German Silva, *Auge y Ocaso de Augusto Pinochet: Psicohistoria de un liderazgo* (Santiago: Ediciones del Ornitorrinco, 1988), 18.

7. Correa and Subercaseaux, *Ego Sum,* 53–54.

8. Souza and Silva, *Auge y Ocaso de Augusto Pinochet,* 74–75.

9. Interview with Elinor Comandari Kaiser, *Revista Cosas,* 14 September 1993.

10. Interview, *El Mercurio,* 28 December 1986.

11. Souza and Silva, *Auge y Ocaso de Augusto Pinochet,* 27. For a view that stresses Pinochet's power-driven personality, see Alfredo Jocelyn-Holt Letelier, *El Chile perplejo: Del avanzar sin transar al transar sin parar* (Santiago: Editorial Planeta, 1998).

12. Interview with Sergio Villalobos, *La Nación,* 18 January 1998. Villalobos is a well-known Chilean historian.

13. *Mitología militar chilena: Surrealismo desde el superego* (Minneapolis: Institute for the Study of Ideologies and Literature, 1989); Dauno Totoro, *La cofradía blindada Chile civil y Chile militar: Trauma y conflicto* (Santiago: Editorial Planeta, 1998).

14. Sergio Marras, *Palabra de Soldado* (Santiago: Ediciones del Ornitorrinco, 1989), 128–29.

15. Estado Mayor del Ejército, *Historia de Ejército de Chile* (Santiago: 1985), vol. 9, p. 329; quoted in Totoro, *La cofradia blindada,* 25. This is the official text used by the military schools.

16. Coronel Carlos Castro, quoted in Totoro, *La cofradia blindada,* 25.

17. Florencio Infante Diaz, *La Segunda,* 6 June 1997.

18. Brian Loveman, *The Constitution of Tyranny: Regimes of Exception in Spanish America* (Pittsburgh: University of Pittsburgh Press, 1993), 403.

19. See Brian Loveman and Thomas Davies, Jr., eds., *The Politics of Antipolitics: The Military in Latin America,* 3d ed. (Wilmington, Del.: Scholarly Resources, 1997), and Brian Loveman, *For la Patria: Politics and the Armed Forces in Latin America* (Wilmington, Del.: Scholarly Resources, 1999).

20. Department of State, Briefing Memorandum, secret, from Jack Kubisch to the Secretary of State, available at www.seas.gwu.edu/nsarchive/ NSAEBB8/ch10–02.

21. For a detailed analysis of the human rights abuses, see *Report of the Chilean National Commission on Truth and Reconciliation,* trans. Philip E. Berryman, 2 vols. (Notre Dame, Ind.: University of Notre Dame Press, 1993).

22. See, for instance, Bando No. 5, 11 September 1973, and Decreto-Ley No. 1, Junta Militar de Gobierno, 11 September 1973.

23. Declaración de Principios del Gobierno de Chile, Santiago, 1974.

24. Pamela Constable and Arturo Valenzuela, *A Nation of Enemies: Chile under Pinochet* (New York: W.W. Norton, 1993), 91. Constable and Valenzuela's book contains the most vivid account of the Pinochet regime and the actions, goals, and intentions of Pinochet's police state.

25. Ibid., 99.

26. Pamela Lowden, *Moral Opposition to Authoritarian Rule in Chile: 1973–1990* (New York: St. Martin's Press, 1996).

27. See, for instance, Cardinal Silva's 1982 Working Paper entitled "Solidarity" in which he criticized not only the repressive policies and system, but the economic policies that had led to a concentration of wealth, individualism, etc.

28. See, for instance, Hernán Montealegre's poem "Passion for Chile" (manuscript, no date). Montealegre led the Viacaría's legal office and was detained several times by the police.

29. Gustavo Leigh, in a speech, 21 March 1978. The occasion for the speech was the celebration of the anniversary of the establishment of the Air Force. General Leigh used the occasion to delineate the nature of the new institutionality envisioned by him and his supporters.

30. Sergio de Castro, in a speech before the Sesion Inaugural Comité Interempresarial Chile-Japón, 8 September 1980.

31. For an analysis, see Edgardo Boeninger, *Democracia en Chile: Lecciones para la gobernabilidad* (Santiago: Editorial Andrés Bello, 1997), 267–76, and Borzutzky, "Chilean Politics and Social Security Polices."

32. The following is the text of the statement that appeared in the ballot. "In the face of the international aggression unleashed against our country, I support President Pinochet in his defense of the dignity of Chile, and I reaffirm the legitimacy of the government of the republic as sovereign head of the process of institutionalization of the country." Under the text appeared the word "yes," followed by a Chilean flag, while the word "no" was accompanied by a black box.

33. *Latin American Political Report* 12, no. 29, 28 July 1978, p.226.

34. Manuel Garretón, "La institucionalización política del régimen militar chileno: 1973–1981," *Mensaje,* no. 310, (July 1982): 329–33.

35. Sergio Fernández, *Mi lucha por la democracia* (Santiago: Editorial Los Andes, 1994), 146–51; Boeninger, *Democracia en Chile,* 279.

36. Interview with former minister Madariaga, August 1986.

37. Articles 8, 16 No. 6, and 82 Nos. 7, 8, and 90–96.

38. Declaration of Principles of the Chilean Government, p. 29.

39. Ibid., 30.

40. Interview with former minister Madariaga, August 1986. The words are attributed to Jorge Guzmán.

41. Sergio de Castro, in a speech, "El estado de las finanzas públicas," *El Mercurio,* 8 October 1980, p. 1.

42. Sergio de Castro, in a speech before the Sesion Inaugural Comité Interempresarial Chile-Japón, 8 September 1980.

43. José Piñera, in a speech, 7 November 1979.

44. Jorge Cahuas, "Exposición sobre el Estado de la Hacienda Pública," Ministerio de Hacienda, Santiago, October 1974.

45. T. Moulián and P. Vergara, "Política económica y proceso de hegemonía," in *Chile: Liberalismo económico y dictadura política,* ed. Sergio Bitar (Lima: Instituto de Estudios Peruanos, 1980); Manuel Garretón, "Institucionalización y oposición en el régimen autoritario chileno," Paper No. 59 (Washington, D.C.: Woodrow Wilson Center).

46. For an example of that kind of presentation, see Jorge Cahuas and Sergio de la Cuadra, "La política económica de apertura al exterior en Chile," *Cuadernos de Economía* 54–55 (December 1981): 195–231. Both Cahuas and de la Cuadra had been Ministers of Finance during the present regime.

47. For an excellent analysis of the origin of the Chicago Boys and their history, see Juan Gabriel Valdés, *La escuela de Chicago: Operación Chile* (Buenos Aires: Grupo Editorial Zeta, 1989); see also Pilar Vergara, "Las Transformaciones de las funciones económicas del Estado en Chile bajo el régimen militar," *Coleccion Estudios CIEPLAN,* no. 5 (July 1981).

48. U.S. Congress, *Covert Actions in Chile*; Arturo Fontaine, *Los economistas y el Presidente Pinochet* (Santiago: Editorial Zig-Zag, 1988).

49. W. J. Samuels, "Further Limits to the Chicago Doctrine," quoted in Valdés, *La escuela de Chicago,* 102.

50. Ibid., 101.

51. Although some analysts have correctly called this model neo-conservative, the majority has called it neo-liberal. See Alejandro Foxley, *Latin American Experiments with Neo-Conservative Economics* (Berkeley: University of California Press, 1983). On the importance of Hayek in Chile, see Alejandro Foxley, "Perspectivas económicas," *Mensaje,* no. 301 (August 1981): 411–15; R.O.W., "Chicago en Santiago: El poder invisible," *Mensaje,* no. 301 (August 1981): 416–19; J. J. Brunner and E. García, "Chile: Un nuevo paisaje cultural," *Mensaje,* no. 302 (September 1981): 487–94; R. Cristi and C. Ruiz, "Hacia una nueva moral de mercado?" *Mensaje,* no. 299 (June 1981): 241–45. The importance and influence of Hayek was reflected in his participation in a conference in Santiago in April 1981 entitled "Fundamentos de un sistema social libre."

52. Brunner and García, "Chile: Un nuevo paisaje cultural," 490.

53. The former Ministers of Economy Pablo Barahona, Fernando Leniz, and Alvaro Bardón, the former Minister of Labor and Mines José Piñera, and the former Minister of Finance Rolf Luders were some of the most important figures in their group.

54. Jorge Cahuas, "Estado de la Hacienda Pública, 1975," November 1975, p. 5.

55. For an explanation, see Sergio de Castro, speech before the Asociación Latinoamericana de Instituciones de Desarrollo, 29 March 1977, published in *Chilean Economic Policy*, ed. Juan C. Méndez (Santiago, 1978), 233–42. The government continued to intervene in some important areas such as forestry, sugar beets, selected industries, and traditional agriculture.

56. Vergara, "Las Transformaciones," 128–33; H. Cortés and L. Sjaastad argue that in the decentralized administration the reductions were even larger, reaching 10 percent per year. See their "Protección y empleo," *Cuadernos de Economía*, nos. 54–55 (August-December 1981): 384. See also Foxley, *Latin American Experiments*, 40.

57. *The Economist*, 2 February 1980. For an analysis of those policies, see A. Bardón and F. Bacigalupo, "Algunos puntos referentes al manejo monetario en Chile," paper presented to the Twenty-second Meeting of Governors of Latin American Central Banks, Buenos Aires, September 1980.

58. The government policies have been explained by Sergio de la Cuadra, "Apertura al mercado financiero de capitales," paper presented in the School of Economics, Universidad Católica de Chile, 2 April 1980, and Cahuas and de la Cuadra, "La política económica." For a critique, see J. Herrera and J. Morales, "La inversión financiera externa: El caso de Chile, 1974–1978," *Estudios CIEPLAN*, no. 35 (July 1979): 103–150.

59. Augusto Pinochet, speech, 28 June 1976, published in *Chilean Economic Policy*, ed. Juan C. Méndez (Santiago, 1978), 194.

60. See, for instance, Jorge Cahuas, "Estado de la Hacienda Pública, 1975."

61. Karl Polanyi, *The Great Transformation: The Political and Economic Origin of Our Times* (Boston: Beacon Press, 1944).

62. Cristina Hurtado-Beca, "Chile 1973–1981: Desarticulación y reestructuración autoritaria del movimiento sindical," *Boletín de Estudios Latinoamericanos y del Caribe*, no. 31 (December 1981).

63. See D. L. 2345, 2346, and 2347.

64. See D. L. 2657.

65. José Piñera, speech at the Segundo Simposio Latinoamericano y Europeo de Cooperación Económico, August 1979.

66. After creating the Plan Laboral and enacting the social security reform, Minister Piñera was moved to the Ministry of Mines to reform the mining property system.

67. The average number of hours worked each week had increased from 45.2 in 1970 to 48.8 in 1980. Laws 18018, 18019, 18020, 18032, and 18044.

68. D. L. 3648, 10 May 1981.

69. See, for instance, interview with Juan Díaz Salas, Professor of Labor Law, *La Tercera de la Hora,* 30 March 1981, p. 9.

70. Data for 1970–1980, CEPAL, *Chile: Principales Indicadores Económicos* (1981; 1982).

71. Foxley, *Latin American Experiments,* 32; Anibal Pinto arrives at a similar conclusion when he argues that the average growth rate for those same years was 1.2 percent, in "Chile: El modelo ortoxo y el desarrollo nacional," *Trimestre Económico* 47, no. 192 (October-December 1980): 855; Thomas Edwards, *Economic Development and Reform in Chile, Progress under Frei, 1964–1970,* Latin American Studies Center, March 1972, Michigan State University, 17.

72. Banco Central de Chile, *Boletín Mensual,* No. 657 (November 1982): 2562.

73. Vergara, "Las Transformaciones," 132.

74. Ffrench-Davis, *Políticas económicas,* 19.

75. Foxley, *Latin American Experiments,* 41–42.

76. Fernando Dahse, *El mapa de la extrema riqueza: Los grupos económicos y el proceso de concentración de capitales* (Santiago: Editorial Aconcagua, 1979), 22 and 176–78.

77. Roberto Zahler, "Repercusiones monetarias y reales de la apertura financiera al exterior," *Revista de la Cepal* (April 1980): 147.

78. Dahse, *El mapa de la extrema riqueza,* 188–93.

79. Ibid., 194–200.

80. Vicent Parkin, "Economic Liberalism in Chile, 1973–1982: Model for Growth and Development or Recipe for Stagnation and Impoverishment?" *Cambridge Journal of Economics* 7 (1983): 101–24. For an official statement on the nature of the "adjustment mechanisms," see Rolf Luders, *Towards Economic Recovery in Chile: A Report on the Economy and Public Finances of Chile by the Minister of Finance and Economy* (Santiago: Rolf Luders, Imprenta Ine., December 1982).

81. Banco Central de Chile, *Indicadores Económicos y sociales, 1960–1982,* Santiago, April 1982, p. 24.

82. *Latin American Weekly Review* (LAWR), 11 September 1983.

83. Banco Central de Chile, *Indicadores Económicos y sociales, 1960–1982,* p. 24.

84. Eduardo Silva, "The Political Economy of Chile's Regime Transition," in *The Struggle for Democracy in Chile,* rev. ed., ed. Paul W. Drake and Ivan Jaksic (Lincoln, Neb.: University of Nebraska Press, 1995), 110.

85. S. Edwards and A. Edwards, *Monetarism and Liberalization: The Chilean Experiment* (Cambridge: Balinger, 1986), 80.

86. Silva, "Political Economy," 110, 112.

87. Ibid., 116.

88. Manuel Délano and Hugo Translaviña, *La herencia de los Chicago Boys* (Santiago: Ediciones del Ornitorrinco, 1989), 127.

89. The protest movement has been analyzed by Gonzalo de la Masa and Mario Garcés, *La explosión de las mayorías, protesta nacional 1983–1984* (Santiago: Editorial ECO, 1985); Rodrigo Baño, *Movimiento popular y política de partido en la coyontura en 1983–1984* (Santiago: FLACSO, 1985); Cathy Schneider "Mobilization at the Grasroots: Shantytowns and Resistance in Authoritarian Chile," *Latin American Perspectives* 18, no. 1 (Winter 1991); Manuel Antonio Garretón, "Popular Mobilization and the Military Regime: The Complexities of the Indivisible Transition," in *Power and Popular Protest*, ed. Susan Eckstein (Berkeley: University of California Press, 1989); Barbara Stallings, "Political Economy of Democratic Transition: Chile in the 1980's," in *Debt and Democracy in Latin America*, ed. Barbara Stallings and Robert Kaufman (Boulder, Colo.: Westview Press, 1989); Kenneth W. Roberts, *Deepening Democracy? The Modern Left and Social Movements in Chile and Peru* (Stanford, Calif.: Stanford University Press, 1998).

90. Fernández, *Mi lucha*, 204.

91. See Silvia Borzutzky, "The Pinochet Regime: Crisis and Consolidation," in *Authoritarians and Democrats: Regime Transition in Latin America*, ed. James M. Malloy and Mitchell Seligson (Pittsburgh: University of Pittsburgh Press, 1987).

92. Boeninger, *Democracia en Chile*, 307–12.

93. Fernández, *Mi lucha*, 207.

94. Ibid., 198.

95. Boeninger, *Democracia en Chile*, 330.

96. The process of socialist renovation has been analyzed by Ignacio Walker, *Socialismo y Democracia: Chile y Europa en perspectiva comparada* (Santiago: CIEPLAN-Hachete, 1990); Carlos Bascuñan Edwards, *La izquierda sin Allende* (Santiago: Planeta, espejo de Chile, 1990); Lois Hecht Oppenheimer, "Democracy and Social Transformation in Chile: The Debate within the Left," *Latin American Perspectives* 12, no. 3 (Summer 1985); Ricardo Lagos, *Hacia la democracia: Los Socialistas en el Chile de hoy* (Santiago: Ediciones Documentas, 1987); Alexis Guardia, *Chile, pais centaúro: perfil del socialismo renovado* (Santiago: Ediciones BAT, 1990); Jorge Arrate, *La fuerza demócratica en la idea socialista* (Barcelona: Ediciones Documentas, 1985); Silvia Borzutzky and Aldo Vacs, "The Impact of the Collapse of Communism and the Cuban Crisis on the South American Left," in *Cuba after the Cold War*, ed. Carmelo Mesa-Lago (Pittsburgh: University of Pittsburgh Press, 1994).

97. Manuel A. Garretón, "The Political Opposition and the Party System under the Military Regime," in *The Struggle for Democracy in Chile*, rev. ed., ed. Paul W. Drake and Ivan Jaksic (Lincoln, Neb.: University of Nebraska Press, 1995), 236.

98. Boeninger, *Democracia en Chile*, 337.

99. Luis Corbalán, "Rebellion popular: Camino de nuestro partido," mimeo (Santiago, 1982).

100. For an analysis, see Boris Yopo, "Las relaciones internacionales del Partido Comunista de Chile," and Osvaldo Puccio, "La política del Partido Comunista de Chile: Elementos para su evolución y permanencia en el último período," in *El Partido Comunista en Chile*, ed. Augusto Varas (Santiago: CESOC-LACSO, 1988); Carmelo Furci, *The Chilean Communist Party and the Road to Socialism* (London: Zed Press, 1984); Hernan Vidal, *FPMR: El tabú del conflicto armado en Chile* (Santiago: Mosquito Editores, 1995). For a comparative analysis with other South American Communist parties, see Borzutzky and Vacs, "Impact of the Collapse of Communism."

101. Fernández, *Mi lucha*, 262, 272.

102. Enrique Cañas Kirby, *Proceso político en Chile: 1973–1990* (Santiago: Editorial Andrés Bello, 1997), 251.

103. Ibid., 255.

104. For interviews with leading members of the right, see Maria Luz Benavente, *La nueva derecha* (Santiago: Teorema Gráfica Integral, 1994); see also Andrés Allamand, *La centro-derecha del futuro* (Santiago: Editorial Los Andes, 1993).

105. Manuel A. Garretón, *Las condiciones sociopoliticas de la inauguaración democrática en Chile*, Hellen Kellogg Institute for International Studies, Working paper #142, June 1990, University of Notre Dame.

106. The constitutional reforms are analyzed by Francisco Cumplido et al., *La reforma constitucional* (Santiago: CESOC, 1989).

107. Fernández, *Mi lucha*, 311.

108. The role of Minister Cáceres and other key figures in the process has been analyzed by Ascenio Cavallo, *Los hombres de la transición* (Santiago: Editorial Andrés Bello, 1992). See also Luciano Vasquez Murúaga, *Transición a la chilena* (Santiago, Editorial Barcelona, 1990).

109. Karen L. Remmer, *The Chilean Military under Authoritarian Rule, 1973–1987*, Occasional Paper Series N1, Latin American Institute, 1 March 1988, University of New Mexico, 34.

110. Apuntes CIEPLAN, N1 16, Balance Económico y Social del Regimen Militar, December 1988.

111. Analisis Económico, Informe bimestral, November-December 1991, p. 6.

Notes to Chapter 8

1. Sistema de seguridad social, Observaciones de la Junta de Gobierno, confidential document.

2. Esquema preliminar integrado sobre la reforma de la seguridad social, Ministerio del Trabajo, Santiago, August 1974, p. 3.

3. Ibid., 2.

4. For a detailed analysis of this process, see Borzutzky, "Chilean Politics and Social Security Politics."

5. I had the opportunity to read these letters while doing research in 1982.

6. For a complete summary of those laws, see José Camurúaga, "Modificaciones legales del sexenio 1973–1979 en la seguridad social," unpublished manuscript; see also *Hoy,* 16–22 August 1978, p. 6.

7. For an analysis, see Superintendencia de Seguridad Social, "Significado e importancia del D.L. 2448" (mimeo).

8. *El Cronista,* 18 December 1978, p. 5.

9. Interview with Luís Larraín, former Superintendent of Social Security and member of the Commission.

10. ODEPLAN, "Plan de fomento del empleo y eficiencia en la acción social" (Santiago: 1979).

11. José Piñera, "La reforma previsional," Informe económico 1976–1977, Colocadora Nacional de Valores, October 1979, pp. 39–45.

12. Ibid., 39 and 46.

13. *La Nación,* 20 June 1981.

14. José Pablo Arellano, "Elementos para el análisis de la reforma previsional chilena," *Colección Estudios CIEPLAN,* no. 6 (December 1981): 11.

15. Carmelo Mesa-Lago, *La reforma de la seguridad social y las pensiones en América Latina: Importancia y evaluación de las alternativas de privatización* (Santiago: United Nations, Comisión Económica para América Latina y el Caribe, 1994), 18.

16. Arellano, "Elementos para el analisís," 15. The elimination of the *perseguidoras* does not have a direct influence on the amount of the employer contributions since they were financed directly from General Revenues. See Martín Cóstabal, "Efectos económicos de la reforma previsional," *Gestión* 6, no. 64 (1981): x.

17. Ibid.

18. Exposición del Ministro del Trabajo, José Piñera, "Seminario sobre Reforma Previsional y evaluación del Plan Laboral," Santiago, 29 June 1980, p. 2.

19. Ibid., 6.

20. Cóstabal, "Efectos económicos," 64.

21. For an analysis, see Ernesto Illanes, "Inversión de recursos del sistema de pensiones," *Gestión* 6, no. 63 (1981): 48–52; D.L. 3500, articles 37–45.

22. See "Texto Actualizado de las leyes que rigen la Previsión Social derivada de la Capitalización Individual," published in Superintendencia de Administradoras de Fondos de Pensiones [henceforth SAFP], *Boletín Estadístico* (November 1987).

23. SAFP, *Boletín Estadistico*, no. 12 (1987): 55. According to Minister Kast the speed of change was four times faster than that the one predicted by the government (*El Mercurio*, 19 May 1981, p. 26).

24. Grafimatic reports that the cost of the publicity campaign in the first two months was around U.S.$8 million (*Hoy*, no. 213, 19 August 1981, p. 26).

25. *Hoy*, no. 213, 19 August 1982, p. 26.

26. The remaining three belonged to the Copper Workers Association, the Teachers Association, and to the Chilean Builders Association.

27. Carmelo Mesa-Lago, *El desarrollo de la Seguridad Social en América Latina* (Santiago: United Nations, Estudios e Informes de la Cepal, 1985), 114. SAFP, *Boletín Estadístico Mensual*, no. 74 (December 1987): 17, and no. 148 (December 1998): 57.

28. Piñera, "Seminario sobre Reforma Previsional," 12.

29. *La Segunda*, 10 March 1981, p. 23.

30. Piñera, "Seminario sobre Reforma Previsional," 12.

31. Carmelo Mesa-Lago, "Pension Reform around the World: Comparative Features and Performance of Structural Pension Reforms in Latin America," *Brooklyn Law Review*, no. 64 (Fall 1998): 782.

32. SAFP, *Boletín Estadístico Mensual*, no. 148 (December 1998): 373–74; data for 2000 obtained from Osraldo Macías, Technical Director, SAFP, June 2001.

33. CEPAL, *Balance Preliminar de las Economías de América Látina y del Caribe*, Santiago, December 1998.

34. SAFP, *Boletín Estadístico Mensual*, no. 77 (March 1988): 13, and no. 148 (December 1998): 340.

35. SAFP, *Boletín Estadístico Mensual*, no. 74 (December 87): 42, 43, and 53, and no. 148 (December 1998): 142, 402. Data on the average value of a pension in the old system was not found.

36. Alberto Arenas de Mesa and Verónica Montecinos, "The Privatization of Social Security and Women's Welfare: Gender Effects of the Chilean Reform," unpublished manuscript, University of Pittsburgh 1996, 24.

37. Informe Sernam, *El Mercurio*, 8 June 2001, p. B2.

38. Alberto Arenas de Mesa and Verónica Montecinos, "The Privatization of Social Security and Women's Welfare: Gender Effects of the Chilean Reform," *Latin American Research Review* 34, no. 3 (Fall).

39. SAFP, *Boletín Estadístico Mensual,* no. 73: 5, 6 and 11, and *Boletín Estadístico Mensual,* no. 148 (December 1998): 42–47.

40. SAFP, *Boletín Estadístico Mensual,* no. 148 (December 1998): 28, 32.

41. Mesa-Lago, "Pension Reform around the World," 786.

42. C. Mesa-Lago, "La reforma estructural de pensiones en América Latina: tipología, comprobación de presupuestos y enseñanzas," in *Pensiones en América Latina: Dos décadas de reformas,* ed. Alejandro Bonilla and Alfredo Conte-Grand (Ginebra: Organización Internacional del Trabajo, 1998), 120.

43. Data provided by Osvaldo Macias, Director of Technical Studies, SAFP, June 2001.

44. Centro de Estudios Públicos, "Estudio social y de opinión públic en la población de Santiago, Dic 1986-Enero 1987," Santiago, Documento de Trabajo No. 83, May 1987.

45. A. Iglesias, A. Echeverría, and P. López, "Proyección de los fondos de pensiones," in *Análisis de la Previsión en Chile,* ed. S. Baeza (Santiago: Centro de Estudios Públicos, 1986), 115–17. Data for 2000 obtained from Osraldo Macías, Technical Director, SAFP, June 2001.

46. Ibid., 117–18.

47. SAFP, *Boletín Estadístico Mensual,* no. 148 (December 1998): 405.

48. Alejandro Bonilla, "Informe de Misión Santiago de Chile," Ginebra, OIT, 5–12 October; Carmelo Mesa-Lago, "Review of Chile, SAL III Condition: Pension System," Washington, D.C., World Bank, 1988; Colin Gillion and Alejandro Bonilla, "Analysis of a National Private Pension Scheme: The Case of Chile," *International Labour Review* 131 (1998):2, among others, argue that the pension program has not had the expected impact. For the opposite argument, see Hernan Cheyre, *La previsión en Chile ayer y hoy: Impacto de una reforma* (Santiago: Centro de Estudios Públicos, 1991); Augusto Iglesias and Rodrigo Acuña, *Chile: Experiencia con un regimen de capitalización 1981–1991* (Santiago: CEPAL/PNUD Sistemas de Pensiones en América Latina, 1991).

49. Robert Holzmann, *On Economic Benefits and Fiscal Requirements of Moving from Unfunded to Funded Pensions* (Santiago: United Nations, Economic Commission for Latin America and the Caribbean, 1997), 41, 43, and 46.

50. Alberto Arenas de Mesa, "Learning from the Privatization of the Social Security Pension System in Chile: Macroeconomic Effects, Lessons, and Challenges," doctoral dissertation, University of Pittsburgh, 1997, cited by Mesa-Lago, "Pension Reform around the World," 787.

51. *The Economist*, 3 July 1999, p. 30.

52. Interviews with Professor Patricio Novoa, Ramón Covarrubias, and Luis Orlandini. See also José Pablo Arellano, "Reformas al sistema de seguridad social chileno," *Mensaje*, no. 291 (August 1980): 412–13; for estimates on the deficit, see "Mas eficiencia en la Seguridad Social," *Gestión* 6, no. 64 (1981): 19.

53. José Pablo Arellano, "Evaluación de la reforma previsional," and Juan Alfredo García, "Mercado de renta vitalicia y bono de reconocimiento," in *Analísis de la reforma previsional*, ed. S. Baeza (Santiago: Centro de Estudios Públicos, 1986), 88, 89, and 176.

54. Mesa-Lago, *La Reforma de la seguridad social*, 22.

55. Alberto Arenas de Mesa, "Efectos fiscales del sistema de pensiones en Chile: Proyección del déficit fiscal 1999–2037," presented at the Seminario sobre responsabilidades fiscales en sistemas de pensiones, Santiago, September 1999.

56. *Que Pasa*, 28 August 1999, p. 62.

57. Ibid., 63.

58. Mesa-Lago, *La Reforma de la seguridad social*, 22–23.

59. Ibid.

60. Ibid., 62.

61. Interview with Patricio Mardones, Undersecretary of Labor, Santiago, August 1981.

62. Silvia Borzutzky, "Chile: The Politics of Privatization," in *Do Options Exist: The Reform of the Pension Systems in Latin America*, ed. Maria A Cruz-Saco and Carmelo Mesa-Lago (Pittsburgh: University of Pittsburgh Press, 1999).

63. Piñera, *El cascabel al gato: La batalla por le reforma previsional* (Santiago: Zig Zag, 1991), 14.

64. Ibid., 114.

65. Mesa-Lago, *El desarrollo de la seguridad social*, 127.

66. Patricio Aylwin, Mensaje Presidencial, 1990.

67. M. E. de la Jara, *Que Pasa*, no. 538, 30 July 1981, pp. 19–21; D.L. 2575, 15 May 1979.

68. D.L. 2575, 15 May 1979. The reforms in the health area have been analyzed by Joseph L. Scarpacci, *Primary Medical Care in Chile: Accessibility under Military Rule* (Pittsburgh: University of Pittsburgh Press, 1988); *La salud en Chile: evolución y perspectivas*, ed. Ernesto Miranda (Santiago: Centro de Estudios Públicos, 1994); *Health Services Privatization in Industrial Societies*, ed. Joseph L Scarpacci (New Brunswick, N.J.: Rutgers University Press, 1988); Brian Cartin, "Chile: The Effectiveness of the Reform," in *Do Options Exist? The Reform of Pensions and Health Care Sys-*

tems in Latin América, ed. María A. Cruz Saco and Carmelo Mesa-Lago (Pittsburgh: University of Pittsburgh Press, 1999).

69. Cartin, "Effectiveness of the Reform," 211–12.

70. D.L. 2575, 15 May 1979.

71. Cartin, "Effectiveness of the Reform," 210.

72. Matthew P. Ligozio, "Analysis of Health Care: A Closer Look at Chile," unpublished manuscript, University of Pittsburgh, 1998, 15–16.

73. Ibid., 11.

74. Law Decree 18,933, March 1990.

75. Ligozio, "Analysis of Health Care," 12–14.

76. Interview with Juan Aristía, Director, Superintendencia de Fondos de Pensiones, Santiago, August 1981.

77. Balance Económico Social del Regimen Militar (Apuntes CIEPLAN, no. 76, December 1988), Section II.

78. J. Rodríguez, *Distribución del ingreso y del gasto social en Chile—1983* (Santiago: ILADES, 1985), 103.

79. *La Tercera* en Internet, 30 January 1998, see www.latercera@copesa.cl.

80. Ibid., 1 September 1998.

81. Ibid., 7 May 1998.

82. Ibid., 23 August 1998.

83. Ibid., 7 May 1998.

84. Eugenio Droguet, "Se vislumbra acuerdo para modificar la ley de Isapres," *El Mercurio* Electrónico, 29 May 2000, see www.elmercurio.cl. See also Superintendencia de Institutos de Salud Previsional (SISP), "Annual Statistics," at www.sisp.cl/estd/e-sintes.

85. *La Tercera* en Internet, 19 August 1999.

86. Ibid.

87. Ibid., 23 May 1997.

88. *El Mercurio* Electrónico, 29 May 2000.

89. Interview with Patricio Mardones, Undersecretary of Labor.

Epilogue

1. Pamela Constable and Arturo Valenzuela, "Chile's Return to Democracy," *Foreign Affairs* 68, no. 15: 177.

2. Ibid., 176.

3. *Análisis,* 6 July 1992, pp. 10–14.

4. *Report of the Chilean National Commission on Truth and Reconciliation,* 461.

5. Ibid., 756.

6. Human Rights Watch, Americas (New York: Humans Rights Watch, 1994), p. 1.

7. *Análisis,* 17 February 1992, pp. 17–18.

8. Ibid.

9. *Qué pasa,* no. 1189, January 1994, p. 23.

10. *El Mercurio,* International Edition, 13–19 July 1995, p. 2.

11. This quote is reported for 6 September 1995 at www.clari.news.

12. Elizabeth Lira and Maria Isabel Castillo, *Psicología de la amenza política y del miedo* (Santiago: ILAS, 1991), and "Trauma político y memoria social," *Psicología Política,* no. 6 (1993); Elizabeth Lira et al., "El miedo: un enfoque psicósocial," *Revista Chilena de Psicología* 8, no. 1 (1985–86); Elizabeth Lira, "Las consecuencias de las violaciones de derechos humanos en Chile y la política de derechos humanos del gobierno de la transición: Que ha gando la gente?" paper presented at Seventeenth Congress of LASA, and "Consecuencias psicósociales de la represión politica en Chile," *Revista de Psicología del Salvador* 7, no. 28 (April 1988).

13. Nancy Caro Hollander, *Love in Time of Hate: Liberation Psychology in Latin America* (New Brunswick, N.J.: Rutgers University Press, 1997), 93.

14. *Clari News,* 14 September 1995.

15. For a very insightful analysis of the legacy of the Pinochet regime, see Tomás Moulián, *Chile actual: Anatomía de un mito* (Santiago: LOM Ediciones, 1997).

16. United Nations, Oficina Internacional del Trabajo, *Chile: Crecimiento, empleo y el desafío de la justicia social* (Santiago: OIT, 1998), 19. Henceforth this source will be identified as OIT, 1998.

17. Ibid., 21.

18. Ibid., 28. See also Patricio Aylwin, *Un desafío colectivo* (Santiago: Editorial Planeta, 1988).

19. OIT, 1998, 62.

20. Ibid., 69.

21. According to one study in 1995 only Brazil, Guatemala, Honduras, and Panama exhibit a distribution of income that is worse than Chile's. See José Bengoa, "Distribución de los ingresos," *Temas Sociales,* no. 11 (1996).

22. OIT, 1998, 65. Other studies point to even higher disparities; see, for instance, Mario Marcel and Andrés Solimano, "The Distribution of Income and Economic Adjustment," in *The Chilean Economy: Lessons and Challenges,* ed. Barry Bosworth et al. (Washington, D.C.: Brookings Institution, 1994), 219. These authors report that the income of the highest 20 percent captures 61.5 percent of the income while the lowest 20 percent receives 3.4 percent.

23. Boeninger, *Democracia en Chile*, 483–92.
24. Ibid., 477–83.
25. *Análisis*, 17 August 1992, pp. 27–28.
26. *El Mercurio*, International Edition, 3–9 August 1995, p. 6.
27. Human Rights Watch, *The Limits of Tolerance: Freedom of Expression and the Public Debate in Chile* (New York: Human Rights Watch, 1998), p. ix.
28. Moulián, *Chile actual*, chs. 1–4.
29. Loveman and Lira, *Las suaves cenizas del olvido*, 18.

Index

Acuerdo por el No. *See* No campaign
AD. *See* Democratic Alliance
Administadores de Fondos de
    Pensiones (AFP), 203, 215–28,
    235
Agrarian Reform Law, 80, 84, 102,
    111, 113–14, 128
Agreement for the No. *See* No
    campaign
Aguirre, Cerda Pedro, 27–28, 30–33,
    39
Alessandri, Arturo, 10–14, 16, 20–21,
    27, 43, 47, 73, 78, 80, 83, 122
Alessandri, Jorge, 34, 66, 98, 124, 141,
    147
    administration of, 38, 40, 97–98,
    105
Allende, Salvador, 16, 24, 122, 153,
    155, 174, 183
    administration of, xiii, xiv, 86,
    93–94, 96, 121–22
    changes to political system,
    127–36. *See also* Chile,
    Congress, balance of power
    with Executive
    conflicts within coalition, 129–34
    disintegration of, 135–39,
    148–51, 153–56
    economic program, 124–28
    formation of coalition, 123–24
    health care policies, 143–45

nationalization policy, 132–33
    social security reform, 139–45
    transition to socialism, 126–28.
    See also income redistribution;
    socialism; social property
    area
    —failure of, 128–33, 148–51
    political development of, 123–24
Alliance for Progress, 76
Altamirano, Carlos, 123–24
Alywin, Patricio, 194, 198, 232, 253
    administration of, 236, 243,
    245–47, 249–52
Anaconda, 73, 138
Andean Common Market, 77–78
Anteproyecto del Estatuto Funda-
    mental de Principios y Bases
    del Sistema de Seguridad
    Social, 205–8
Anteproyecto de Reform de la
    Seguridad Social, 112–13, 115
apertura, 178, 184
Armed Forces Fund, 48
Armed Forces Law, 198
Asociación de Empleados Fiscales, 39
Asociación de Empleados Semi-
    fiscales, 39
Association of Retirees, 141, 146

Balmaceda, José Manuel, 2, 46
Beneficiencia Pública, 63

Blue-Collar Workers Fund, 48–49, 53, 56–57, 63, 66, 141, 217, 233, 266n21
Buchi, Hernán, 190–91, 197, 201, 242, 250

Cáceras, Carlos, 199
Caja de Empleados Particulares. *See* White-Collar Workers Fund
Caja de Empleados Públicos. *See* Civil Servants Fund
Caja de los Comerciantes Minoristas. *See* Retailers Fund
Caja de Seguro Obligatorio. *See* Blue-Collar Workers Fund
Cajas. *See* social security system, funds
Cajas de Compensación de Asignación Familiar, 115, 209
callempero, 82
campesinos, 86
Castillo, Velasco Eduardo, 74–75
Catholic Church, 76, 164–65, 192–93, 202
CEFA. *See* Special Committees of Rural Control
Central Bank, 77, 198, 250
Centralized Fund for the Leveling of Family Allowances, 140
Central Unica de Trabajadores de Chile (CUT), 40–41
Central Valley, 2, 3, 73
Chacarillas speech, 166–67
Chicago Boys, 166, 174–76, 182, 189, 210, 214, 225, 232. *See also* "economic team"
Chile
  agrarian reform, 80–81, 86. *See also* Frei, Eduardo, administration of, agrarian policies
  authoritarian government, 153–203. *See also* Pinochet, Augusto, regime of
  capitalism, 166, 172, 215–16. *See also* neoliberalism

civil servants, 46, 103, 105, 108, 113, 181, 230. *See also* social security system, and civil servants
Congress, 9, 11, 13–14, 16–17, 20–23, 30, 43, 47–48, 60, 72–73, 78–81, 83–84, 89–90, 93–94, 98–102, 106, 108, 112–16, 118–20, 145–47, 151, 153, 160, 198–99, 230, 235
  balance of power with Executive, 128, 133–34, 136, 143, 169
  economic crisis, early 1980s, 185–89
  economic development, early twentieth century, 10–11, 19, 27–31
  economic development, nineteenth century, 2–4
  electoral system, 19, 21–23, 42, 84, 127, 136, 242–44, 261n5
  apportionment, 22–23, 72
  labor movement in, 6–10, 16, 19, 33, 36–41, 81, 124, 140, 206, 229
  labor policies, 1, 9–10, 12–13, 36–38, 88–91, 109, 180–83, 252
  unionization, 14–15, 36–37. *See also* unions
  political crisis, 1960s, 72–73
  political crisis under Allende, 127–39, 145–51
  political development, early twentieth century, 10–13, 16–18
  political development, nineteenth century, 2–4
  political party system, xii, 23–26, 28, 38–43, 45, 49, 67–68, 72, 89, 118, 134–35, 153, 160–61, 167, 187–89, 193, 243, 253. *See also* individual names of parties
  political violence in, 130–31, 133, 136–37

rural problem, 74, 93, 95
social crisis, 1960s, 73–74
as socialist state, 121–39, 148–51.
    See also Allende, Salvador,
    administration of; income
    redistribution
social legislation, 14, 18, 106
social narrative of, xiii–xv, 1, 17–18,
    20, 36, 43, 46, 69, 96, 120, 122,
    139, 150–51, 154, 158,
    160–61, 172, 176, 202, 204,
    213, 231, 238, 240, 254, 257n4
tax system, 32, 34–35, 77, 252
transition of democracy, xiii, 153,
    191–202, 241–55
welfare state, 113, 125, 139
Chilean Development Corporation
    (CORFO), 28, 30–31
Chilean Lawyers Association. *See*
    Colegio de Abogados
Chilean Medical Association. *See*
    Colegio Médico de Chile
Chilean Road to Socialism, 125–26,
    146, 148
Chilean Telephone Company, 138
Chilean Workers Confederation (CUT),
    89, 95, 116–18, 139–40
CHILECTRA, 31
Chiribono affair, 90, 92, 95
Chonchol, Jacques, 85–86, 90, 132
Christian Democratic Party (PDC),
    23–24, 28, 41, 68, 71, 91,
    113–14, 116–18, 124, 133–34,
    151, 164, 188, 191, 193–95,
    198, 244, 270n12. *See also*
    Frei, Eduardo, administration of
economic program of, 76–79
failure of, 92–96
philosophy of, 74–76
political reforms of, 80–81
social reforms of, 81–91
Civil Code, 3, 52
Civil Servants Fund, 48–49, 55, 58,
    106–7, 142, 147, 227
clientelism, xi–xii, 25–26, 42, 45, 60,

65–68, 72, 74, 89, 91, 93, 106,
    118–19, 214, 231
CNI. *See* National Information Center
Colegio de Abogados, 135
Colegio Médico de Chile, 105–8,
    143–44, 236–37
Comando de Acción Gremial, 135
Commission on Truth and
    Reconciliation, 246–47
Committee on Social Legislation, 9
Communist Party, 7, 23, 39, 41, 50,
    123, 129–30, 160, 162,
    191–92, 195, 244–45
communitarian state, xii, 71, 75–76,
    79–91, 95–96, 122, 132. *See
    also* Christian Democratic Party;
    Frei, Eduardo, administration of
Compensatory Fund, 100
Concertación de los Partidos por el No.
    See No campaign
Concha, Juan Enrique, 12
Concha, Malaquías, 11
Confederación de Empleados
    Particulares, 39
Confederación Democrática, 134–136
Confederación de Trabajadores de
    Chile (CTCH), 38–39
Confederation of Production and
    Commerce, 189
Consejería de Promoción Popular, 83
Consejo de Estado, 193
Conservative Party, 3, 22–24, 34, 72,
    74, 80
constitutionalists. *See* military, Chile,
    constitutionalists
Constitutional Reform (1970), xii,
    134–35, 141, 143, 149
Constitutional Reform Bill (1964), 98
Contreras, Manuel, 162–63, 248
Copper Agreements, 113–14
copper industry, 73, 77, 80. *See also*
    social security system, and
    copper workers
nationalization of, 124–25, 127–28,
    137–38, 142, 201

CORFO. *See* Chilean Development Corporation
Corporation of Agrarian Reform (CORA), 84, 110
corporatists, 165–66, 206–7, 239
Cóstabal, Martín, 210, 213, 215
Covarrubias, Alvaro, 100
COVEMA, 164
Cruz, Luis, 38
Cruz-Coke, Eduardo, 62
CTCH. *See* Confederación de Trabajadores de Chile
Cuban Revolution, 82–83, 122
CUT. *See* Central Unica de Trabajadores de Chile *or* Chilean Workers Confederation

de Castro, Sergio, 166, 172, 174, 210
Declaración de Principios, 161, 167
Decree Law 520, 131–32
Decree Law 3500, 212, 215–16. *See also* social security reform, 1980
Decree Law 2448, 209–10, 213, 239
Democratic Alliance (AD), 188, 191–92
democratic model (of 1980 Constitution), 169–70
Democratic Party, 11–12, 259n21
Democratic Popular Movement (MDP), 191–92
Díaz, Nicanor, 165–66, 180, 206–7
DINA. *See* National Directorate of Intelligence
Durán, Julio, 135

ECLA. *See* United Nations Economic Committee for Latin America
Economic Active Population (EAP), 51, 66, 140, 217
"economic team," 180–81, 204. *See also* Chicago Boys
1833 Constitution, 2–4
El Mercurio, 84–85, 115, 138
empate social. See "social tie"

espontaneísmo, 130–31
Estado Communitario. See communitarian state
Estatuto de Garantías Constitucionales, 133–34

Family Allowance Funds, 115–16
Federation of Chilean Workers (FOCH), 7–8, 27, 38
Fernández, Sergio, 169–70, 172, 180, 193, 199, 206
Fernández Commission, 193–94
Figueroa, Alex, 237–38
Figueroa, Emilio, 27
First National Health Program, 102–3
FOCH. *See* Federation of Chilean Workers
FONASA. *See* United Health Fund
Fondo Unico de Nivelación de la Asignaciones Familiares, 140
Fondo Unico de Salud. *See* United Health Fund
FPMR. *See* Frente Patriótico Manuel Rodríguez
Free Choice System. *See* Sistema de Libre Elección
Frei, Eduardo, xii, 73–74, 91, 93, 95, 123, 134, 141
  administration of, xiv, 91, 121–22, 127–28, 147, 184, 236, 238, 243, 247, 251–52
  agrarian policies, 80, 84–87, 93, 95, 97, 103–4, 123–33, 136
  economic program, 76–79, 96
  integration of marginals, 81–84, 93, 103–4
  social security reform, 98–100, 148, 209. *See also* social security reform, and Frei administration
  —failure of, 102, 106–9, 114–20
  working class policies, 81, 87–91

Frente Patriótico Manuel Rodríguez
    (FPMR), 195–96
Fresno, Juan Francisco, 192
Friedman, Milton, 176, 179
Fuentealba, Renán, 134

García, Ricardo, 192
González, Cortés Exequiel, 47–48
González, Videla Gabriel, 33, 39
gremios, 135
grupos económicos, 185, 189
Gumicio, Rafael Agustín, 74, 90–91
Guzmán, Jaime, 197

Haberger, Arnold, 174
hacendado. See haciendas
haciendas, 52–54, 73, 82, 84–85
Henríquez, Silva, 165
human rights, xiii, 161–65, 170, 193,
    198, 201, 241, 242, 245–49,
    253–55

Ibañez, Carlos, 38
ILO. *See* International Labor Office
import substitution model, 19, 27–31,
    42, 45, 67, 71, 73, 77, 81, 173,
    179, 184, 200
income redistribution, 126–29, 154
INDAP. *See* National Institute for
    Agricultural Development
inflation, 5, 19–20, 31–36, 40, 43, 71,
    73, 76–77, 79, 89–90, 118,
    127–28, 141, 146–47, 177–78,
    183, 186, 190–91, 208, 250–51
institutionalists. *See* military, Chile,
    institutionalists
Instituto de Normalización Previsional,
    216, 218–19
Instituto de Salud Previsional
    (ISAPRE), 234–38, 240
International Labor Office (ILO), 88,
    102, 251
interventores, 132
ISAPRE. *See* Instituto de Salud
    Previsional

Izquierda Cristiana, 124
Izquierda Unida, 195

Jarpa, Sergio Onofre, 188, 192
Junta de Gobierno, 160–61, 167–68,
    205, 208

Kast, Miguel, 182–83, 210–11, 225
Kennecott, 73, 138
Klein-Saks Mission, 34

Labor Code, 13, 37–38, 52–53, 89,
    140, 180
Labor Courts, 37, 53, 183
Land Reform Law, 81, 85, 119, 124,
    132, 262n13
la via Chilena al socialismo. *See*
    Chilean Road to Socialism
Law 4051. *See* Obligatory Insurance
    Fund
Law 4052. *See* White-Collar Workers
    Fund
Law 4053, 16
Law 4054, 48, 61
Law 6174, 61
Law 8811. *See* Peasant Unionization
    Law
Law 8987. *See* Law of Permanent
    Defense of Democracy
Law 15020, 110–11
Law 16250, 111
Law of Permanent Defense of
    Democracy, 39
Leftist Democratic Participation. *See*
    Participación Democrática de
    Izquierda
Leftist Revolutionary Movement
    (MIR), 94, 130–32, 155, 162,
    191, 195
Leigh, Gustavo, 165–68, 180,
    207–8
León, Eduardo, 114
Ley de Medicina Curativa, 103, 108
Ley Maldita. See Law of Permanent
    Defense of Democracy

Liberal Alliance, 12, 16
Liberal Party, 11, 22–23, 34, 72, 74, 80

mancomunal, 6–7
MAPU. *See* Movimiento de Acción
    Popular Unido
marginals, 74, 82–84, 93, 96, 103,
    127. *See also* Frei, Eduardo,
    administration of, integration of
    marginals
Maritain, Jacques, 24, 74–75
MDP. *See* Democratic Popular
    Movement
Melo, Galvarino, 141
Merchant Marine Workers Fund, 55
"metropolization," 82. *See also*
    marginals
military, Chile, 8, 13–17, 20, 46, 48,
    105, 113, 122, 139, 244–46,
    249. *See also* social security
    system, and military
    and Allende regime, 135–37,
        150–51, 153, 155–56, 161
    constitutionalists, 135, 155
    institutionalists, 135, 155
    narrative of, 157–58
    under Pinochet, 159–61, 169–70,
        173, 178–79, 198–201, 205,
        241
    and religion, 158–59
MIR. *See* Leftist Revolutionary
    Movement
Modernización de la Previsión. *See*
    social security reform, 1980
modernizaciones. See "modernizations"
"modernizations," 178–79, 200,
    202–4, 210, 219, 240, 250
monetarist school, 173–76, 183, 186,
    188
Movement Fatherland and Liberty, 131
Movimiento de Acción Popular Unido
    (MAPU), 90, 92, 124, 132
Movimiento de Izquierda
    Revolucionaria. *See* Leftist
    Revolutionary Movement

Movimiento Patria y Libertad. *See*
    Movement Fatherland and
    Liberty
mutual aid societies, 6, 259n6
mutualidades. See mutual aid societies

National Directorate of Intelligence
    (DINA), 161–64, 248
National Fund of Family Benefits, 101
National Health Service (SNS), 64,
    103–8, 143–44, 233, 236,
    271n16
National Information Center (CNI),
    163–64
National Institute for Agricultural
    Development (INDAP), 84–86,
    110
nationalization, 128, 132, 140, 142.
    See also copper industry,
    nationalization of
National Party, 124, 134
National Planning Office
    (ODEPLAN), 57, 205–6, 210
National System of Health Services,
    233
neoliberalism, 154, 165, 167, 171,
    173–76, 200, 203, 205–8, 218,
    229, 232, 239
    failure of, 185–89
    goals of, 176–79
    health care reform plan, 231–38
    labor policy, 180–83
    pragmatic, 189–91
    results of, 183–85, 196–97
    and social security reform, 205–8,
        210–19, 238–40
1980 Constitution, xiii, 167–72, 175,
    188, 192–93, 197, 199–200,
    241, 243, 245, 248–49
1978 Amnesty Law, 163, 241, 245–47
1933 Constitution, 21
1925 Constitution, xi, 17, 19, 21,
    28–29, 33, 42–43, 48, 66–67,
    79, 121, 165
nitrate industry, 3–5, 8, 11, 16, 47

Nixon, Richard, and Allende
government, 128, 138, 150
nivelación de salarios, 29
No campaign, 194, 196–98, 244, 248
Novoa, Patricio, 100, 112–13, 115
Novoa Commission, 100, 112, 209
Nuñez, Ricardo, 194–95, 244

Obligatory Insurance Fund, 15–16
ODEPLAN. *See* National Planning
Office
Operation Condor, 163–64

Parada, José Manuel, 165
Participación Democrática de
Izquierda (PDI), 196
Patria y Libertad, 94, 166
patrimonialism, 156–67, 201, 231,
239–40
patronato, 12
PDC. *See* Christian Democratic Party
PDI. *See* Participación Democrática
de Izquierda
Peasant Unionization Law, 53, 84–85,
102, 111, 114
perseguidora, 56, 60, 65, 115, 209
Piñera, José, 181, 207, 210–11,
213–14, 219, 225, 231, 252,
279n53, 280n66
Pinochet, Augusto, xiii, xiv, 137, 156,
208, 241–42, 249
regime of, xv, 96, 243, 254–55
and Catholic Church, 164–65
consolidation of power, 161–67,
175
economic crisis, 185–89
economic policy, 166–67,
170–73, 200–203, 229, 250,
253. *See also* "modernizations";
neoliberalism
—results of, 183–85, 196–97
health care reform, 231–38
ideology of, 157–60
labor policies, 180–83
legitimacy of, 167–69, 187

and Nazi Germany, 163
political crisis, 187–88
political policy, 167–72, 175–76,
200–203
preparation for plebiscite,
191–200
and religion, 156–57, 159, 163
and repression, 154, 161–64,
187–89, 191–94, 200, 202
rise to power, 155–56
social security reform, 203–4,
238–40
—Anteproyecto del Estatuto
Fundamental de Principios y
Bases del Sistema de Seguridad
Social, 205–8
—Decree Law 2448, 209–10
—family allowances, 209–10
—health and maternity benefits,
212, 231–38
—1980 reform, 210–19
—pensions, 209–10
—results of, 219–31
transformation of political system,
154, 160–67
war against Marxism, 158,
161–62, 166, 172, 194
Plan Decenal de Salud, 103, 105
Plan Laboral, 181, 252, 280n66
Poblaciones Callampas, 82
Poblete, Moisés, 12, 47
Police Fund, 48
política and políticas, relationship
between, ix–x, xiii, 68, 203, 213,
255
Popular Democratic Movement, 188
Popular Front, 28, 30, 32, 39, 68, 139,
148
Popular Unity. *See* Unidad Popular
coalition
populist politics, 19–43, 45, 51, 67,
76, 96, 121
Prat, Jorge, 98, 266n26
Prat Commission/Report, 51, 56, 66,
98, 266n26

Prats, Carlos, 136–37, 155–56, 164, 276n2
Preventative Medicine Law, 62–63
Previsión para todos, 139–43
Promoción Popular. *See* Consejería de Promoción Popular
Promoción Popular Bill. *See* Consejería de Promoción Popular

Radical Party, 4, 11, 23, 28, 33, 39, 41, 74, 94, 133, 259n21
rebeldes, 90, 92
Recabarren, Luis Emilio, 6–7, 38, 40
Reforma Previsional. See social security reform
Renovación Nacional (RN), 197, 199, 243
Retailers Fund, 140
Rettig Commission. *See* Commission on Truth and Reconciliation
Rios, Juan Antonio, 39
RN. *See* Renovación Nacional
Rodríguez, Pablo, 166
Rural Unionization Law, 87

Salud para todos, 139, 143–45
Schneider, René, 155
Servicio Médico Nacional de Empleados (SERMENA), 63, 105–8, 140, 143, 233, 236
Servicio Nacional de Salud, 144
Servicio Unico de Salud. *See* United Health Service
Si campaign, 194, 196
sindicato unido, 50
Sistema de Libre Elección, 106, 108
Sistema Nacional de Servicios de Salud. *See* National System of Health Services
Sistema Unico de Prestaciones Familiares, 208
SNA. *See* Sociedad Nacional de Agricultura
SNS. *See* National Health Service

socialism, 121–39, 148–51. *See also* Allende, Salvador, administration of; income redistribution
Allende plan for transition to, 126–38
failure of, 128–33, 148–51
Socialist Party, 23–24, 41, 50, 123, 130–31, 133–34, 136, 149, 155, 160, 162, 191, 194, 244
social property area, 126, 131–32
social question, 2–6, 10, 12–16
social security reform. *See also* social security system, administration of; social security system, family allowances; social security system, funds; social security system, health and maternity benefits; social security system, pensions
and Allende administration, 139–48
Anteproyecto del Estatuto Fundamental de Principios y Bases del Sistema de Seguridad Social, 205–8
Decree Law 2448, 209–10
and Frei administration, 97–121, 148
failure of, 102, 106–9, 114–20
1980, 210–19
and Pinochet regime, 203–40
results of, 219–31
social security system, 26, 29, 35–36, 38–39, 42, 75, 81, 122, 255
administration of, 64–65
reform of, 214–16
benefits, 51, 57–64, 68. *See also* social security system, family allowances; social security system, health and maternity benefits; social security system, pensions; social security system, workman's compensation
expansion of, 139–41, 147

and blue-collar workers, 47, 55, 57–58, 63, 140–42
and civil servants, 56–60, 63, 105, 113, 209–10
and copper workers, 49–50, 52, 60
costs of, 56, 65–66, 98, 145–48, 205, 223, 226–28
development of, 45–51, 66–69
early basis of, 15–16
family allowances, 45, 51, 61, 252–53
reform of, and Allende administration, 140–42, 145
reform of, and Frei administration, 98–102, 111, 115
reform of, and Pinochet regime, 208–10, 212
financial structure, 55–57, 212–14
funds, 48, 63, 112, 147. *See also individual names of funds*
fragmentation of, 48–51, 64
reform of, 212–14, 219, 233
groups covered, 51–55. *See also* social security system, and blue-collar workers; social security system, and civil servants; social security system, and copper workers; social security system, and military; social security system, and race track workers; social security system, and railroad workers; social security system, and rural population; social security system, and white-collar workers; social security system, and women
health and maternity benefits, 46, 51, 61–64, 75
reform of, and Allende administration, 143–45
reform of, and Frei administration, 98, 102–9, 112, 143
reform of, and Pinochet regime, 212, 231–38

and military, 47, 55–57, 59–60, 64, 105, 113, 140, 142, 212, 214, 220, 229
pensions, 46, 51, 57–62, 65, 252–53, 255, 266n21
reform of, and Allende administration, 139–41, 145–47
reform of, and Frei administration, 98, 100, 109–18
reform of, and Pinochet regime, 208–10, 212, 216, 230–31
—impact of, 220–28, 239
privatization of, xiii, 203–40, 255
and race track workers, 49–50, 57, 60, 145
and railroad workers, 47
and rural population, 52–55, 67–68, 266n21
and white-collar workers, 47, 56–58, 63, 140
and women, 221–22, 235, 238, 240
workman's compensation, 64, 98, 100, 234
"social tie," 35–36
Sociedad Nacional de Agricultura (SNA), 53, 87
Special Committees of Rural Control (CEFA), 110
statism, 171
subsidiarity of the state, 167, 170, 175–77, 206, 210, 214, 226, 228, 232, 239–40
Superintendencia de Administradoras de Fondos de Pensiones, 216, 218–19, 221, 228
Superintendencia de Seguridad Social, 56, 64, 110, 204–9, 218–20

Ten-Year Health Plan. *See* Plan Decenal de Salud
Thayer, William, 88, 100–101, 114
toma, 130, 132–33, 148
Tomic, Radomiro, 124
transitional model, 169, 172

UDI. *See* Unión Democrática
    Independiente
Unidad Popular coalition (UP),
    121–51, 161, 179, 194. *See also*
    Allende, Salvador,
    administration of
    conflicts within, 129–34
    disintegration of, 134–39, 149–51
    economic program, 124–28
Unified Command of Gremial Action.
    See Comando de Acción
    Gremial
Unión Democrática Independiente
    (UDI), 191–92, 197, 243
Unión Nacional, 192
unions, 48, 50, 75, 87–89, 93, 140,
    160, 178, 180–82, 187–88,
    194, 252
    peasant, 84–87
United Health Fund (FONASA), 233,
    237
United Nations Economic
    Commission for Latin America
    (ECLA), 125, 174

United States
    and Allende administration, 124,
        128, 137–39, 149–50
    and Pinochet regime, 160, 174
United/Unified Health Service, 103,
    143
U.S.S.R., and Allende administration,
    145–50
UP. *See* Unidad Popular coalition

Vekemans, Roger, 82–83
Vicaría de Solidaridad, 165, 193
Vicuña Subercaseaux, Benjamín, 12
Vuscovic, Pedro, 132

Wage Readjustment Bill, 93
White-Collar Workers Fund, 16,
    48–49, 55, 106–7, 233
Workers Capitalization Fund,
    89–90

Yañez, Eleodoro, 12

Zorrilla, Américo, 141–42